BRITISH MILITARY POLICY IN INDIA, 1900–1945
Colonial Constraints and Declining Power

BRITISH MILITARY POLICY IN INDIA, 1900–1945

Colonial Constraints and Declining Power

ANIRUDH DESHPANDE

MANOHAR
2005

First published 2005

ISBN 81-7304-583-6

Published by

Ajay Kumar Jain for
Manohar Publishers & Distributors
4753/23 Ansari Road, Daryaganj
New Delhi 110 002

Typeset at

Digigrafics
New Delhi 110 049

Printed at

Lordson Publishers Pvt. Ltd.
Delhi 110 007

To
Anu,
Shefali, and
Urvashi

Contents

Preface

This book examines the implications of British military policy in India in a period marked by declining British power. British military doctrine had evolved into a set of seemingly inflexible principles at the beginning of the twentieth century. Between the late eighteenth and the closing decades of the nineteenth century Britain's naval mastery on the high seas inculcated a belief in British military invincibility in British imperial ruling circles. In the second half of the nineteenth century weaknesses in Britain's military position surfaced and led to the policy of appeasement. Appeasement stayed with Britain till 1939 and was symptomatic of the undercurrents of the changing British military position between 1850 and 1950. British military policy was located in a context in which war became increasingly unprofitable.

Between the Crimean and the Great War technological developments transformed the meaning of strategy and sea power. Trains meant growing land power. The motorization and timely concentration of divisions rendered a seaborne invasion of the continent obsolete. Land power was demonstrated in the wars of German unification. Following this, in the twentieth century, air power became equally, if not more, important. British responses to these developments were late. The Great War demonstrated the hiatus between Britain's strategic interests and her economic and ideological capacity to attain them. Above all, modern warfare meant that fleets had to develop in consonance with land and air power. This required the support of a vigorous, versatile, and innovative industry which the British colonial empire did not possess.

Between the two World Wars Britain's military planning was governed by the Ten Year Rule and the so-called 'peace hypothesis'. In the 1930s Britain fell back on treaties aimed at limiting the arms race and gaining time. But diplomacy is rarely a substitute for power. In these circumstances the Indian armed forces felt the effects of British military policy. But British policy was not merely a product of official attempts to grapple with imperial decline. It was conditioned by the economic, social, and political factors peculiar to colonial India. Increasingly, and against their will, the British contended with Indian opinion in military matters. This was a prelude to their experiencing the consequences of changing Indian social realities during the Second World War.

The British and Indian perspectives on military reform, the inter-War retrenchment, the issues of Indianization and modernization, the change in recruitment due to the demands of war, and finally the harsh realities of demobilization are the salient features of Indian military history studied in this book. The first three chapters—preceded by a comprehensive introduction to British policy, strategy, and *colonial over-stretch* in the nineteenth and twentieth centuries—analyse the reform process, retrenchment, Indianization, and modernization affecting the Indian armed forces in detail. Chapter 4 examines military recruitment in India. It focuses on recruitment changes and their consequences during the Second World War. It also compares the process of demobilization after the Great War with what happened after the Second World War. The Conclusion criticizes 'decolonization' and reiterates the central problematic of imperial systems: *all empires decline sooner or later because the costs of maintaining them ultimately exceed the material and mental resources they generate.*

The modern Indian Army dates back to the nineteenth century. The three Presidency Armies of the eighteenth century changed during the course of the nineteenth century. The greatest transformation occurred in the Bengal Army. The Indian Army was later reorganized into nine divisional commands and its regiments were re-numbered under the leadership of Lord Kitchener. Earlier the Mutiny proved to be a watershed event in Indian military history. It led to the exclusion of Indians from the artillery, the construction of cantonments to segregate the Army from the *bazaar*, and greater racial distance between the European and Indian components of the Army in India. From the 1880s onwards and till the Second World War the *martial races* theory governed the recruitment of Indians in general. This was done to keep the Indian Army manageable and loyal.

India assumed a new geo-political significance for the British imperial interests between the two World Wars. The consolidation of the USSR in the 1920s and the growing Axis threat of the 1930s gave India a new importance in British imperial strategy. However, this was rarely expressed in policy affecting the Indian services. In sum, even a certain appreciation of India's position in the Empire after the Great War *did not bring about large increases or modernization* in the Indian armed forces. The reforms contemplated after 1918 were predicated upon the experience of the Great War and the changing international position of the British Empire after it. But the economic limitations of the Raj put paid to them.

The Esher recommendations, with their limitations, were destined to be wasted in the 1920s. After all, the Victorian discourse which corsetted the Indian services contradicted the demands of modern warfare. The modernization of the colonial military establishment between 1900 and 1945 was also related to the social reform of the armed forces. At the heart of all this lay the matter of economies and Indianization. While the Esher recommendations bypassed practicable Indianization, the colonial state betrayed the wartime promises made to Indians. This led to an interesting contest of identities between the Indians and the colonial state on the Indianization question in the 1920s and 1930s. In the 1930s, besides Indianization, military policy had to confront the problem of technological modernization. Here, once again, the economic legacy of the 1920s played a crucial role in deciding budgets and technological change. Consequently, when the policy makers tried to modernize the Indian services on the eve of the Second World War they ran into the chronic problems of the Raj in India. This is not to say that their perspectives, as late as 1938, were free of colonial prejudices inimical to Indian cooperation in the impending War. Following this, the Indian armed forces remained unprepared for a major war in 1939. In the event the Second World War imposed fresh imperatives on the Indian military establishment while signalling the end of British colonialism in India. Our study of recruitment, demobilization, and discontent in this volume attempts a more nuanced understanding of this process.

ANIRUDH DESHPANDE

Acknowledgements

This book is a revised version of my Ph.D. thesis. Between 1991 and 1994, when the Ph.D. drafts were being written, several individuals and institutions helped me. I am grateful to my supervisor Professor Majid Hayat Siddiqi for guiding my M.Phil./Ph.D. programme at the Centre for Historical Studies (CHS), JNU. My M.Phil. dissertation 'The Royal Indian Navy Uprising and Popular Protest, 1946' was also submitted under his supervision to the CHS in 1987. This led me to a larger history of the colonial military establishment. Professor Stephen Cohen, who needs no introduction, gave generous comments as an external examiner of my thesis. In May 1993 the military historian and Keeper of the Churchill Archives Centre (Churchill College, Cambridge) Mr Correlli Barnett discussed issues of military policy with me. I gratefully acknowledge his advice. Professor Sumit Guha went through a draft and gave valuable comments during the summer of 1994. A version of Chapter 2 received the Partha Sarathi Gupta Award in the 'Modern India and Countries other than India' section at the Indian History Congress, Calcutta, 2–5 January 2001. Drafts of this chapter were presented at JNU (1997) and NMML, Teen Murti Bhavan (1998), where the late Professor Partha Sarathi Gupta was present. His comments are gratefully acknowledged. The support and encouragement generously offered by members of our Teen Murti 'lunch group'—Dr Amiya Prasad Sen, Dr Pralay Kanungo, and Dr Dhirendra Dangwal—is gratefully acknowledged.

I thank the University Grants Commission of India for awarding me a Junior Research Fellowship (JRF) in December 1986 after I passed the newly instituted UGC fellowship exam. Dr U.P. Thaplial, Director of the Historical Section of the Ministry of Defence, R.K. Puram, New Delhi, and his staff were ever helpful. I thank them for their hospitality. I am also grateful to the members and staff of the Centre for Historical Studies, the Dean's Office, School of Social Sciences (JNU), JNU Library, the National

Archives of India (NAI), the United Services' Institute of India Library (USII), the Nehru Memorial Museum & Library (NMML), the Central Secretariat Library (CSL), the Cambridge University Library with its Official Publications Section (CUL), and the Churchill Archives Centre, for their invaluable assistance.

In large measure I owe this book to my wife Anu. Without her support my enterprise, would have collapsed. All the necessary distractions have been provided at various stages by our daughters Shefali and Urvashi. This volume, *sans* limitations, is dedicated to them. Thanks are also due to Anjali and Anand for their encouragement. In the end I would like to express my gratitude to Maa for all that she has done for me. I regret that she did not live to see this volume.

The people and institutions mentioned above are not responsible for any mistake this book might contain.

ANIRUDH DESHPANDE

Abbreviations

ADP	*Army Department Proceedings*
CER	*The RIN Mutiny Commission of Enquiry Report*
CID	Committee on Imperial Defence
CSL	Central Secretariat Library, New Delhi
CUL	Cambridge University Library, Cambridge, U.K.
EC	Esher Committee
ECR	Esher Committee Report
ECO	Emergency Commissioned Officer
FOCRIN	Flag Officer Commanding, Royal Indian Navy
HS	Historical Section, Ministry of Defence, New Delhi
IRC	Indian Retrenchment Committee
KCO	King's Commissioned Officer
MC	Military Council
NCO	Non Commissioned Officer
NMML	Nehru Memorial Museum & Library, New Delhi
RIAF	Royal Indian Air Force
RIM	Royal Indian Marine
USII	United Services' Institute of India, New Delhi
VCO	Viceroy's Commissioned Officer

Important Committee Reports referred to in the book:

1. *Army in India Committee Report 1920* (Esher Committee Report). The recommendations of this Committee were spread over nine parts and dealt with questions related to the overall organization of Indian defence in detail. The Committee was led by Lord Esher and worked in the context of a presumed evolution of Dominion Status for India after the Great War but it was unpopular in India.
2. *Report of the Indian Retrenchment Committee, 1923* (*IRC*). The job of this committee was to suggest measures to balance the budget in the 1920s. Since the public and war debt of the GOI was already very high, economic orthodoxy dictated a steep decline in state expenditure. In the event the severe

recommendations of the IRC countered the ambitions spelt out by the Esher Committee in much of the 1920s.

3. *Shea Committee Report 1922.* This is the report of a committee appointed by the Commander-in-Chief to enquire into initial questions related to the Indianization of the Indian Army's Officer Corps. It was headed by Lt. Gen. Shea acting Chief of the General Staff. The Shea Committee projected a time frame and a unit scheme for Indianization for the first time.
4. *Report of the Indian Sandhurst Committee 1927.* Also called the Skeen Committee Report, it resulted from a need to review the process of Indianization in the mid-1920s. The aim of the Committee was to study the viability of establishing an Indian Sandhurst. This the committee did on the basis of a sweeping criticism of military education in India.
5. *Chetwode Committee Report 1931.* The Chetwode Committee was formed under the leadership of General Chetwode, the Commander-in-Chief in India, after some Indian pressure prevailed on the matter of Indianization in the Indian Round Table Conference of 1930-1. Though the Chetwode Committee admitted that the Indian Sandhurst would open shortly, the divisional scheme suggested by it provoked interesting 'dissertations' of dissent from its Indian members.
6. Committee on the Indianization of the Officer Ranks of the Indian Army—Draft Report 1939. Also known as the *Indianization Committee Report 1938-9*, it contains a valuable history of Indianization besides advocating more Indianization.
7. *Secret Report of the Expert Committee on the Defence of India 1938-9 (Chatfield Committee Report).* During the late 1930s the need to survey Indian defence in relation to the new international situation was finally felt by the British government. The Chatfield Committee led by Lord Chatfield arrived in India in 1938 for the purpose of making recommendations regarding Indian defence. However, the Committee ended up highlighting the drawbacks of the Indian military position in 1939 and its recommendations were generally seen as inadequate from the point of view of both Imperial and Indian defence.
8. *The Royal Indian Navy Mutiny Commission of Enquiry Report 1946 (CER).* After the large-scale and violent mutiny of February 1946 in the RIN, a Commission of Enquiry was

instituted by the GOI to study the causes and nature of the popular mutiny. The CER reached its conclusions on the basis of examining witnesses, correspondence, locations, and the reports compiled by the RIN authorities.

9. *Mowatt Committee Report.* The unsuccessful British operations against the Afridis on the North-West Frontier in 1897-8 raised questions of expenditure on the Army in India. Matters of expenditure also emanated from the Kitchener Scheme designed to remedy defects in the Indian Army organization after 1904. The Mowatt Committee Report was the Report of Committee on Special Military Expenditure formed in 1907 by the British Government. The Committee suggested a reduction in military expenditure.

INTRODUCTION

The Contours of British Military Policy in India

A British military historian describes the colonial Indian Army in the following words:

> The Indian Army seemed a splendid asset: hearts warmed at the sight of those dusky lancers, gaudy as jungle birds, who trotted beside the viceregal carriage, and at the thought of British and Indian brothers-in-arms with mule and mountain gun carrying peace up the valleys of the North-West Frontier. The squeal of the bugle, the crunch of ironshod ammunition boots on the dusty road, red coats and khaki, turban and topee, tents under a sky of brass—it was in these terms, *touching the heart rather than the critical intelligence*, that the British tended to see the power which they believed India gave them.[1] (emphasis added)

It is apposite to begin a book on British military policy in India with reference to the imperial myth of the Indian Army. One of the aims of this book is to explore the historical intricacies of this carefully cultivated myth. Myths apart, at another level, without the Indian Army there would have been no British rule in India. It was such an important constituent of the British Raj that it is taken for granted by most scholars of colonial India. This has produced unfortunate consequences for the study of modern Indian military history. The glorification of the armed forces in independent India and the sacrosanct status they enjoy in nationalist ideologies of all shades have not helped the emergence of substantial critical military thinking in India. It is true that Indian historiography of the colonial military establishment has, in general, remained unaffected by the epistemological developments which have revolutionized the study of military history elsewhere. Perhaps this is explained by the fact that most histories of the modern Indian Army, to borrow Heathcote's phrase, in its 'classical period' stress the continuities characteristic of its famous regiments. Official accounts and written histories from within the services are more guilty on this account. This narrative is different from other histories of the Indian Army because of the following reasons. It is neither an over-arching discourse on the colonial Indian armed forces nor a specialized monograph comprising regimental and battle trivia.[2] Unlike a standard textbook, it does not contain mandatory sections on all aspects of the colonial military. Although it touches upon various aspects of the colonial Indian armed forces, its aim is to explore the dialectic of military policy, military organization, and imperial fortunes in British India during the first forty-five years of the twentieth century.

This volume departs from certain long-established traditions of Indian military history in asserting that regimental histories are not academically central to military history in the age of nuclear weapons and computerized warfare. Indeed, many would claim that the regiment had become militarily obsolete even before the Second World War. Several authors have noted the drawbacks of the regimental system. Barnett has even called it an outdated eighteenth-century institution unsuited to the compulsions of modern warfare. According to critics, the regimental system narrows the vision of an army and creates unnecessary diversity. In practice, because modern armies are deployed in large formations, the regiment ceases to be an operational unit.[3] In the context of an increasing dichotomy between conventional and contemporary warfare in the twentieth century, characterized by the rise of low-intensity conflicts and the declining importance of the infantry as it is, this criticism assumes greater importance. However, fortunately or unfortunately for the Indian Army and its historians, the institution with its strong colonial roots and usefulness lends itself easily to regimental valorization. This is also helped by the fact that the Indian regimental system has remained truly untested in a substantial war after 1945. Its post-Independence record, contrary to official and public opinion, is not particularly distinguished. In 1962 due to several reasons it failed to deliver. In 1965 in several areas of conflict its combat record was generally average. In 1971, when the Indo-Pak War was decided in East Bengal, the conditions favouring India were exceptional. A similar combination of factors is unlikely to obtain in future.

The IPKF operations in Sri Lanka (1987-9) were disastrous and ultimately led to the assassination of Rajiv Gandhi. Earlier, even during the Great War, and more so the Second World War, only *major departures* from the existing system of recruitment and organization enabled India and her normally Frontier-oriented armed forces to participate in these international conflicts.[4]

In independent India the regiment, rightly or wrongly, is often perceived as the nucleus of the army. Since this repository of discipline and control is also cultivated by nationalist ideology, it is difficult, if not altogether impossible, to be openly critical of it. The Indian armed forces have managed to create a special place for themselves in a republic where the military peagent is an essential ingredient of prevalent nationalist discourses and iconography. Since 1947 the glorification of the Army has also been reinforced by its increasing importance in a fractured civil society. Many would contend, especially in the context of growing communalism in India, that the Indian armed forces are the only genuine secular institutions left in the Republic. All this only goes to show that Indian military history can be studied from a variety of perspectives. However, my assertion against considering the regiment as the focal point of the army is predicated upon military realities peculiar to the twentieth century. For the colonial period this contention is also sustained by the indisputable fact that the days of a mythical Frontier, *shikar* (generally as part of the hospitality offered to senior army officers by local elites), pig sticking, polo, and the cavalry had become numbered even before the Great War exposed imperial Britain's military weaknesses. The Great War ushered the Indian armed forces into an era of official and nationalist criticism. An examination of this reveals the most important aspects of British military policy in India. This book bypasses the regiment in favour of highlighting these aspects and examines their relationship with the Indian armed forces roughly between 1900 and 1945. Furthermore, this is done with reference to the important indices of British colonial over-extension evident in India between 1919 and 1945. In sum, therefore, this is an attempt to present a synthesis of military, political, and socio-economic history of the British Raj with reference to the major developments in British military policy. Hopefully, it will satisfy the interested readers' demand for a military history which is comprehensive in scope and removed from the banalities of the battlefield.[5]

BRITISH IMPERIAL STAGNATION AND DECLINE

Those seriously concerned with the history of colonial India are aware of the salient features of British military strategy in the nineteenth and twentieth centuries. The most important and holistic in scope amongst these was the systemic crisis of the British Empire which undermined British power in the inter-War period. The rapid and unexpected decline of British power after the Great War cast a gloom not only over its contemporary apologists, many of whom searched in vain for prescriptions to stem the rot, but also the historiography documenting it. The descriptions of inter-War Britain are almost universally pessimistic. For instance, the Marxist economic and social historian Eric Hobsbawm has described inter-War Britain as a foundering ship with an 'ignorant' and 'impotent' captain and crew.[6] It is important from the viewpoint of Indian history to note that most historians locate the genesis of this crisis in the nineteenth century.

British military doctrine and strategy in the nineteenth century was governed to a large degree by British naval supremacy. This strategy, which was rooted in the latter half of the eighteenth century and the Napoleonic period, had assumed a certain inflexibility towards the end of the nineteenth century. After researching aspects and areas of colonial warfare and the overall British direction of war, historians assert that between the late eighteenth and nineteenth centuries, despite the rise of imperialist rivals like Germany and Japan, Britain's naval supremacy remained unaffected in general. A global naval history of the nineteenth century also suggests that the widespread belief in British naval pre-eminence was predicated upon the fact that between 1850 and 1914 major naval battles of the Nelson era were not fought. In this scenario, effective British military thinking and policy was dominated by the Admiralty, the Royal Navy, and the illusions spawned by Pax Britannica.[7]

Traditionally speaking, British strategy was also predicated upon Britain's geographical and colonial position and domestic conditions. The gradual expansion of franchise, a growing disapproval and unpopularity of conscription, and a small army characterized the age of liberalism in which Indian revenues, the Cardwell System,[8] and Her Majesty's Navy played their respective roles in British history and military development. The typical British way of warfare was an outcome of historical factors peculiar to the eighteenth and nineteenth centuries. Above all, till the lessons of the Crimean War were learnt, Britain was the world's first and foremost modern industrial country. In the British scheme of things, the assertion of naval supremacy with and a naval blockade against a Continental power came first. After this came the formation of coalitions against countries disturbing the balance of power in Europe. Translated into real military action, and in the ultimate analysis, this meant a limited Wellington-style continental commitment by a conscript British expeditionary force in Europe.

In the colonies, where garrisons of the British Army monopolized artillery, protected imperial interests and simultaneously countered and stiffened colonial troops, the cost of war was borne by the colonial revenues, resources, and manpower reserves.[9] The success of this arrangement was also based on several favourable factors such as a balance of power in Europe, the industrial, commercial, and naval supremacy of Britain over her European rivals, adroit diplomacy, and the easy availability of colonial troops led by British officers. After 1815 Britain's continental liability generally remained small. However, the British continued to intervene vigorously in Asia and Africa in the greater interest of their far-flung empire with the help of overseas resources throughout the nineteenth century. Nonetheless, and somewhat ironically, these colonial wars most probably ended up strengthening the British naval convictions because the timely imperial deployment of troops was supported by the British domination of the major international sea lanes.[10] But, in general, the colonial resources remained unrepresented in the British metropolitan vision of modern warfare despite the crucial role they played in the creation and maintenance of the British Empire. The sum total of all this constituted the theory and practice of the traditional way of British warfare, which was finally destroyed by the Great War.

In the second half of the nineteenth century, while the British Empire looked stronger than ever, flaws in the British military arrangement started surfacing. Britain's preference for appeasement, especially after the costly Crimean adventure, reflected a weakness in the imperial chain of assets. One influential author submits that the policy of appeasement, which became a subject of intense criticism during the 1930s, can actually be traced back to the 1860s. The policy of appeasement, in short, meant the settlement of international and domestic disputes by 'admitting and satisfying grievances through rational negotiation and compromise' to avoid expensive conflicts.[11] This argument is not entirely devoid of value given the changing nature of the British state in the nineteenth century. The near-continuous recourse to appeasement dogged Britain till 1939 and was symptomatic of the undercurrents of the changing British military position between 1850 and 1950. The history of the Second World War suggests that appeasement was one of the causes responsible for the military ascendancy of Nazi Germany in the late 1930s.

The preponderance of appeasement in British policy should be viewed in a context of opinion which did not favour war. Over the course of a century Britain had become the centre of world commerce and her most important stakes lay in trade. Exports from the Empire played a crucial role in the British metropolitan balance of payments. Major wars harmed this political economy which was enmeshed in a complicated imperial-colonial grid comprising trade, insurance and shipping. This transition of Britain from the first industrial country to a nation heavily dependent upon colonial trade greatly influenced the course of the British Empire. This was the predicament of Empire which, combined with rising social welfare costs and a public distaste for war, ultimately led to the 'guns *v.* butter' debates of the twentieth century. The works of Hobsbawm, Barnett, Gamble, and Kennedy show why and how in the late nineteenth and early twentieth centuries the comparative decline of British industry set in. This was the prelude to the final crash of the 'Victorian economy' between the two world wars. In such circumstances it was inconceivable that Great Britain would be able to defend its vast colonial empire all by herself. Therefore, the process of leasing out defence to Japan in the East and the United States in the West began before the Great War.[12] The economic problems of managing and defending the empire was reflected in the consciousness of the British ruling class. Hence, even before the Great War began, a 'fundamental loss of will in British ruling circles' and their inability to resolve the British strategic dilemma had become crystal clear to contemporary observers.[13] Ultimately, the Great War drove home the lesson that despite its far-flung empire Britain could no longer dominate the world.[14] Indeed, as the years passed the largely backward empire became a strategic burden.

The naval decline of Britain in the twentieth century was both symbolic and absolute. Since the method of deploying expeditionary forces was based on sea power, a resumé of the latter is called forth here.[15] By 1815 the British had created an overseas empire based on naval and industrial supremacy and the international significance of naval power had been realized by British statesmen during the second half of the eighteenth century. Though the 'command of the sea' began to be understood in this period, the transition from the obsolete Fighting Instructions of 1691 to Kempenfelt and Howe's revised Fighting Instructions of 1781-2 occurred slowly, and available evidence does not suggest that colonial naval forces like the Bombay Marine derived benefits from these instructions.[16] However, it is clear that despite the differentiated nature of warfare preceding the Industrial Revolution, in the eighteenth century British policy began to consciously inculcate some consistency as far as maritime supremacy was concerned. In short, the concept of sea power belonged to the century in which British financial and trading interests began to promote an orthodoxy according to which 'maritime commerce and naval power were indissoluble'.[17] In the late eighteenth and most of the nineteenth century the Royal Navy reigned supreme while British maritime hegemony was buttressed by the establishment of British rule in most of Asia and Africa. This made for much of British overconfidence in military matters. The token East India Squadron of the Royal Navy stationed in India was an apt expression of this feeling. But real matters were more complicated. There is sufficient reason to believe that in the long run an uncritical dependence on the Navy undermined British security. It is a different matter that in much of contemporary British thinking the unprecedented maritime hegemony of the Royal Navy probably bred an illusion of permanence. It is understandable why a prosperous Victorian Britain, led by reasonable statesmen and protected by a most formidable navy as it was, appeared invincible. But despite the optimism generated by free trade principles, and the presumed immortality of the Raj, faults were beginning to appear in the British position towards the end of Queen Victoria's reign. Graham substantiates a trend of military economies, matching the history of appeasement, stretching from the nineteenth to the twentieth century. Paradoxically, the naval superiority of Britain in this period was itself partially responsible for generating these economies and retarding the growth of military science in Britain.[18]

Outside the British Empire things were changing and new military standards had evolved. With the spread of the Industrial Revolution military technology began to develop in new countries. It is equally important to note that the ideological orientation of these latecomers was different from the Victorian world-view of the British ruling classes. Between the Crimean War and the Great War new applications of modern technology began to transform military strategy. Sea power and its notions could hardly remain unaffected by these new developments. The growing importance and use of railways gave generals a command over land which offset Britain's command over the seas. Enhanced mobility on land, due to faster trains and later thanks to the motorization of infantry divisions, assisted the timely concentration of large bodies of fresh, well-equipped, and battle-ready troops at strategic points. A small expeditionary force had little chance against these odds. In the development of military technology, staff training and strategy united Germany, and reformed Japan registered impressive advances after 1870. It was on the road to Dunkirk that generals like Moltke felt confident of dealing with any serious landing within twenty-four hours. This exposed the limitations of the expeditionary force concept and formed the background of the awesome demonstration of land power in Europe first during the Great War and then the German offensive against France in 1940. Soon thereafter the fall of Singapore to the Japanese and the sinking of the *Repulse* and the *Prince of Wales* mocked the Royal Navy. The scale of the Second World War, and the role which the Red Army played in it, proved that navies could do little to influence the decisive battles fought in central and Eastern Europe. Evidently the military focus had shifted from sea power to land power in the period when the

British Empire was declining apace. Furthermore, while growing land power played a decisive role in the wars of German unification, air power, especially after the Great War, quickly became a significant factor in national strategic thinking in Europe.

It would be simplistic, of not altogether incorrect, to say that the British did not respond at all to the changes mentioned above but often their responses, which were individually articulated, were either too late or ran up against Blimpish attitudes. A critical view of the subject tells us that between 1870 and 1939 time and resources ran out for the British Empire. The Great War demolished the basis of nineteenth-century liberal democracy and capitalism and exposed the drawbacks of an economically uneven colonial empire and an over-dependence on sea power. It totally changed the world of the nineteenth-century politicians and highlighted the gap between Britain's strategic interests and her economic and ideological capacity to satisfy them. Above all, modern warfare, which also meant that naval fleets had to develop in relation with land and air power, demonstrated the indispensability of a versatile and innovative industry. The British colonies, it is almost universally acknowledged, were industrially primitive. Its most populated colony ranked amongst the poorest countries of the world. In terms of military technology and strategy the Empire, which showed little sign of economic rejuvenation, had become a vast British liability by the turn of the century. In the period of total war this meant weakness, not strength.

While materially the British Empire fell behind its competitors, in the field of military thought the British unwillingness to learn from history assumed legendary proportions. The Afghan and Boer experiences of the nineteenth century had underlined important military lessons of recruitment, training, and deployment but, by and large, in the 1920s strategic and tactical doctrines in Britain remained negative. The British national and imperial defence perspective in this period was governed by the Ten Year Rule[19] and the 'peace hypothesis' which had emerged from the Armistice. Combined with persistent economic problems, this perspective caused an irreparable military decline. The 'Two Power Standard' for the Royal Navy, a symbol of British military might, was adopted by Salisbury's cabinet in 1889 only to be modified many times before the Great War. Finally, the burdens of the Great War eliminated the Two Power Standard in favour of a 'One Power Standard' in 1920.[20] Naval decline, however, was only the symptom of a deep-seated malaise. During the entire inter-War period the British position on major international issues illuminated the fact that 'there was still a wide gap between a statement of principles and an acceptance of the implications of those principles in practice'.[21] The Admiralty obviously grumbled against the line of naval retreat but large-scale naval expenditure, like increased expenditure on the modernization of colonial services, was pre-empted by the economically depressed 1930s. Furthermore, the economic factor was compounded by the failure of the imperial and colonial services to imaginatively innovate in the changed circumstances which followed the Great War. In this context, Brian Bond's observation on the British Army can easily be applied to the entire British Empire between the wars.[22]

In the 1930s Britain, in the hope of gaining time, responded to international rearmament by falling back on treaties aimed at limiting the European arms race. But, as historians of the period point out, diplomacy was no substitute for economic and military power. The situation had become so alarming that the Chiefs of Staff, in their annual review for 1937, noted with concern that the British Empire was threatened at both ends by strong military powers and 'only very great military and financial strength could give the Empire security'.[23] But despite warnings, and the lessons of the Great War, policy changes occurred very slowly. The Ten Year Rule was finally revoked in 1932 but by the time Hitler came to power in Germany Britain's 'palsied military stance' was already evident as 'the result of thirteen years of untroubled international security and the imperatives of budget balancing to maintain economic stability'.[24] In British history the decade of the 1920s was marked by a 'draconian disarmament' carried out obviously at the expense of the armed services.[25] In July 1935 a Defence Policy and Requirements Committee was appointed to recommend a rearmament programme but effective rearming began only after 1939. Even then, critical imbalances between the services remained because there simply wasn't enough for everyone. For instance, between 1934 and 1939, the RAF was preferred in resource allocation to counter the highly overrated

Luftwaffe. By the mid-1930s the perceived strategic balance had swung to air power and the growing importance of the island metropolis in imperial military reckoning became clear. Later when greater financial restrictions became necessary the overseas commitments were often 'sacrificed in the interests of the metropolitan force'.[26] These imperial constraints had drastic repercussions on the Indian military scenario, to which we must now turn.

THE INDIAN CHAPTERS

The British and Indian perspectives on reform of the Indian armed forces, the prevalence of retrenchment in the inter-War period, the questions of Indianization and modernization, the continuity and change in recruitment, and Finally, the grim realities of demobilization are the salient features of this book. The first three chapters analyse the policy and process of reform, retrenchment, Indianization, and modernization affecting the Indian armed forces. Chapter 4 examines the intricacies of military recruitment in India with a specific focus on recruitment during the Second World War and the change it brought about in the Indian services. It also studies and compares the process of demobilization of the Indian armed forces after the two world wars respectively. Finally, the Conclusion adds an extra theoretical dimension to the study of British military policy in India by placing the policy themes of this book in the context of over-extension and possible decolonization.

The story of the modern Indian armed forces, including British policy affecting their future, began in the nineteenth century when most of India was disarmed by a colonial state desirous of achieving and maintaining its military superiority over Indians. Simultaneously, Indians were also divided and classified into the so-called martial and non-martial races to suit British interests in India. The three Presidency Armies, established in the eighteenth century and recruited from the respective Presidencies, experienced changes in the nineteenth century. However, the greatest transformation occurred in the Bengal Army. After the Mutiny of 1857, and following the Peel and Eden Committee recommendations, the Bengal Army and its recruitment pattern was reorganized on the well-known colonial principle of 'divide and rule'.[27] In 1895 the Presidency Armies were integrated into a single Army under a unified command. This Indian Army was further reorganized into nine divisional commands and its regiments were re-numbered under the influence of Lord Kitchener, the Commander-in-Chief in India, between 1902 and 1909. In the late nineteenth and the early twentieth centuries the orthodoxy of the *martial races* theory reigned supreme over the Indian military establishment, while recruitment languished among the so-called non-martial peoples of India. The Great War caused some changes but while Cohen's favourable account of the Indian Army shows these to be temporary, Bond is totally dismissive of them.[28] The continuity of nineteenth-century thought and practice in the Army is also substantiated in other sympathetic works by V. Longer, P. Mason, and B. Farwell (1974, 1974, and 1989) cited earlier. However, the trend of appreciative history writing continues. In fact, Professor Cohen's general view, contained in the revised version of his much-read *The Indian Army,* has remained unchanged despite the effects of the Indian blunder in Sri Lanka.[29] In sum, and as noted earlier, general histories praise the Indian Army and point out the continuities characterizing its history. Regimental histories, rather predictably, draw upon the continuity in the socio-geographical recruitment, tradition, and valour of especially selected regiments.[30]

From the viewpoint of this book, it is important to note that India assumed a new geo-political significance for the British Empire in the inter-War period and perceptive British officials appreciated this fact. Indian troops and agricultural supplies were also evaluated as useful war potential by most contemporary military analysts despite conservative assertions to the contrary.[31] The consolidation of the USSR in the 1920s and the Axis threat of the 1930s also made India more important to Britain's strategic position in the East, although the latter was rarely reflected in the policy decisions affecting the Indian services. The study of modern Indian military history must be placed with in a context formed by these historical realities. We should also concentrate on the fact that even the belated official appreciation of India's changed position in the Empire after the Great War did not, and indeed could not, lead to the enlargement or modernization of the Indian armed forces. This is documented in Chapter 3 of this book. In short, the chapter argues that the specificities of the

Indian military establishment constituted an index of arrested development in the 1930s.[32]

The official appreciation of military reform in India in the 1920s is analysed in Chapter 1 of this book. The reforms contemplated after 1918 were predicated upon the experience of the Great War and the changing international position of the British Empire after it. The chapter also shows why and how the historical limitations of the Raj put paid to large-scale military reform in India in the 1920s. Before reforms could be put into practice London and Delhi had to resolve many problems, political agreement being one of them. This remained a problematic of British policy in the inter-War period because of the intrusion of the Indian nationalism in Indian, and, therefore, by implication imperial, military matters and the economic crisis of the Raj. The official intention of military reform emanating from London is to be found in the usually under-examined *Esher Committee Report* (*ECR*). However, I must add that in the 1920s the pattern of reform and retrenchment in India followed the process initiated in England where, after the mutinies caused by faulty demobilization, a Committee on the Organization of the After War Army under the chairmanship of Lt. Gen. Sir Alexander Hamilton-Gordon was set up in 1919. In 1921-2 drastic reductions were recommended by the Report of the Committee on National Expenditure, better known as the Geddes Report or Geddes Axe after Sir Eric Geddes, Chairman of the said Committee.[33]

The Army in India Committee Report (1920), also known as the *Esher Committee Report ECR*, outlined the agenda of British military policy in India after the Great War. The Esher Committee recommendations were spread over nine parts with two separate minutes by its Indian members, Sir Krishna Gupta and Sir Umar Hayat Khan. The drawbacks of the *ECR* are mentioned in Chapter 1 of this book. But, to begin with, it should be stated that the Esher Committee had tried framing its recommendations in a spirit which was supposed to be consistent with the gradual approach of India towards Dominion Status. However, the Committee had to proceed on the basis of existing institutions and conditions in India in 1919-20. This automatically bred a respect for tradition in the Esher recommendations. In general, the pursuit of a 'sound Imperial military system' led to three crucial Esher recommendations. First, the Committee advocated greater control of the Government of India (GOI) over Indian military affairs. Second, it wanted the GOI to be given a voice in matters of Imperial defence. Third, to escape the implications of the preceding suggestion, it wanted the Imperial General Staff to exercise 'a considerable influence' on the military policy of the GOI. It goes without saying that the third recommendation, which seemed to replace the India Office by the Imperial General Staff in policy making, became controversial in India. The Esher Committee also made recommendations regarding other aspects of the military in India such as the setting up of an *advisory* Military Council, the decentralization of the command system, improvement in service conditions, the viability of a 'Kitchener College' to encourage the Indian Viceroy's Commissioned Officers (VCO), a possible Indian Sandhurst, and the development of the Royal Indian Marine into a regional navy.

Developments in the first half of the twentieth century proved that the Indian services were unprepared for modernized warfare. The modernization of the existing Indian military establishment between the wars was related at least to the successful social reform, if not a complete transformation, of the armed forces. At the heart of this was Indianization, an issue taken up by the Indian nationalists soon after the Great War. Since the Esher recommendations failed to incorporate a clear and firm commitment to Indianization, and the GOI was inclined towards a betrayal of the wartime promises made to Indians on this account, the Indian nationalists launched a spirited campaign to achieve an accelerated Indianization of the Indian Army in the 1920s. Consequently, during the Indianization debate of the 1920s the nationalist engagement with colonialism produced a lasting critique of the prejudiced and divisive recruitment policy followed in India by the British. As a result, the insufficient Indianization between the Wars, for which the British were largely to blame, and the reluctance of young Britons to join the Indian, or for that matter the British, Army, created a severe shortage of officers in the Indian Army on the eve of the Second World War. Chapter 2 examines the issue of Indianization and the identitarian conflict reflected in it.

While Chapters 1 and 2 examine the issues of military reform in the 1920s and 1930s, Chapter 3 looks at the modernization of the Indian services in the inter-War years. It comments upon a variety of policy matters related to the much-needed refurbishing of the Indian services. The chapter also studies the economic climate informing British policy and military processes. It also includes an examination of the modernization-related Chatfield recommendations which immediately preceded the Second World War. On the whole, the chapter contends that some factors aborting the reform drives of the 1920s were also simultaneously active in stalling modernization. The chapter has collectively described these factors as the legacy of the 1920s.

Chapter 4 studies/examines/looks at the theory and practice of military recruitment followed by the British up to 1939 in India, evaluates the experience of the Great War, and observes the changes in policy and the armed forces during the Second World War. It also studies the 'martial races' theory on the basis of interpreting the *Caste Handbooks* of the Indian Army and asserts that despite the experiences of the Great War recruitment theory and practice in India remained unchanged till 1939. The chapter also includes an analysis of the propaganda, political dynamics, and the socio-economic context of wartime recruitment in India. On the whole, my account of wartime recruitment argues that the pressure of mass recruitment practically swept away the 'martial races' concept and brought new recruits with new expectations into the Indian armed forces. In the event, these new aspirations proved difficult to satisfy after 1945.

Chapter 4 also looks at demobilization, the final policy theme of this book. Demobilization, with major social implications, initially appeared on the official agenda at the conclusion of the Great War. The chapter underlines the process of demobilization which followed the Great War. It also emphasizes the debate between the Home and the Finance Departments of the GOI on the matter of adequately rewarding the demobilized soldiers. This study emphasizes the emergence of discontent in the Indian Army as a result of inadequate demobilization in the 1920s. In studying demobilization in the 1920s, the chapter also points to the economic limitations of the process and the influence of nationalist propaganda on disaffected soldiers. After comparing the demobilization process of the 1920s with demobilization in the late 1940s, the chapter suggests that the British were alarmed at the widespread and visible discontent in the Indian Army at the end of the Great War. The social consciousness of Indian soldiers had been enhanced due to their experience of an international war for the first time. This fact was hardly hidden from the British, but due to the economic limitations of demobilization the Raj failed to satisfy the aspirations of a large number of *jawans* returning from the front.

The process of demobilization during the late stages of the Second World War and the immediate post-War period was overshadowed by the omnipotent economic question and the Indian National Army (INA) issue. This study reveals that the armies of war in India were demobilized haphazardly in an atmosphere not conducive to Indian expectations which, like those of the British Army after the Great War, had assumed unprecedented proportions in 1945. This fuelled discontent on a large scale. The case of the Royal Indian Navy (RIN) and the Royal Indian Air Force (RIAF), and the sympathy the INA garnered in the post-War Indian Army, proved that the failed process of demobilization, in combination with service grievances like racial discrimination in the Indian services, significantly eroded British hegemony in India even as negotiations for the Transfer of Power and Partition were taking place.[34] Demobilization was another aspect of military organization in India which the British failed to handle properly. It was one thing to raise a volunteer army of some millions to tide over an imperial crisis but quite another to satisfy its post-War demands. As a result, the unsuccessful demobilization and resettlement of troops in 1945-6 lent credibility to the predictions of officers like Cariappa who were usually not known for their 'political' views:

> When the war is over, when we have settled with the Axis Powers once and for all, and have put them in their proper places, this vastly expanded Indian Army will have to be brought down to a reasonable size compatible with the requirements of defence. There will therefore be thousands of men, who are not professional soldiers, being demobilised. On demobilisation it is not within the practical ability of ANY Government in this world to provide suitable jobs to every one of these demobilised soldiers immediately. There will be the inevitable 'disease' of unemployment with its attendant discontent. This will indeed be a very serious problem to the authorities concerned later UNLESS everyone concerned gets down to tackling the problem seriously NOW.[35] [emphasis as in original]

Chapter 4 underscores the fact that a significant number of the volunteers of 1939-45 were different men compared with the peasant recruits of 1914-18. But even if all the recruits participating in the Second World War had been peasants, it is doubtful whether the British Empire could have satisfied their land hunger in 1945. The failure of demobilization, like the drawbacks of Indianization and modernization, demonstrated the inability of the British to come to terms with an important Indian military matter in the 1940s. As a consequence, the mixing of these military causes with the explosive political situation of 1945-6 led to a significant decline of British control over the Indian services not seen since the Mutiny of 1857. This, and much more, was evident in the Naval Uprising of 1946.[36]

NOTES

1. Correlli Barnett, *The Collapse of British Power*, London, 1972, p. 79.
2. Roger Perkins, *Regiments of the Empire: A Bibliography*, Devon, 1989, lists most Indian regimental histories. The following comprise a valuable historiography: Philip Mason, *A Matter of Honour: An Account of the Indian Army, Its officers and men*, London, 1974; Victor Longer, *Red Coats to Olive Green*, New Delhi, 1974; Stephen Cohen, *The Indian Army*, New Delhi, 1971 and revised without much change in 1990; T.A. Heathcote, *The Indian Army: The Garrison of British Imperial India 1822-1922*, London, 1974 and *The Military in British India: The Development of British Land Forces in South Asia*, Manchester, 1995; Boris Mollo, *The Indian Army*, Dorset, 1981; C.C. Trench, *The Indian Army and the King's Enemies, 1900-1947*, London, 1988; Byron Farwell, *Armies of the Raj*, London, 1989; S.L. Menezes, *Fidelity and Honour: The Indian Army from the Seventeenth to the Twenty-First Century*, New Delhi, 1993; David Omissi, *The Sepoy and the Raj*, London, 1994; and the recent collection of essays by some South Asian scholars on the British Indian Army in P.S. Gupta and A. Deshpande (eds.), *The British Raj and Its Indian Armed Forces, 1857-1939*, New Delhi, 2002. Besides these are the volumes of the *Official History of the Indian Armed Forces in the Second World War 1939-45*, published by the Combined Inter-Services Historical Section India and Pakistan.
3. Brian Bond, *British Military Policy between the Two World Wars*, Oxford, 1980, pp. 60-2.

4. The limitations of the Indian Army have been examined in some detail by Stephen Peter Rosen, *Societies and Military Power: India and Its Armies*, New Delhi, OUP, 1996.
5. Arthur Marwick, *War and Social Change in the Twentieth Century*, London, 1974 offers a 'four-part analytical framework' for the historical sociology of war comprising a study of destruction, the test of society under war, the effects of social participation in war, and the psychological ramifications of war. A re-statement of the model is found in Marwick, *Total War and Social Change*, London, 1988. For an analysis of the inter-action between war, politics, society, and economy, see the Fontana volumes of Geoffrey Best, *War and Society in Revolutionary Europe, 1770-1870*, Suffolk, 1982; Victor Kiernan, *European Armies from Conquest to Collapse*, London, 1982; and Brian Bond, *War and Society in Europe, 1870-1970*, London, 1984. Geoffrey Parker, *The Military Revolution: Military Innovation and the Rise of the West, 1500-1800*, Cambridge, 1988; and Paul Kennedy, *The Rise and Fall of the Great Powers*, New York, 1987 provide a technological and economic angle to the study of military history.
6. Eric Hobsbawm, *Industry and Empire*, Harmondsworth, 1983, p. 212.
7. A forceful argument underscoring the risks of over-extension emerges from C. Barnett, *The Collapse of British Power*, London, 1972; A. Gamble, *Britain in Decline*, Boston, 1981; S. Roskill, *Naval Policy between the Wars*, London, 1968; R.P.S. Junior, *British Rearmament in the Thirties: Politics and Profit*, Princeton, 1977; B. Bond, *British Military Policy between the Two World Wars*; V. Kiernan, *European Armies from Conquest to Collapse*, London, 1982; Callender and Hinsley, *The Naval Side of British History 1485-1945*, London, 1952; M. Howard, *The Theory and Practice of War*, London, 1965; P. Kennedy, *Strategy and Diplomacy 1870-1945; Eight Studies*, London, 1986; and *The Rise and Fall of the Great Powers*, New York, 1987; and G.S. Graham, *The Politics of Naval Supremacy: Studies in British Maritime Ascendancy*, Cambridge, 1965, and *Great Britain in the Indian Ocean: A Study of Maritime Enterprise 1810-1850*, Oxford, 1967.
8. The Cardwell System of the nineteenth century was designed to provide a permanent garrison for India which normally constituted one-half of the British Regular Army. The system provided a balance between units of the British Army inside and outside Britain so that drafts to the latter could be regularly replenished and troops rotated. Over time it was found that the system worked to the benefit of overseas garrisons at the cost of the units at home. According to Bond (1980: 100), by the 1920s the Cardwell System was creating and not solving more problems.
9. See Chandler and Beckett (eds.), *The Oxford Illustrated History of the British Army*, London, 1994, for details.

10. A. Deshpande, 'The Bombay Marine: Aspects of Maritime History 1650-1850', *Studies in History*, Vol. 11, No. 2, N.S., 1995, examines these aspects of imperial history with reference to the geopolitics of the Arabian Sea region.
11. Kennedy, *Strategy and Diplomacy*, p. 16. Although there is some merit in Kennedy's assertion, British policy often changed in response to circumstances. The Afghan policy of the nineteenth and early twentieth centuries, for instance, does not fit into the scheme of appeasement. In our opinion, appeasement was most probably related to the capacity of rivals to damage British interests. This might explain how Britain chose to interact with Nazi Germany *before* the Second World War.
12. Hobsbawm, *Industry and Empire*, p. 207.
13. Gamble, *Britain in Decline*, pp. 58-9.
14. For more on this see Eric Hobsbawm, *Age of Extremes: The Short Twentieth Century*, New Delhi, 1995, *passim*.
15. For the concepts of sea power and 'military revolution', see Parker, *The Military Revolution*. A critical assessment of the 'military revolution' in the context of naval warfare in India between AD 1650 and 1800 is attempted in A. Deshpande, 'Limitations of Military Technology: Naval Warfare on the West Coast, 1650-1800', *Economic and Political Weekly*, 25 April 1992. Readers interested in the concept and history of sea power can also refer to S. Subrahmanyam, *The Career and Legend of Vasco Da Gama*, New Delhi, 1997; and the works of Paul Kennedy cited earlier.
16. D.B. Horn and M. Ransome, *English Historical Documents 1714-1783*, London, 1957, pp. 579-80, 605-8.
17. Graham, *The Politics of Naval Supremacy*, p. 18.
18. Ibid., pp. 57-8.
19. A rule adopted in 1923 according to which defence preparation was to be planned on the assumption that there would be no major military conflict in the ten years following the year in which decisions were taken.
20. The Two Power Standard had meant that the Royal Navy be as strong as the two largest navies below it. The One Power Standard implied parity with only the next best navy in the world.
21. N. Gibbs, 'British Strategic Doctrine 1918-1939', in M. Howard (ed.), *The Theory and Practice of War*, op. cit.
22. Bond, *British Military Policy*, p. 71 writes: 'Although the Army's character between the wars was greatly influenced by external circumstances such as political indifference and lack of money for new weapons and equipment, nevertheless it seems reasonable to maintain that the Service remained primarily responsible for its own style of life and morals. Like most armies at most times it was conservative but with

a strong element of the reactionary apparent in its deep-rooted reluctance to adapt to both technological developments and changes in the society in which it lived. The Army's profound attachment to horses, for example, though admirable in terms of sentiment, was professionally costly in a world increasingly dominated by the petrol engine.'

23. Barnett, *The Collapse of British Power*, p. 440.
24. R.P.S. Junior, *British Rearmament in the Thirties*, p. 19.
25. Bond, *British Military Policy*, p. 27.
26. Gibbs, 'British Strategic Doctrine', op. cit.
27. The Peel Commission Report, officially called the *Report of the Commissioners Appointed to Inquire into the Organisation of the Indian Army, 1859,* investigated military matters after the Mutiny of 1857. The Eden Commission of 1879 contemplated further reform of the Army organisation in India in the light of the Afghan experience. The most important changes in the armed forces of the British Raj between 1857 and 1939 have recently been surveyed in Gupta and Deshpande (eds.), *The British Raj and Its Indian Armed Forces*, op. cit.
28. See Cohen, 'The Untouchable Soldier: Caste, Politics and the Indian Army', *Journal of Asian Studies*, Vol. XXVIII, No. 3, May 1969; Bond, *British Military Policy*, pp. 105-6, in a scathing review of the Indian Army in the 1920s, writes that it was a 'depressing backwater still living in the atmosphere of the Victorian era. The First World War had bequeathed little to the Indian Army in the way of either new equipment or ideas.' Some economic dimensions and 'multiplier effects' of military spending in north-western Punjab especially in terms of the link between military remuneration and the creation of rural demand have been noticed, rather optimistically, in Clive Dewey, *Arrested Development in India*, Delhi, 1988.
29. Cohen, *The Indian Army.*
30. Praise of the Indian Army often appears exaggerated. For instance, D.C. Ellinwood and S.D. Pradhan (eds.), *India and World War I,* New Delhi, 1978, p. 65 fail to note the temporary nature of changes in the Army during the Great War. Instead, they claim, contrary to the assertions of this volume, that by 1939 the Indian Army 'had become capable of fighting against European armies without the assistance of any of the services of the British Army'.
31. Marwick, *War and Social Change*, p. 6, identifies four main categories of 'serious historical writing' on the effects of war, i.e. Tory, Liberal, economic, and sociological. In our view, it is extremely difficult to make neat divisions like these. This is true more in the case of countries like India where an *integral* military history is yet to be written. Barnett, *The Collapse of British Power,* is critical of the use of Indian resources in the period of total war and this goes against much of the nationalist

and imperialist thought on the matter. However, it strengthens the argument that India remained an economic backwater under British imperialist rule.

32. B. Prasad (ed.), *Official History of the Indian Armed Forces in the Second World War: Expansion of the Armed Forces and Defence Organisation 1939-45*, New Delhi, 1956; the introduction makes a similar point.
33. Bond, *British Military Policy*, pp. 20-1, mentions that mutinies occurred in the British Army soon after the Great War. There was a full-fledged mutiny at Calais (27-31 January 1919). Remedial measures, including the peaceful dissolution of the armies of war were swiftly taken by Churchill, who became Secretary of State for War and Air in January 1919. The situation had become very serious as morale and discipline plunged due to the combination of the natural though 'unrealistic' expectations of many soldiers, the proliferation of communist propaganda, and the threat of large-scale strikes by the working classes.
34. This has been explored earlier in Anirudh Deshpande, 'The Royal Indian Navy Uprising and Popular Protest, 1946', unpublished M.Phil. thesis, Centre for Historical Studies, JNU, New Delhi, 1987. Also see Deshpande, 'Sailors and the Crowd: Popular Protest in Karachi, 1946', *Indian Economic and Social History Review*, Vol. 26, No. 1, 1989, and 'Hopes and Disillusionment: Recruitment, Demobilisation and the Emergence of Discontent in the Indian Armed Forces after the Second World War', *Indian Economic and Social History Review*, Vol. 33, No. 2, 1996.
35. 'Welfare of Indian Troops', Broadcast by Brigadier Cariappa, 18 April 1945, Group XXII (Part II) Se. No. 10, Cariappa Papers, NAI. The official view of the RIN, shorn of important contradictions, is present in B. Prasad (1964). The following works have studied the RIN Mutiny in some details; S. Banerjee, *The RIN Strike*, New Delhi, 1954 is a Communist perspective on the RIN Mutiny; R.C. Dutt, *Mutiny of the Innocents*, Bombay, 1971 is a semi-autobiographical work describing the RIN Mutiny in detail; S. Singh, *Under Two Ensigns*, New Delhi, 1985 contains an interesting account of the causes of the RIN Mutiny; P.S. Gourgey, *The Indian Naval Revolt of 1946*, 1996 also presents an insider's view of the event.
36. On the popularly supported RIN Uprising see the following two articles by A. Deshpande: 'Remembering the RIN Revolt: Popular Celebration of Nationalism Fifty Years Ago', *Mainstream*, 24 February 1996, and 'Crowd Intervention in Indian History: An overview of popular resistance coterminous with the 1946 RIN Mutiny', *Mainstream*, 22 February 1992.

ONE

Reform and Retrenchment Following the Great War

INTRODUCTION

At the end of the nineteenth century the Indian armed forces were organized in accordance with the principles and recommendations of the Peel and Eden Commissions.[1] The naval forces of colonial India after 1863 comprised the Royal Indian Marine (hereafter RIM). This was essentially a survey-cum-transport service maintained on policy guidelines laid down after the Mutiny of 1857. The RIM, quite different from the Bombay Marine of the East India Company, was subordinated to the Army by the Marine Service Acts of the late nineteenth century.[2]

Between 1895 and 1914, under the lasting influence of the Army Organization Commission of 1879 assembled by Lord Lytton to suggest a reorganization of the Indian Army on the basis of the aukward experiences of the Second Afghan War (1878-80), some departments of the Indian Army were re-organized and the separate Presidency Armies were abolished. Reforms based on the Eden Commission recommendations highlighted the 'endeavour . . . to carry out the principles of segregation' by separating the Punjabis and Hindustanis in units and prohibiting the enlistment of lower-caste Hindus. The Presidency Armies were ostensibly abolished to develop efficiency and loyalty in the Indian Army. The danger of the unwieldy Bengal Army 'becoming homogeneous' due to its 'fusion into one huge body of soldiers' was cited as a reason for the reforms of 1895.[3] But in the event these reforms did not result in great efficiency.

For instance, the Sub-Committee on the Military Requirements of the Empire, chaired by Morley and having Lord Esher among its members, noticed the high rate of wastage in men and animals during the Tirah operations of 1897-8 from wounds and illness. The Tirah operations, which had displayed the manifold vulnerability of the army in India on the North-West Frontier, were described as a defeat before the Committee of Imperial Defence in 1907 by senior Indian Army officers.[4] The Tirah frontier failure of 1897-8 exposed several deficiencies of army organization in India and in 1911 Lord Hardinge thought of 'pruning' the Native Army of its useless branches and 'hopeless duffers' in the higher commissioned ranks. In fact, the Viceroy asked the Commander-in-Chief (hereafter C-in-C) not to promote these 'duffers' and wherever possible retire them on pensions. Drawing Morley's attention to the slowness of promotion in the Indian Army, he mentioned how the climate of India and long service made most officers 'quite unfit' to take command of their regiments. In Hardinge's view, which was vindicated later, a younger class of colonels was needed to secure efficiency in the Native (read Indian) Army.[5] The growing criticism of the Army in India led to the appointment of an Army in India Committee under the presidency of Field Marshal Lord Nicholson in 1912. This body was supposed to recommend changes in the numbers and constitution of the Indian military establishment in the context of contemporary Indian military obligations. However, the Great War prevented the implementation of the Nicholson Committee recommendations and postponed military reform in India.[6]

The Great War and the Russian Revolution of 1917 brought geo-political changes near India and revived the old Russophobia of the British Empire. Soon after the Armistice, the GOI spoke of the 'formidable menace of Bolshevik ideas' threatening India and Lord Chelmsford extended full support to Afghanistan against Bolshevism in 1918. Nonetheless, exaggerated British fears provoked the Third Afghan War in the summer of 1919. While the border was disturbed mass nationalism began to pose a serious challenge to colonial authority in India. The Indian demand for colonial reform and the fulfilment of British wartime promises was becoming more insistent. It was also important to involve the armed forces in the political reforms with an eye on the gradual development of self-government in India. During the Great War the Indian Army's organization and administration came under severe strain and criticism. The indictment of the

Indian Army by the Report of the Mesopotamia Commission prompted the Secretary of State Montagu to send a reform-related despatch to the GOI dated 10 August 1917. During the Afghan War of 1919 'allegations of incompetency in medical and transport arrangements' were levelled against the GOI and this remained unmitigated by the fact that in 1919 the GOI was generally 'passing through a period of great difficulty and acid criticism'.[7] The experience of the Expeditionary Force in Mesopotamia had been wretched. The Force 'D', for instance, suffered the 'crime of non-provision of transport' and a beriberi epidemic. Matters were made worse and operations jeopardized due to the 'appalling sick rate from debility and scurvy'. In fact, 'acid criticisms' of the Army medical services had been made as early as 1915 without effect, and ultimately predictions that during prolonged deployment the troops would suffer from cholera, typhus, and paratyphoid came true.[8]

After the Third Afghan War the GOI made it clear that for some time large forces would be kept on the North-West Frontier. It was also stated that 'money in unprecedented quantities' would be spent on the improvement of Frontier roads and railways to help future military operations. But first this money had to be found and the Indian Army modernized to execute the new Frontier policy. In the meantime public criticism of the Indian Army had assumed alarming proportions. As a prelude to the setting up of the Army in India Committee under Lord Esher, the press drew public attention to another 'Mesopotamian muddle' ostensibly perpetrated by the Army HQs on the Frontier. Consequently, the GOI was forced to admit after the Afghan War that the press coverage of the badly planned Afghan campaign had 'very seriously affected the reputation of the Indian Government both in Great Britain and in India'.[9] The recommendations of the Mesopotamia Commission had raised questions of 'great complexity and magnitude' and the British Government wanted to investigate matters related to the Indian Army before reforms in India were seriously contemplated. The great impact of the Mesopotamia Commission's Report on British policy can be gauged by the fact that in 1918 the War Office was even thinking of assuming direct administrative control over the Indian Army.[10] In short, the Indian experience of the Great War, the 'Mesopotamian muddle', and the criticism of the Indian Army during the Afghan campaign of 1919 together led to the creation of the Army in India Committee of 1919. The first section of this chapter examines its report. The second analyses the reaction of the GOI to the *ECR*, the third looks at the retrenchment which reduced reform to an academic matter in the 1920s, and the fourth concludes the chapter.

THE ACCENT OF REFORM

The Esher Committee (EC) considered the financial and political conditions prevalent in India in 1919 before submitting its report.[11] In tune with the Montagu-Chelmsford reforms its suggestions kept in mind the proposed but still largely theoretical evolution of India towards Dominion Status. Since the armed forces were to be the ultimate guarantors of any reform scheme in India, the EC recommended improvements in the internal military administration of India primarily to make the armed forces contented:

> We are impressed by the necessity of maintaining this instrument, placed as it always must and should be in the hands of the civil power, in the highest state of efficiency. Whatever form the future Government of India may take, however it may be democratised, and whatever advance may be made on the part of the various sections of the Indian community towards national and imperial unity, the army cannot fail to remain a vital attribute of government in the hands of the dominant authority.[12]

The EC wanted the Indian authorities to establish a system which would be simple, economical, and 'adaptable, without undue friction and disturbance' in conditions imposed by a world war because the obvious shortcomings of the Indian military organization had surfaced during 1914-18.[13] Simultaneously, domestic pressures were influencing British policy in India. Reforms were necessary because new political factors such as the rising labour question and growing trade unionism in India were threatening production in the Government factories and 'indeed, all sources of production'.[14] Since the nineteenth century new military standards had evolved in Europe and the Great War underlined the importance of making countries militarily self-sufficient. Men's eyes had 'opened to the vastness of the requirement of modern warfare, to the necessity of organising the Empire's resources in peace time in such a way as to be capable, on the outbreak of war, of expansion with a rapidity and to an extent never contemplated before'.[15] To fight a future war India needed modern transport and communications, a professional military establishment, and above all industrial development. But all this had to be achieved under British hegemony which was dependent upon the continuation of loyalty in the Indian armed forces and the happiness of the British regiments stationed in India. In pursuit of this the EC was 'convinced of the necessity of raising the standard of living for British and Indian soldiers of all ranks' because the 'spirit of both' was 'to be maintained at the high level which the interests of the Indian Empire' demanded.[16]

The EC suggested a reform of the military organization in India in the context of Indian political conditions and infrastructure. Since political unrest in India was growing, to counter it effectively the military had to develop a closer liaison with civilian authority. Reports had made it clear that despite the regimental tradition Indian soldiers could be influenced by hostile propaganda. Their experiences in Egypt, Palestine, Mesopotamia, and Persia, 'where movements and influences hostile to the British Government in India' were at work, called for alertness in military and civil intelligence about potential mutinies. Hence, to preclude rebellion it was necessary to quickly inform the civil authorities about 'an unhealthy spirit among the troops'.[17] The EC took a serious view of several 'seditious and revolutionary movements in India' which were undermining the fidelity of Indian troops. In this connection it was satisfactorily noted that copies of the Fortnightly Reports prepared by the civil administration of each province were being forwarded regularly to the Army authorities at the HQ, command, division, and sometimes even to brigade levels.[18]

At the end of the War, discontent in the British and Indian Armies was rampant. Service conditions in the British Army, which withdrew into a 'self-conscious isolation' after the War, became exceedingly unattractive between the wars. The peace-training routine and regimental life with the accent on turn out, drill, and polish came back after the War, which was widely perceived as an abnormal event in any case. Conditions of promotion improved late and far-reaching proposals were announced only after the purge of the Army Council under Hore-Belisha in 1937 and the Willingdon Committee's examination of the issue in 1939. The 1920s were marked by a shortage of young men from the gentry to fill the 650 commissions offered each year due to the poor public image of the Army. Before 1914 an average of 80 university graduates were commissioned each year but by 1924 this figure had fallen to 12.[19]

In India, as the *ECR* observed, discontent was caused no doubt 'in great part due to the war and its aftermath, such as frequent transfers, the prevalence of high prices, and the fluctuations in the exchange value of the rupee, and also to changes in the political organisation in India'.[20] Service grievances within the officer corps were serious and had to 'be removed at once'. There were discrepancies in pay between the Indian and the British Armies. Red tape had lengthened during the War and delays were occurring in giving the men their 'just dues'. Nothing less than a 'complete revision' and simplification of procedures was needed to restore confidence amongst the troops. Service conditions in India belonged to the nineteenth century, the state of accommodation and hospitals left much to be desired, and rank-and-file grumbling about these was 'legitimate'.[21] Officers of the Indian Army generally believed that their service was inferior to that of the British Army and quite obviously technologically less efficient. Furthermore, the problems faced by the Indian Army in Mesopotamia and Palestine attached a 'stigma' to Army administration in India and justified this widely prevalent opinion. Discrimination faced by British officers of the Indian Army competing with others in the European theatre was real.[22] The officers were also angry because all important proposals were sent by the GOI to the Secretary of State in Council for approval and this caused needless delay. The military authorities in India, for their part, had adopted 'an attitude of undue reticence' towards service conditions.[23] The Indian Army had become so unattractive that reluctance on part of the good Sandhurst cadets, supported by their parents, to elect for it was openly expressed in England. More alarmingly, such tendencies were 'particularly noticeable in the case of those families' which had 'a long and honourable connection with the Indian Army'.[24] Therefore, improvements in accomodation, health care, travel, pay, and allowances were deemed necessary for British officers of the Indian Army.

A 'conspicuous difference' existed between the standards of British officers and the British NCOs and their families. Crowded, ill-ventilated troop decks in troopships were often situated below the water line. Family quarters were cramped, afforded little privacy, militated against the 'spirit of the times', and exposed Englishwomen to Indians. This deprecated imperial prestige significantly.[25] In the tropical climate of India several improvements were necessary to make Indian barracks approximate to acceptable British standards. Soldiers, who could no longer be treated as servants, demanded proper lighting, space, libraries and writing, and spacious bathrooms. The accentuation of class differences between Britons had to be discouraged and improvements in barracks could not be 'postponed without the risk of undesirable consequences'.[26] Married soldiers were really hard-pressed because their families lived in 'conditions not differing much, except in the matter of fresh air, from slum lodgings in London'.[27] But in England a system of making military service socially tolerable had already been inaugurated in Aldershot and the King had written to General Henry S. Rawlinson (C-in-C) about this: 'I have been struck by the advance made in providing for the recreation and advancement of the troops. The Queen and I were especially pleased to find that steps are being taken to include the married families in these schemes. The provision of clubs for the married women and playgrounds for the children is a new and admirable development.'[28]

It was noted with some accuracy and concern that in the absence of recreational facilities many younger soldiers were falling prey to external sources of amusement. This endangered the myth of self-sufficiency cultivated by regimental life. Hence, to reassert ideological control the demand of soldiers for clubs like the officers' gymkhanas could not be overlooked. Furthermore, the development of sports and cinemas attached to clubs and dancing rooms were culturally significant for European socializing:

> We wish, in conclusion, to point out that the outlook of the present-day soldiers upon life is widely different from that of their predecessors of the old army. They have neither their deep-seated discipline nor their long-suffering patience. They and their wives look for a higher level of

comfort and a somewhat different class of recreation. Their reasonable aspirations must be met, and their idiosyncrasies must be sympathetically studied, if they are to be a contented army while serving in India.[29]

The British Army was a counterpoise against civil and military unrest in India and had to be satisfied irrespective of the costs involved. However, as the *ECR* noted with concern, the Great War had deeply influenced the Indian soldiers and their experiences in Europe had affected their views on a number of important social and cultural issues. Soon after the war, with dim promotion prospects, they began to feel the brunt of rising prices. During the War, with many nationalist leaders urging Indians to volunteer, military service had assumed a much wider significance which was reflected in the tremendous expansion of the Army during 1914-18. Simultaneously, due to government promises expectations in the ranks had risen and Indian officers had started comparing themselves unfavourably with their brothers in the civil service and the police. Therefore, an increase of pay for Indian officers, i.e. VCOs on conditions of efficiency and the discretion of their commanding officers, criteria not applied to British personnel, was urged. The NCOs incurred heavy expenses on new outfits to the tune of Rs. 250 in the infantry and Rs. 400 in the cavalry on promotion to jamadar rank whereas their pay was only Rs. 60 and Rs. 70 respectively. This often led to indebtedness at the hands of moneylenders, and to the cost of *izzat,* for years.[30] The GOI was asked to subsidize these officers whose pensions were also to be calculated as a certain proportion of their pay.[31]

Even the badges of rank expressed racial discrimination and caused discontent amongst Indians. In 1920 it was impossible to distinguish the difference between Indian officers holding the King's Commission (KC), and were therefore entitled to salutes from British as well as Indian soldiers, and similar British officers. It was also difficult to recognize an Indian Company officer entitled to salutes only from Indian soldiers. Uniform badges, with parity between Indian and British KCOs, were desirable if racial friction in the day-to-day functioning of the Army was to be avoided. Up to 1919 Indian officers were disallowed soldier servants *by regulation*. Obviously such archaic rules had been laid down to initially preserve British exclusivity in the services.

To lessen resentment servants had to be permitted for status-conscious upper-class Indian KCOs and regulations needed standardization.[32] Social consciousness amongst Indians of all ranks was growing and this was reflected in the VCOs' desire to educate their sons. An insidious movement of upward mobility was to be witnessed in such contemporary demands. Indian VCOs, who came from villages, openly criticized the elitist bias in colonial education which was engineered to produce the Indian KCOs:

> Our investigations have left us in no doubt that the education of their sons is a matter which is greatly troubling the minds of all Indian officers today. They see the sons of wealthy zamindars and others reaping the advantages of an education which costs more than they can afford, and which enables the former to go up for Sandhurst and a King's Commission, or to compete for the many good civil appointments now open to Indians. They represent with much force that, as Indians are now admitted to positions in the army which were not open to themselves, they have a right to expect that Government will not overlook their services and will make it possible for their sons to enter where the doors are shut to them.[33]

These demands had to be taken seriously because the progeny of these 'gentlemen' were perceived as good recruiting material for the future. It would be 'to the benefit of their country if the sons of these brave and loyal gentlemen' were 'given opportunities to fit themselves to compete on something approaching equal terms with the sons of the more wealthy classes'.[34] However, this was easier said than done in the two decades following the Great War. In the inter-War period the military finances of the Raj continued to deteriorate and the use of limited funds was complicated further by the cultural stereotypes guiding military policy in general in India. The lighting of barracks, and the British attitude towards it, makes for a good example. As late as 1927 the cost of the electrification of Indian barracks was estimated to be one lakh rupees. Considering this the idea was dropped and instead lamps, with their oil allowance, were transferred to the Indian lines from the British units which were being provided electricity. The electrification of Indian lines had to await a new re-building plan. However, apart from the argument for economy, it was stated at the time by C-in-C Birdwood that since Indian soldiers never complained about the lighting arrangements in their barracks, the problem could not be considered a part of service grievances in the same way as pay, pension, and leave. Irwin, with complacency barely hidden, rejoined in observing that Indian soldiers hardly read anything and were accustomed to village lighting arrangements. In his opinion electricity was of no use to the Indians: 'It is indeed doubtful if the Indian soldier will read much, even when he gets electric light in his barracks.'[35]

Before 1920 a scheme had been prepared to establish a Kitchener College to educate the sons of Indian officers to enable them to gain a direct promotion to jamadar rank. It was thought that incidentally this college would prepare some bright pupils for Sandhurst and indirectly reserve the Indian KCO ranks for the trusted sons of the Army. The idea was to keep the 'political' Indian middle class out of the military services. The EC wanted these reforms carried out quickly or else 'the earnest desire of the risaldars or subedars, to see a road by which their sons can climb higher than the fathers' would 'be doomed to disappointment'.[36] A network of such military colleges to serve vested interests in the Army could be developed later. Indian members of the EC argued for an Indian Sandhurst but finally agreed with the majority that the time for it was not ripe in 1919-20.[37]

Even the *jawans* were demanding better education. It was well known that Army schools were inefficient, there was no education policy regarding regimental schools, and the teachers in regimental schools were ill paid. The headmasters drew a paltry Rs. 25 (2 pounds, 10 shillings) a month. The grant for textbooks, prizes, stationery, and other equipment was only Rs. 30 a month. Accommodation, libraries, and lighting were conspicuous by their absence, with Rs. 10 per month being sanctioned for these. Obviously an army of peasants dependent upon village networks for employment had neglected education as an avenue of upward social mobility. As politics assumed greater social importance, and nationalism became popular even in rural areas, it began to be understood that badly paid teachers could undermine loyalty in the Army. In fact, the EC neatly concluded that there was 'little to prevent the regimental school being a centre for discontent and even disloyalty'.[38]

But alarm gave rise to unrealistic policy prescriptions. The adoption of a system similar to that prevalent in England was recommended. Since education was considered integral to military training, the commanding officers were asked to take charge of regimental education. An Indian wing of the proposed Army Education Corps was required with the personnel comprising Indian officers and NCOs trained as teachers to foster invaluable traditions. In fact, education had to be made a *recruitment incentive* for a peasantry facing limited opportunities in a colonial economy. However, the EC could not anticipate that the armed forces, with budgetary constraints ruling supreme during the inter-War years, would themselves curtail the opportunities for the peasantry.[39]

The economic demands of Indian officers were considered equally important. The VCOs, for instance, maintained that family pensions were insufficient to keep their widows 'from the borders of starvation'. Significantly, the social criteria for granting family pensions in India and Britain were different. In England the pension was given to the widow. In India it was a 'contribution to the family generally by way of compensation for the loss of one of its bread winners'. According to the EC, those who wanted Indian pensions to be placed on par with English pensions failed 'to recognise the connection of the Indian family pension with the land, and its corporate organisation and system of mutual support'.[40] Much of this had changed in recent times. During the War the number of widows and orphans had risen substantially, especially in Punjab, economic conditions had worsened and in numerous instances older customs had failed to safeguard dependants from poverty and hunger. Therefore, in 1919-20 the government was asked to shoulder the responsibilities earlier handled by the Indian joint family. That the government knew so little of Indian social institutions was cause enough to correct official misconceptions:

> The veil which hides Indian family life from outside intrusion is a bar to that perfect knowledge which should precede decision; but we feel strongly that any government which sends a married soldier of any race to a war in which he loses his life should be actually responsible for providing a pension sufficient to keep his widow and children from want, and should not make its contribution dependent upon the intricacies of a family system into which it cannot penetrate.[41]

Pay, due to post-War inflation, was a crucial issue in 1920. The *jawan's* pay had only been Rs. 11 per month since 1911. Added to this, he received a monthly war bonus of Rs. 4 and those serving overseas and in the NWFP received an additional field *batta* of Rs. 5 per month. Thus, some jawans received Rs. 15 and some Rs. 20 a month. Before the War soldiers got free rations only on service but during and after it rations became forever free. The much mentioned war bonus was actually declared in 1918 and it represented 'the increase in prices, or the fall in purchasing power, of the sepoy's basic rate of pay'. Furthermore, this bonus was neither permanent nor incorporated in the overall pay. Making this permanent but ruling out further increases was the paternal recommendation of the Esher Committee.[42] The cost of maintaining a sepoy was officially calculated in the following manner. Before 1917 when the monthly pay was only Rs. 11, Rs. 3.80 of this was calculated as the cost of food. Sepoys received cash compensation when prices of staples rose. Hence, Rs. 7.20 was the net pay of the sepoy.[43] During the War free rations were granted but the troops retained the allowance of Rs. 3.80 originally earmarked for food. Later a war bonus of Rs. 4 was declared, making the total pay Rs. 15.00. This was almost double the net pay received in 1914. The real cost of living was higher. Rations at 1919-20 prices came to Rs. 14.00 per month for a sepoy and this meant that actually the government was spending Rs. 29.00 (14 + 15) on each soldier per month. Feeding the men was the government's responsibility and jawans were not likely to sympathetically consider the official calculations based on 1919-20 prices:

> The Indian soldier has seen the world during the last six years in a way he never has before. His ideas of comfort have risen, and he has acquired certain tastes to which he was previously a stranger. He is well aware of what has been done for the British soldier in the way of amelioration of conditions of life and pay since the war began, and he is now apt to compare his own pay with that of his British comrades.[44]

Despite rank-and-file grumbling recruiting did not languish in 1918-19. But this did not merit complacence because recruitment continued due to worsening domestic conditions. However, new factors began working against the armed forces. Many Indian soldiers, especially the Sikhs, were becoming mechanics in large numbers. This led the EC to ruefully observe that 'pay far beyond that which the army can offer is obtainable now by Indians with even a small knowledge of machinery'. This reference to the competition between the armed forces and civilian society for technicians remained valid even during and after the Second World War.[45] Several enterprising Indians were also taking advantage of lucrative openings in the Far East and trends indicated that this outflow of men trained in the services would continue. India had 'before her a period of industrial and agricultural' growth which would attract thousands of young men of the 'martial classes'.[46] The fear of losing the 'martial classes' was paramount because the official mind could not come to grips with the fact, despite the experience of the War, that ultimately the supply of recruits and later more suitable recruits would dry up in the favoured classes. The government gave several reasons for not raising the pay of *jawans* beyond the 1918 levels. It assumed that a pay double of what was given up to 1916 was sufficient for the soldiers' needs. The increase in the cost of living was, rather hopefully, considered transient. It was observed that all sepoys were not married and in future the proportion of unmarried sepoys would grow. It was never contemplated that the pay of a youth of 18 to 25 'should suffice for the entire maintenance of a wife and family, who in practice usually rely for support largely upon their share in an agricultural holding, cultivated by other members of the family'.[47] More convincingly, however, finance militated against a raise because it 'would inevitably result in an increase to the pay of other employees of the Government such as police and forest subordinates and the like'.[48] Indian revenues were in no position to shoulder this burden.

Nonetheless, the Esher Committee, informed by the peculiar conditions of 1920 as it was, called for a raise. An increase at a time when political agitators were trying to undermine service loyalties was justified in its view. Improved service conditions were imperative to keep the martial races from lucrative civilian jobs in future. In fact, long before 1919 a reconstruction programme for the troops' lines had been initiated by General Sir O'Moore Creagh and its speedy implementation was recommended by the EC in the disturbed 1920s. Significantly enough, the two Indians on the EC, following the changes in the British Army, wanted the abolition of corporal punishment in the Army. The EC, however, concluded that Army HQ would hopefully tackle the question with sympathy![49]

The scope of the Esher recommendations was broad and included the RIM. In fact, before the EC took up the matter of military reform in India Lord Hardinge in 1911 had been hopeful of obtaining economies in the Indian Marine with an eye on 'future shrinking revenue'.[50] Soon after the Great War, Admiral of the Fleet Lord Jellicoe had carried out an extensive survey of Indian naval defence and needs in April 1919. In 1920 the Indian Marine Service Act of 1884 defining and establishing the auxiliary nature of the RIM was in force. The Marine Regulations of 1886 and 1918 did little to change matters and India had no navy virtually from 1863 when the Indian Navy of the East India Company was formally abolished.[51] In 1920 the Marine had 225 officers of all ranks in its executive and engineering branches nominated from training ships and the mercantile marine by the Secretary of State. The Marine managed the substantial dockyard of Bombay and the smaller ones at Kidderpore and Mandalay. It also handled the work of marine survey, a legacy of the nineteenth century. The officers of the service had their commissions signed by the King and recognized by the Admiralty. The 'subordinate part' of the service comprised some 2,000 Indians who manned the ships and numerous others in charge of the several dockyards.[52]

In 1919 Lord Jellicoe advocated the expansion of the RIM into an Indian Navy in the near future. The GOI considered this proposal but was unable to implement it although it was understood that in future the RIM would have to be expanded even to 'undertake certain fresh responsibilities' like policing the Persian Gulf. The Director of the service in 1920 was a senior officer of the Royal Navy (RN) and was nominated by the Admiralty the usual concurrence of the Secretary of State. The Director submitted his proposals to the Secretary in the Army Department, who in turn as a soldier took orders on Marine questions from the Army member. The Admiralty was not responsible for training the service even though according to law it could take over the RIM during war if necessary. The budget of the RIM was controlled by the Army authorities as a separate section of the military budget. The making of Indian naval matters completely subservient to the Admiralty and the Army had developed during the nineteenth century with the abolition of the East India Company.[53] The EC wanted the

Admiralty to help the service keeping in mind the larger imperial interests. Since the RIM was an Indian service paid for and maintained by the GOI, the EC wanted its Director to be a rear admiral on the active list having the status of a secretary to the GOI. In this way the Director subordinated to the C-in-C would simultaneously have direct access to the Viceroy. This change was ostensibly suggested to make administrative reform in future easy.

Since the nineteenth century the system of employing and maintaining lascar crews had remained unchanged. The syrang (native petty officer) often controlled the lascars and it was his responsibility to see that the men assembled rapidly and performed their duties. Syrangs as jobbers and caste seniors established a code of conduct for the crews and were important enough to perform as gunners in the latter's absence.[54] They performed the role of VCOs in the Marine. In the Bombay Dockyard Establishment in 1930 syrangs were earning Rs. 80 per month in the Artificer grades. In the Marine Transport Establishment of Bombay and Karachi lascar pay ranged from Rs. 15 to Rs. 31 per month. Sukhanis and tindals, placed between lascars and syrangs, usually received Rs. 56 and Rs. 40 per month respectively. At the lowest level were the topasses and lascar boys who now performed menial duties and were no longer soldier-sailors as their names suggested. Placed slightly above these were the stokers and lascars called native seamen. Surprisingly, the rates paid to the syrangs and the tindals were equal to those paid to English petty officers and leading seamen respectively.[55] This underlines their importance to British shipping in the East in general.

Obvious improvements had taken place since the Great War. A comparison with the rates of 1917 shows that the pay of syrangs, who were also given pensions since 1871, improved between 1917 and 1930 rising from Rs. 30-40 to Rs. 80 a month. Lascars received Rs. 25 per month in 1917 which was more than what most sepoys got in 1919. The pay of sukhanis and tindals remained the same between 1917 and 1930 although in some establishments tindal rates improved slightly. On the whole, the wages of syrangs, tindals, and skilled artificers rose over time whereas the pay of lascars and topasses showed stagnation.[56] This underscores the growing significance of technicians and their bargaining power in terms of remuneration in general between the two World Wars.

For reform the RIM, essentially a nineteenth-century organization like the Indian Army, had to be 'radically altered' and 'much improved'. In 1919 recruitment was unsystematic. Stokers and crews were engaged haphazardly in Bombay and usually syrangs were asked to collect crews. Since it became difficult to assemble crews after the war, the setting up of a regular recruitment agency with its HQ at Ratnagiri, presumably to continue traditional recruitment, was thought crucial. Lads had to be taken on young for training. Pay, pension, leave rules, and maintaining reserves had to be considered afresh. Experimental Indianization was also called for, with suitable candidates availing of education in the higher branches of seamanship and marine engineering. It was recommended that the RIM finally handle the Persian Gulf and free the expensive British sailors from duty. The Esher Committee, echoing Malcolm's sentiment of the early nineteenth century, was confident that the 'Indian, trained and led by British officers, will be a match for any enemy that he is likely to encounter there'.[57]

The contentment of the armed forces in India was the guarantee of British rule in the subcontinent and the British strategic position in the East in general but the achievement of higher military standards in India not only called for substantial resources but also a political will to overrule several historical continuities governing the armed forces in 1919. The EC recommendations touched upon a broad agenda of reform thought necessary after the War. But in the first place the Esher recommendations were predicated upon a naive hope that a liberal climate after the War would create the space and official mentality for military reform in India. However, given India's political, industrial, and agrarian conditions in 1919-20 years would pass before the Esher recommendations could even be taken seriously. Second, on several issues the Committee upheld the *status quo* and proceeded on the lines laid down by British fears and colonial caution. Thus, on the politically crucial issue of Indianizing the officer corps, the ideology and policy of recruitment from the 'martial races', or even the simple demand to abolish corporal punishment in the Army, the Esher Committee displayed a lack of foresight and firm commitment. Divided

Indian opinion in the Committee probably helped this slackness. For instance, Sir Krishna G. Gupta took the nationalist position on Indianization which stated that Dominion Status would be incomplete without Indianization. In this view, the post-1857 British distrust of Indians and the consequent reliance on the 'martial classes' had to give way to a growing confidence in the educated middle classes. Gupta went far enough to advocate an end to the concept of the martial races. This was consistent with the nationalist demand that in training and education self-sufficiency was of paramount importance to India because the import of men and materials from England constituted an economic drain. The 'only way of introducing economy without impairing efficiency' was to gradually 'increase the Indian element in the ranks as well as superior positions'.[58] The views of Sir Umar Hayat Khan, a conservative Punjabi landowner and a social representative of the officially favoured Punjabi Musalmans, presented a contrast. He tersely stated that because reform could not be allowed to undermine military tradition, the right type of men had to be sent up to Sandhurst. Partaking of current Russophobia, he also inveighed against a possible combination of the military, revolutionary movements, and foreign aggression against the Raj in the near future. Hence, the wavering sepoys at all times had to be stiffened with British troops. Alluding to the Bengali Battalion, he also suggested that the policy of recruiting the 'martial classes' was time tested and sound.[59]

THE GOI AND THE ESHER RECOMMENDATIONS

The Esher recommendations provoked a great deal of scepticism in India, and Keith Jeffery has drawn our attention to the tension they caused between London and Delhi.[60] According to the GOI, in 1920-1 'Indian opinion did not understand that the structure contemplated by the Esher Committee, in which the Army in India was to play its part as one unit of a co-ordinated whole, had not yet come into full existence'.[61] This was largely true because no concrete plan of arranging India in a system of self-governing Dominions had emerged prior to the framing of the Esher recommendations. There were policy statements no doubt, but no real movement towards the implementation of war-time policies. In these circumstances the omnipresent fear of the GOI losing control over the Army in India and becoming saddled with unaffordable increases in military spending naturally arose. Soon after receiving the *ECR*, a Committee of the Indian Legislature examined it and, as a result of this, the Legislative Assembly in 1921 passed some important resolutions defining the attitude of the GOI towards Army reform in the 1920s. The Assembly, also under considerable Indian pressure, clearly stated that the primary purpose of the Army in India was the defence of, and the maintenance of internal order within, India. For other purposes 'the obligations resting on India should be no more onerous than those resting on the self-governing dominions, and should be undertaken subject to the same conditions as are applicable to those areas'. The Assembly also recommended the deployment of the Indian Army outside India only 'with the previous consent of the Governor General in Council in very grave emergencies'.[62]

These Assembly Resolutions can be traced to the mounting public criticism of military expenditure in India, the growing demand for Indianization, and the pressure brought upon the Raj by the anti-Rowlatt uprising and the Non-Cooperation Movement. The discussions on the Esher recommendations in the Viceroy's Council preceding 1921-2 also say a lot about the predicament of a besieged government as far as military reform was concerned. The Viceroy circulated the copy of Parts I and II of the *ECR* with his comments to the members of his council in March 1920. Admittedly, the conditions in India were not 'normal' when the *ECR* was received by the GOI and on several points in it a conflict of opinion was noticeable between London and Delhi.[63]

The recommendations of the Esher Committee were based on the following three principles of policy. The first was the assertion of the control of the GOI over Indian military affairs. The second was the importance given to imperial affairs in the reckoning of Indian defence, and the third was the exercise of a considered influence of the Imperial General Staff upon the 'military policy' of the GOI. These principles, except the first, led several critics in the GOI to suspect the designs of the Esher Committee. It was thought the *ECR* was an 'attempt to deprive India of control of her own armed forces and to make them a tool for Imperial aggression in Central Asia'. Later on the GOI also admitted that the 'phraseology of certain parts of the Report combined with some isolated *obiter dicta* unessential to the main project, was such as to lend these suspicions an air of verisimilitude'.[64] Indian political circles misconstrued the central argument of the *ECR*, which stated that Indian military policy after 1918 could not be divorced from the general coordination of Imperial resources, requirements, and organization if India was to become a self-governing Dominion in the British Commonwealth of nations. In the debate on the Esher recommendations, the GOI defended itself on the basis of the fundamental British principle 'of control by the civil power over military matters', although there was little in the *ECR* to suggest a replay of the Curzon-Kitchener debate in the 1920s. The Indian political position on military matters was also important because 'under no circumstances, of course' could 'Indian political leaders be expected to look with favour upon any policy which seems, however remotely, either to deprive the Indian Government, over which they have legitimate aspirations for control, of unfettered direction of the Indian Army; or to hint at the possible employment of Indian forces for ends in which India herself is but partly concerned'. These disapprovals were also caused by the military conditions in the troubled Middle East:

> The troubles in Mesopotamia, and the rumoured agreement for the reorganisation of Persia seemed in India to involve the continued employment for an indefinite period of Indian troops overseas. . . . Hence, it was that the recommendations of the first part of the Esher Committee's Report, which had as their aim the determination of the place of the Army in India in a future scheme for the military organisation of the whole Commonwealth, excited a storm of reprobation.[65]

The GOI could hardly consider matters of military reform in India without keeping an eye on its treasury in the first place and misunderstandings regarding military finance between the GOI and the Secretary of State dated back to the pre-Great War period. For instance, in 1908, following the Mowatt Committee's recommendations regarding the reduction of military expenditure in India, the Viceroy had criticized the Secretary of State's interference in Indian military expenditure. Trouble arose over expenditure undertaken on redistribution and accommodation of troops and other scheduled measures. In his criticism the Viceroy mentioned that the despatch from the Secretary of State to him regarding these matters in 1907 'wholly abrogated' the building powers of the GOI, which were ordinarily limited to 67,000 pounds, in the redistribution schemes then being practised by the Indian Army. The Secretary of State even wanted to approve sanctioned measures, arrived at after lengthy deliberations between London and the GOI, and the Viceroy objected to this.[66]

In 1921 in the press and the Central Legislature questions concerning India's defence assumed great importance because of the 'financial stringency' of the immediate post-War years. The popular demand for economy in the armed forces was rising also because the initial total grant for the military in 1921-2 amounted to some Rs. 622 million, which was a very high proportion of the expenditure of and the revenue raised by the Central Government.[67] On the other hand, attempts at effecting savings in the services were failing. For instance, due to the efforts of Lord Rawlinson a saving of Rs. 12.9 million was effected in the established charges of the Army in the financial year 1921-2. But the cost of operations in Waziristan, consequent upon the Third Afghan War, 'swallowed up this saving' and boosted spending further, with the result that revised expenditure on military requirements during 1921-2 actually came to Rs. 650 million.[68] Furthermore, the hardpressed GOI was continuously being asked to increase military expenditure on hospitals, etc., which was desirable but, as a member pointed out, 'beyond' the government's 'capacity to finance'. The member also noted with some anger that the demands of the India Office on the subject of pensions for British officers in the Indian Army betrayed 'a spirit of great extravagance'.[69] The GOI understood the omnipresent need to reform but in future things were going to be difficult. Hailey touched the nub of the problem in observing that: 'I believe that Army finance and Army economy are going to be far more difficult subjects in the future, and that it is necessary to consider now an organisation which will be effective in the new order of things.'[70]

In London the *ECR* occupied the top priority in the immediate post-War milieu conditioned by the overriding Imperial and military questions. While the GOI discussed its several parts between March and August 1920, the report in full was submitted to the British Government in June 1920. Parts III and IX were submitted on 22 June 1920 and their copies were despatched by mail to the GOI two days later, with the Secretary of State urging the GOI to expedite the process of forming its views. In India delays were occurring because of a growing nationalist movement which demanded government attention. After long and careful deliberations the GOI finally expressed its opinion on Parts I and II of the report in August 1920. In London, on the other hand, opinion was growing to get the *ECR* published as soon as possible.[71]

The Great War imposed on India 'a vastly enhanced permanent military liability' and changed its military position in colonial defence and strategy. 'These added imperial liabilities in effect' represented some 33 per cent of the aggregate military liabilities of the GOI and rendered 'the Army in India an Imperial rather than a purely Indian Force'.[72] Implied in this reading of imperial defence was the Indian search for Imperial resources. Furthermore, this interpretation of contemporary military affairs was underscored by the inadequacy of the Indian military organization in meeting post-1918 demands. The 'apparent lack of co-ordination as between policy, financial liability, and military resources' had led to a series of orders and counter-orders causing confusion at the Army HQ besides leaving the troops disturbed. This experience supported the GOI's case and it demanded more autonomy in Indian military matters although it was willing to bend on crucial policy and strategic issues:

> While, therefore, on questions of policy and strategy we desire a greater degree of direction and control by the Imperial authorities, on *matters affecting the execution of that policy such as the size of and nature of the forces to be provided, their organisation and the system of maintenance and reliefs, we consider that the Government of India should be the deciding authority in order to obviate the interminable delay which occurs under the present system and also because such matters directly affect the finances of the country.*[73] (emphasis added)

But there were areas of industrial and defence planning in which the GOI found the Esher recommendations interesting. For instance, the provision of armaments from within India, to save money spent on imports, was one of them. Since it was widely known in India that the Indian armed forces could not entirely depend on largely obsolete government ordnance, the GOI welcomed the Esher emphasis on the connection between industrial development and military strength. In fact, the Army was supposed to generate a lot of demand for Indian industry. It was believed that the Indian services would also deal in 'the greatest extent possible with private firms'. This was in line with the contemplated reform which sought to 'develop the industries of the country and to render India self supporting'.[74] However, as the 1920s unfolded, much of this was exposed as wishful thinking.

While the Secretary of State, apparently unaware of the problems the *ECR* had raised in India, was pressing for the publication of the report, the GOI took its time over it. To begin with, opposition arose from an overstretched Indian Army. The C-in-C, General Munro, thought that the early publication of the report was 'calculated to force the hands of Government' and, in the peculiar conditions prevalent in India after 1918, this could hardly be overlooked. The GOI had to keep its political options open in a troubled India and, hence, a premature commitment to new policy had to be avoided at all costs. Further, several aspects of the relationship between Imperial foreign policy and the Indian armed forces had to be discussed afresh in the peculiar scenario of the 1920s before reform could be attempted. The war had taught the GOI new military lessons in comparison with which the usual frontier campaigns or a limited war against Afghanistan appeared simple affairs. According to Munro, matters had become more complicated because London usually ignored the GOI while formulating and executing Imperial strategy. This was most unfortunate because more often than not the Indian Army, which was the GOI's armed preserve, was crucial to this strategy. In future the ratio between Imperial policy objectives and requisite armed strength to achieve them had to be understood. As Munro summed up: 'That policy should presumably bear some relation to the latter's (India's) military strength, and if this be true, we ought to be in much closer touch with the Home authorities and some understanding should be arrived at with them as to the role, within the Empire, which India may be called upon to discharge.'[75] After 1914 India had emerged as 'the portion of the Empire' which possessed 'the largest military reserves'. The government commanding them wanted a certain degree of autonomy on issues of policy and strategy.[76]

The increasing deployment of Indian troops outside India, entailing massive financial and social costs, was also causing concern in India. The Imperial government invariably requisitioned Indian troops in countries where neither India nor Indians had interests without truly appreciating the problems this caused for the GOI.[77] Such risks were not faced by the British Army which was a conscript army and better equipped. In comparison the compulsions behind volunteer service were entirely different in India. Costly incentives, which endangered tight budgets, had to be given to volunteers serving abroad. It was difficult to maintain recruitment standards when demands rose and this threatened military traditions. Indian opinion and the views of large bodies of *jawans* opposed the prolonged deployment of Indian troops abroad. In Mesopotamia, and elsewhere, Indians had fought in extremely harsh conditions but were denied the right to settle. This was fodder for large-scale discontent. For publicized reasons various political associations as well as sections of the Indian press opposed the stationing of Indian troops in Islamic countries. Furthermore, there was every possibility of this point being pressed by 'all classes of politicians in future' and, thus, encouraging the politicization of the Muslim-dominated sections of the armed forces.[78] In short, the military problem of impoverished India was immense. As late as August 1920 the GOI funded almost 200,000 combatants in countries where India had 'comparatively little interest save as part of the Empire'. Thus, in the interests of the Raj, the extent of India's Imperial liability compared with the responsibilities of the self-governing dominions like Australia and Canada, which played a comparatively minor part in furnishing troops for purely Imperial purposes, had to be fixed. Furthermore, the GOI, after the War, was meeting its imperial obligations in the teeth of nationalist opposition and severe economic problems. It was only fair, felt its representatives, to determine and fix realistic Indian liabilities if she was to ever become a Dominion.

The GOI was weighed down by financial limitations and a milieu heralding militant nationalism. For it treading the path between growing domestic hostility to the Raj and a geo-political commitment to imperial strategy was a delicate affair. On top of this, imperial concessions were not enough in a period symptomatic of imperial crisis. In the words of one official, it was 'clear at once that the mere agreement on the part of His Majesty's Government to pay for forces despatched overseas, or even to re-imburse us for the depots maintained for supplying such forces with the drafts required by them did not compensate' the GOI for the 'financial and general burden' imposed upon it.[79] Beside this, unpredictable imperial decisions often threw normalcy out of gear. For example, after the War the GOI was asked to keep two divisions ready for Mesopotamia. This severely jeopardized demobilization and the disposal of surplus stores. Matters became worse when the War Office later asked the GOI to raise these divisions without incurring extra expenditure, but this was 'not humanly possible'.[80]

Sometimes the War Office almost found excuses to impose extra financial burdens on the GOI, and Hailey cited a 'monstrous claim' of this sort. In his despatch on the Afghan campaign of 1919-21, the C-in-C had referred to the East Persian Force becoming involved in the conflict to cut off Bolshevik assistance to Afghanistan from an outflanking position: 'This remark had a perfectly limited and intelligible meaning. It will perhaps hardly be believed that these words were used by the War Office (with some support from the India Office) as the foundation of a monstrous claim that we should pay half the expenditure on the East Persian Force.'[81] The GOI 'combated' this claim which 'raised at all instances' the danger of its position as a supplier of troops on the following condition: 'We supply troops on demand, and on an implied understanding that they will be paid for. Once they have been supplied, every attempt will obviously be made to get behind that understanding.'[82] The GOI was also afraid of the Imperial General Staff acquiring sweeping powers over Indian military matters. The latter's assistance was most welcome but the control of the Governor-General over Indian matters was more important. Political Indians, unlike their brothers in the nineteenth century, had become conscious of military affairs and their confidence in their ability to criticize military policy was set to grow with the introduction of new constitutional reforms after 1919. Although the new Government of India Act excluded the Army budget from the Assembly vote, caution was necessary because the Government could no longer take Indians for granted. It was 'necessary to avoid any suspicion that the expenditure of funds provided by Indian taxation for the Army in India is subject to any other direction than that of the Governor-General in Council acting under the statutory control of Parliament as exercised through the Secretary of State for India'.[83]

Hence the GOI wanted to be consulted on all questions of policy which indicated the deployment of Indian troops outside India: 'Where each employment is found to be necessary, a definite request should in our opinion be made in advance to the Government of India, and their views on the subject should be fully considered by the Imperial Government.'[84]

Experiences after the Armistice did not warrant the unrestrained deployment of Indian troops at the prevalent political and economic costs of the GOI. Moreover, uneven demobilization enhanced the risks of protest in the armed forces at a time when mass nationalism was growing in India. The fact that considerable units remained outside India after 1918 made planned reorganization on a post-War basis impossible. The discrimination between Imperial and Indian troops in the management of Imperial affairs was another matter of concern. On this the GOI reminded the Imperial Government:

> This called for direct changes in the system of supplying the services if British rule was to be maintained under conditions of widespread social unrest in India. (The) respect of demobilisation and release does not compare favourably (in India) with that accorded to British and Dominion troops, and further that these troops have been retained in territories for which Great Britain has received a mandate, without due regard to our convenience, or to the political situation in India, or to the effect which such action may have had on political opinion in this country.[85]

THE COMPULSIONS OF MONEY

We have already observed that tensions between Delhi and London on matters of Army reform in India were evident before the Great War. The limitations of the British in maintaining or increasing military expenditure in India already had a history before 1914. In the context of that history it would be wrong to assume that the economic effect of the Great War was a factor without antecedents responsible for retarding military reform in India between the two World Wars. However, in the 1920s everyone's attention was focused, with some justification, on the effects of the War on Indian finances. Perhaps a look at the pre-War Kitchener Scheme and the Mowatt Committee's recommendations based on its examination will help place the retrenchment of the 1920s in better perspective.

The Second Afghan War and the Tirah operations of 1897-8, as pointed out earlier, had exposed serious deficiencies in the organization of the Army in India and Lord Kitchener's Scheme of 1904 was an attempt to remove some of them. The scheme was designed primarily to increase the size and efficiency of the Field Army by reducing the numerical strength of the 'obligatory garrisons', i.e. troops tied down in internal security duties. The most economical way of increasing the size of the Field Army was to reduce the burden of internal duties on the regular units and the deployment of mobile units to quell domestic unrest. The overall efficiency of the Field Army was dependent on the development of manpower and material reserves, the imposition of the divisional command system to bring the peacetime organization of the Army in line with wartime organization and the extension of railways in the sensitive Frontier region. Kitchener argued that since Indians were unarmed, efficient policing, with help from the Princely States, could control them. Therefore, to permanently station troops as garrisons for civil purposes was not only outdated, if one took into account the railway factor, but also very expensive. The reduction of these garrisons was the most economical way of increasing the Field Army *without* increasing the total establishment of the Army in India. According to Kitchener's calculations, doing this would have released some 50,000 men for the Field Army at a time when the high command was anticipating a Russian drive to Kabul.

The Mowatt Committee studied all this and appreciated the plan to increase the Field Army but its conclusion in the ultimate analysis signalled an unmistakeable move towards economy. If the Field Army, as a result of these measures, expanded 'beyond what is necessary for the protection of India against external aggression, the natural and economical course would be to reduce the total establishment'. This conclusion was reached despite the fact that the GOI had framed the estimates 'with moderation and economy' when it came to implementing the Kitchener Scheme and preparing India for a possible war against

Afghanistan. The shortage of officers was acute and 950 British officers were required to fit the Indian Army for calculated field duty according to the Scheme. Kitchener called the shortage of officers 'one of the most prominent defects under which the Indian Army' laboured at the time. In 1907 General Duff, the C-in-C, revised the figure to a more economical 567, but even then the shortage was great. The result of the Mowatt survey was strikingly similar to that of the Retrenchment proposals of the 1920s. The probable implementation of the Kitchener Scheme had to wait till 1912-13 or even 1913-14 and unless civil expenditure declined, military expenditure could not rise or even be maintained at the level of 1907. Furthermore, after the Russo-Japanese War the international situation had changed and with the growth of the Anglo-Japanese alliance in the Far East the fear of a Russian attack on India had diminished. This invited some relief for the Indian taxpayer and, by implication, stagnation for the Army in India.[86]

After 1918 military reform was perceived as part of a general shift in British policy designed to guide India towards Dominion Status. But simultaneously retrenchment was an attempt to preserve the Raj. By 1923 the shrill cry of retrenchment began to militate against the recommendations of the Esher Committee. Balancing the budget by curtailing public expenditure and effecting savings became the chief concern of the Retrenchment Committee (hereafter IRC) because during the War government expenditure had soared.[87] The question was, as it still is, whether India could afford substantial military spending in the 1920s. According to an IRC frowning upon the series of huge post-War deficits, this was impossible despite growing taxation. Thus, to balance the budget 'a very substantial reduction in the military estimates' was the order of the day.[88] And according to the IRC, this could be achieved in the near future because the GOI was apparently abandoning its forward policy in Waziristan.[89]

To promote savings the IRC pinpointed several areas of the armed forces in which expenditure could be curtailed as safely as possible. For instance, the cost of the British soldier in India was Rs. 2,500 per annum which was very high compared with the cost of an Indian soldier. Between 1913-14 and 1922-3 the peacetime strength of British battalions in India had increased but during the War the fighting efficiency of these units had increased sufficiently to allow retrenchment. Since in England the peacetime as well as the wartime strength of battalions was lower than in India, the IRC advocated a reduction of 5,700 men. This was important because in future the cost of maintaining British soldiers would increase even if the Esher reforms were not implemented. The cost of the Indian soldier in 1922-3 was Rs. 361 per annum and although this was far below the British average, reductions were advised in active as well as training battalions with the Gurkhas, as usual, remaining an exception. In fact, the GOI was advised to develop cheaper reserves to further lower the peacetime battalion strength.[90] Similarly, the bloated HQs and commands required trimming. Economies were also recommended in the spheres of animal and mechanical transport which had grown during the War.[91]

On the whole, the IRC suggested a saving of Rs. 30.3 million per annum by the reduction of the fighting services and another Rs. 6.3 million by a reduction of 20 per cent in the strength of the Indian battalions. Importantly it wanted the GOI to be given full opportunities to review any 'proposed changes in the administration of British troops involving large expenditure' *before* such expenditures were undertaken.[92] In advising the GOI to limit the Army budget to Rs. 510.47 millions for the year 1923-4, the IRC laid down the framework of the Indian military budget for the inter-War period and ruled out the implementation of the Esher recommendations.[93]

Towards naval defence the IRC recommendations were particularly harsh and contradicted the GOI's position at the Imperial Conference of 1923. In any case, the GOI's commitment to imperial naval defence had overlooked its financial position. The RIM had expanded considerably during the War but the IRC wanted it 'drastically curtailed' with a budget of only Rs. 6.2 million for 1923-4 which was 7.5 million less than the estimates of 1922-3. Several ships were to be laid up and all surplus vessels sold.[94] The IRC, however, said nothing about the subvention of 100,000 pounds per annum which the GOI paid to the Admiralty for the services of the Royal Navy. This drain could otherwise have been utilized in India to help meet the GOI's commitment at the Imperial Conference of 1923. However, the IRC's obsession with economy led to strategic myopia because in the early 1920s, 'It was not anticipated that the Royal Navy might some day be left alone to contend with the German and Italian fleets and to guard the seas of the world at the same time. It was also not foreseen that a war would threaten India from the East.'[95]

In 1921 Gen. C.C. Munro had composed an essay based on facts regarding the Indian armed forces which was probably ignored by the IRC.[96] According to Munro, there were significant differences between Indian and British military problems and many critics did not realize this while criticizing the Indian armed forces. In Britain there were no land frontiers and the naval factor was preponderant, but India had a vulnerable frontier and a 'population subject to outbursts of fanaticism and influenced by the conditions of unrest which are so prevalent throughout the world'. India had no reserves, its police was inefficient, and British soldiers in India were never numerous enough to check massive popular outbursts. After the War, with the rise of mass nationalism and pan-Islamism and danger from the Bolsheviks who were trying to overthrow the Raj, threats to British rule had multiplied. In these circumstances a minimum but efficient force was necessary to protect British interests in India. This would comprise 12.25 brigades for the NWFP, 4 divisions against possible attacks, and 12 infantry brigades in reserve for internal duties. Munro was 'convinced that a small force properly staffed, adequately equipped, well trained, and with the correct proportion of ancillary services' would be more effective than a large ill-equipped force. He warned against further retrenchment while advocating levels lower than those of 1914 but neither naval defence nor the rising cost of modern military technology was considered by him at any stage. Both quality and quantity required funds which the IRC was unwilling to grant.

The provisional budget for 1920-1, calculated in December 1919 by the Military Accountant General, amounted to Rs. 610 million. This was obviously unacceptable as the normal peacetime liability. In January 1920 it was decided to scale down the budget to Rs. 450 million by eliminating non-essentials. In February 1920 the Army estimates were re-examined and it was recommended that Rs. 600 million were necessary for servicing the Army in 1920-1. Extra money was needed for operations. For a while this increased expenditure was unavoidable because of the concessions made to the services soon after the War. The substantially increased cost of British troops in India further strained budgetary provisions. The exchange rate between the pound and the rupee and post-War inflation were other factors to contend with and the fact that Rs. 50 million had been sanctioned for the occupation of Waziristan since 1919-20 did not make matters easy.[97] A diplomatic success against Afghanistan could certainly have helped the financial situation more than the persistence of a jaded Russophobia. Of the gross sum of Rs. 650 million for overall military expenditure in 1920-1, 600 million were for the maintenance of the Army, 45 million for special expenditures in Waziristan, and 50 million for precautionary mobilization, again, on the Frontier. The GOI agreed to provide for operations separately. However, the accepted increases to satisfy the armed forces resulted in the maintenance charges usually exceeding budgetary allocations. This had drastic consequences for the future because it 'necessitated the re-appropriation of the amount set aside for capital expenditure on the purchase of equipment and stores and on various measures of reorganisation'. Despite this, 'concessions granted to British troops' were to 'involve an excess over allotted grants'. Growing charges of the RAF would also add to the financial strain.[98]

The implementation of the proposed Esher reforms at 1920 prices involved an annually recurring expenditure of about Rs. 30 million. Including this the total military expenditure would have been Rs. 680 million during 1921-2. This estimate neither provided for naval defence nor the proposed territorial force nor even for the improvement of defence-related factories. Thus, even before the IRC's recommendations were applied in 1924 allocations for capital expenditures were ruled out. In short Rs. 680 million were far too much for an exhausted colony either in the 1920s or even the 1930s.[99]

While Munro warned against excessive retrenchment, the narrow basis of military finance in colonial India between the Wars was confirmed by the difficulties faced by the Military Council (MC) in its day-to-day functioning. The MC comprised the C-in-C as president, the Chief of the Army Staff (CAS) as vice president, and the Adjutant General, Quartermaster General, Secretary, Army Department and Financial Advisor as members. The MC was an advisory body whose agenda constituted a rough index of daily military affairs in India. Various cases and representations in the armed forces were considered by this body which took decisions on some matters. However, matters involving sizeable financial outlays were referred to the GOI. From cars, ammunition, and bandmasters' allowances to budgets, Indianization, and clothing were discussed in the MC meetings. Limited Indianization received some support and the officials felt the need for proper education and an assessment of the likely troubles arising in India in future.[100]

But even minor expenditure was being avoided by the MC in 1921. For instance, the proposed increase of marriage allowances for British troops in India was referred to the Secretary of State. Similarly, when the issue of lighting military hospitals and troops' lines arose, despite the costs calculated in the budget of 1921-2, the formal approval of the Government was sought. Technological improvements in the Corps of Signals was accepted in principle but left to the availability of funds in 1922-3.[101] The military medical services, which had expanded during the War, were to be reduced significantly after it.[102]

Minor increases and demands were either refused or referred to the Financial Advisor or the GOI. For instance, on the maintenance of a Technical Recruiting Organization during peacetime and its functions, the MC unanimously suggested that such an organization would be 'necessary to meet the requirements of India only'. In fact, in a recommendation to the GOI the MC stated that the British Government be informed that 'in future they must make their own arrangements for the recruitment of technical personnel for employment in Mesopotamia or elsewhere'.[103] At the same meeting three cases relating to an increase in the expenditures of the RAF establishments in India were rejected outright. In the 28th meeting even a paltry increase in the pay of mule driver reservists from Rs. 3 to Rs. 4 per month was accepted only in principle and that too on condition of more retrenchment.[104] The extreme centralization of control and the paucity of resources were reflected in the discussions on the following issues. For example, the supply of fly-proof boxes to hold bed pans and urinals in the wards of British and Indian hospitals was discussed although in April 1921 this demand had been accepted in principle. Even such indispensable sanitary arrangements were to be made in the final instance by the various commanding officers 'only as funds became available from savings under the grant and head of account affected'. As days passed even the HQs suffered. On 17/7/1922 locating the Northern Command HQ in future could not be discussed properly because it was found that adequate funds were 'not likely to be available in the near future'. In 1922, with possibly drastic repercussions, most demands for increasing expenditure were rejected due to financial exigencies. For instance, grants to *pandits* and *moulvis* in the Indian Army and free second-class fare every three years for them were postponed till funds could 'be made available'. In 1922 there were some 524 teachers attached to different regiments and they exerted 'great influence . . . for good or evil' in the services. Financial limitations also ruled out the formation of a new Indian Corps of Clerks supposed to supply clerks to the establishments of Commands, Districts, and the Military Staff Offices.[105] This would hamper administration besides tarnishing the reputation of the services as big employers in a society of limited opportunities.

CONCLUSION

Michael Howard, in his informed text on British military policy, writes that after the Boer War, 'The British Empire was isolated, not particularly splendidly, in a world of highly armed states, with a Navy whose supremacy still depended on the divisions among her adversaries and an Army incapable of taking the field against any single one of them.' In this context, it is not surprising to observe that when the Committee of Imperial Defence sat down to consider the problems of the Empire as a whole in 1902, of the three most important points on its agenda were two concerned with the Indian Empire. The first was the protection of India from Russia and the second was the defence of Egypt and thereby the strategic line to India. This proves that British policy makers were seriously echoing Lord Curzon's following prophesy: 'As long as we rule India we are the greatest power in the world. If we lose it we shall drop straight away to a third rate power.'[106] In the decade before the Great War the need to reform the Imperial military structure, including the Indian armed forces, had been underlined by the military experiences of the late nineteenth century. But the question whether Great Britain and her greatly impoverished colonies had the necessary resources and planning to do so was almost simultaneously highlighted by reports such as the *ECR* and the political reception they inspired in the troubled 1920s. The GOI's response to the *ECR*, not to speak of the Indian reception it got, revealed clearly the hiatus between Imperial armchair perspectives and colonial imperatives. A close reading of the *ECR* tells us that the Imperial planners, despite the wartime promises they made to the Indians, grossly underestimated the capability and desire of educated Indians to accord significance to matters of military expenditure and reform. Consequently, the Esher Committee not only overlooked the possibility of opposition arising to its expressions and schemes from the GOI but also failed to reflect the growing importance of Indian opinion in its recommendations.

The reform of the Army in India had assumed importance after the unhappy experiences of the Second Afghan War and the Tirah operations, and during the Great War political reform in India, including the re-organization of the Indian armed forces in the light of new Imperial needs, emerged as the dominant theme of British policy in India. The formation of the Esher Committee and the subsequent *ECR* constituted the British perspective on Indian military reform with all its limitations. We saw how the EC wanted the GOI, which was grappling with unprecedented military expenditure and nationalist protest soon after the Great War, to consolidate the advantages gained by the Indian armed forces during the War. But keeping the Indian troops loyal in the face of militant mass nationalism was foremost in the mind of the Esher Committee and this explains the *ECR's* respect for Indian military tradition. This deference for tradition and stability created a structural defect, noticeable in the Esher Committee's attitude towards Indianization, in the British reform perspective. On the contrary, while expressing concern about the danger of falling recruitment among the 'martial races', the *ECR* failed to indicate Britain's growing confidence in the Indian middle class. In the Indian atmosphere of 1919-20 this was probably the correct thing to do as far as the British were concerned, but the attitude was inconsistent with the reform perspective guiding the Montagu-Chelmsford Scheme and demanded by Indian opinion. Hence, on many points, the *ECR* appeared self-contradictory. For instance, and despite the shortage of officers in India stressed before and during the Great War, the Esher Committee failed to anticipate that in the 1920s and 1930s the Indianization and modernization of the Indian services would have to go hand in hand. In India, on the other hand, military reform remained focused on Indianization largely due to Indian efforts in the 1920s and 1930s. In short, the Esher Committee argued for reform without considering the social changes in the Indian armed forces necessary to bring it about.

Finally, deteriorating economic conditions put paid to structural reform of the Indian military during the 1920s. Our brief survey of pre-War reform suggests that the tension between the needs of reform and the dictates of economy prevailed even before the Great War. But after the war the need for economy became paramount and while reform was discussed and publicized, the budgetary constraints of the Raj caught up with decision making. The military recommendations of the IRC, which were implemented in the mid-1920s, cancelled the reform and modernization of the Indian services in the 1920s. But even before retrenchment the cost of reform calculated by Munro had suggested the obvious. Finally, the adoption of an inter-War annual Army budget of around Rs. 50 crore ruled out effective material improvement till the Second World War. Our survey of the MC proceedings suggests that minor expenses, which would not have mattered to armed forces placed in more fortunate circumstances, in many instances were either ruled out or made conditional on availability of funds. Under these conditions the capital expenditure required for the social and technological transformation of the Indian armed forces between the Wars became conspicuous by its absence. With expenditure falling and the stagnating services desperately trying to preserve themselves there was little chance of continuities responding to the challenge posed by nationalism in the context of total war. On the whole, official respect for tradition and the continuous preference for revenue over expenditure underpinned British military policy in India in the decade following the First World War:

> Of the imperative necessity of securing financial equilibrium we are convinced, since the alternative will be a progressive deterioration of our financial position, which, if not checked, must have grave consequences. The attainment of our objective can only be secured by, on the one hand, increasing our revenue, and on the other hand, by effecting economies. Although not absorbing a higher proportion of

our total revenues than it has done for the past 20 years, the army does consume now roughly one-half of our central revenues, and clearly offers the widest field for retrenchment. We have, as you are aware, been engaged for weeks past in exploring every possibility of effecting economies without endangering the national safety. While national security must always be the governing factor, financial considerations cannot be ignored. The financial position of the country must indeed have a marked political reaction on the question of national security, since a scale of military expenditure which exceeds our means to a large extent not only adds to the burden of taxation but also renders it impracticable to devote adequate funds to other urgently needed administrative measures, impedes industrial and economic development, raises prices and so creates such discontent in the country as to aggravate seriously the widespread unrest which now prevails in many parts of India.[107]

NOTES

1. Relevant details of the Peel (1859) and Eden (1879) Commission recommendations are found in V. Longer, *Red Coats to Olive Green: A History of the Indian Army 1600-1974*, New Delhi, 1974; Stephen P. Cohen, *The Indian Army*, New Delhi, 1990; C.C. Trench, *The Indian Army and the King's Enemies, 1900-1947*, London, 1988; Byron Farwell, *Armies of the Raj*, London, 1989; S.L. Menezes, *Fidelity and Honour: The Indian Army from the Seventeenth to the Twenty-First Century*, New Delhi, 1993; and David Omissi, *The Sepoy and the Raj: The Indian Army, 1860-1940*, London, 1994. A reading of these works makes it quite clear that the primary aim of the Peel and Eden reforms was to create a secure instrument of power in India involving, above all, a 'counterpoise of natives against natives'.
2. The history of the Bombay Marine has been critically re-examined by Anirudh Deshpande, 'The Bombay Marine: Aspects of Maritime History 1650-1850', *Studies in History*, Vol. 11, No. 2, N.S., 1995.
3. *The Imperial Gazetteer of India, The Indian Empire, Vol. IV: Administrative*, New Edition, Oxford, 1907, pp. 347-53; *The Army in India and Its Evolution, Including an Account of the Establishment of the RAF in India*, Calcutta, 1924 (Government publication), volume in Historical Section of the Ministry of Defence, New Delhi (hereafter the Historical Section is referred to as HS); *Military Handbook of General Information* (Government publication), 1908, volume in the Central Secretariat Library, New Delhi (hereafter referred to as CSL). For a

review of changes in Army organization up to 1914 see Cohen, *The Indian Army*, pp. 22-8, 32-56.

4. Morley Collection (Microfilm), Acc. No. 1615, National Archives of India (hereafter NAI).
5. Hardinge to Secretary of State Morley, 16/3/1911 in Morley Collection (Microfilm), Acc. No. 1614, NAI.
6. *The Army in India and Its Evolution*, p. 33; *Military Handbook of General Information*. From the *Report of the Indian Retrenchment Committee, 1922-23* (hereafter *IRC*), Delhi, 1923, Part I: Military Services, CSL, pp. 7-59, we know the following about the Military Expenditure of the Government of India between 1913-14 and 1922-3. In 1913-14 actual expenditure was Rs. 29,84,41,000, in 1921-2 the revised estimate was Rs. 69,34,69,000 and in 1922-3 the budget estimate was Rs. 67,75,26,000. Of this the Army expenditure showed an increase of 117 per cent between 1913-14 and 1922-3 largely due to rising prices and wartime expansion. In 1913-14 actual Army expenditure stood at Rs. 27,87,45,000. In 1921-2 the revised Army estimate was Rs. 61,82,42,000 whereas the budget estimate for the Army in 1922-3 was Rs. 60,42,30,000. In 1914 the total number of men in the Army was 250,444 of which 76,214 were British and 154,437 Indians. The number of Indian troops serving during the War rose to 573,000 in 1918. In 1922 after demobilization the total was 233,801 of which 68,686 were British and 141,617 Indians.
7. *India in 1919, A statement prepared for presentation to Parliament in accordance with the requirements of the 16th Section of the Govt. of India Act (5 & 6 Geo V, Chap 61)*, pp. 6-19.
8. Colonel Horsley's (Army Medical Service) letter from the Indian Field Ambulance, The Front, Mesopotamia, Force 'D' to Carter of the Indian Medical Service, D/5/71916, enclosed in a letter to the Viceroy by Secretary of State E. Montagu, 3 August 1917 in the Montagu Papers, Acc. No. 1930 (Microfilm), NAI. It was Chamberlain's intention to send a copy of this letter to Chelmsford. The Second Afghan War and the experiences on the Frontier where the Afridis proved formidable opponents underlined the necessity of reforming the Army in India.
9. *India in 1919, A statement prepared for presentation to Parliament . . .*, pp. 15, 19.
10. *Army in India Committee: Table of Meetings, Names of Witnesses & Subjects Discussed; Appendix: Minutes of First Meeting, 28 July 1919; Statement by Lt. Gen. Sir H.V. Cox in the Diaries, correspondence and papers of Viscount Esher*, Churchill Archives Centre, Churchill College, Cambridge. Secretary of State Montagu in a letter to Chelmsford dated 21 Nov. 1918, Acc. No. 1930, Montagu Papers (Microfilm), NAI, stated that he noticed 'increased signs' on the part of the War Office 'of a desire to get control of the Indian Army'. With regard to this he

wanted the Viceroy to get a statement of the Indian case prepared and forwarded to him at an early date. This not only made the GOI really scared of losing control over the Indian Army but also partially explains why the Esher recommendations attracted so much flak in India. For other details of the British involvement and aims in Mesopotamia during the Great War see V.H. Rothwell, 'Mesopotamia in British War Aims', *Historical Journal*, Vol. XIII, No. 2, 1970, pp. 273-94.

11. This section is a critical review of the *Report of the Army in India Committee 1919-20*, submitted to the British and Indian governments in 1920. Also known as the Esher Committee Report. Hereafter referred to as the *ECR*.
12. *ECR*, p. 3.
13. Ibid., p. 3.
14. Ibid., p. 7.
15. Ibid., p. 8.
16. The idea of India gaining Dominion Status in the near future guided this. In fact, an Indian member of the Committee pointed out that without Indianization Dominion Status would be incomplete: *ECR*, letter to E.S. Montagu prefacing parts III and IV and minute by Sir Krishna G. Gupta appended to the *ECR*, pp. 99-100. On issues related to Indianization see Sir Krishna G. Gupta's paper in this volume.
17. *ECR*, pp. 4-5. Mutiny involving the 'martial races' had in fact occurred in Singapore in 1915. For details of this relatively unknown event and the influence of hostile propaganda on Indian troops see Byron Farwell, *Armies of the Raj*, pp. 236-47. Cohen, *The Indian Army*, pp. 68-76 reviews the role of the Indian Army in the First World War but does not mention the Singapore Mutiny. Conditions of warfare, which may be seen at the Imperial War Museum, London and vividly described from the battlefield by C.C. Trench, *The Indian Army and the King's Enemies*, pp. 75-90 could easily have led to discontent. Even Trench overlooks the Singapore Mutiny.
18. *ECR*, p. 5. Ironically such immersion in internal security duties militated against training or even the aquisition of new equipment in the inter-War years, as Brian Bond, *British Military Policy*, op. cit., p. 105, points out.
19. Brian Bond, *British Military Policy*, pp. 54-69.
20. *ECR*, p. 37. A letter to Rufus from Secretary of State Montagu dated 18 Jan. 1922 (PRIVATE), Acc. No. 1934, Montagu Papers (Microfilm), NAI speaks of Indian troops having become unreliable and British troops being demanded in all the areas seriously affected by the Non-Cooperation Movement. Montagu suggested doing away with the services of the Indian Army for internal duties and the creation of a 'mixed gendarmerie' in its place with a proper proportion of Europeans for protecting British interests in India. Speaking of the understandable

Indian demand for the reduction of British troops in India, on 1 Feb. 1922 once again he wrote to Rufus about the necessity of employing British troops in India till a gendarmerie was formed.

21. *ECR*, p. 38.
22. Ibid., p. 38. Officers with 'high reputations . . . found themselves recalled to India, and in many cases on their arrival were assigned posts of less importance than those which they had held in the field, while they lost the opportunities for earning distinction and gaining promotion which were in their grasp in other theatres of war'. A survey of the *War Diaries* of the Indian Army's Expeditionary Force deployed in Mesopotamia makes the point clearer: *Confidential Se. No. 44/2006 Notes from War Diaries, Part ODXLI Mesopotamia Expeditionary Force, General Staff, Army HQ, India, Feb. 1916*, Military Department War Diary, NAI, brings to our notice the extreme shortage of men in the Machine Gun companies. Even the supply of water posed a big problem. Similarly, *Secret Se. No. 9/654 Mesopotamia Expeditionary Force (Force D) Notes from War Diaries, Part CXXVIII, General Staff, Army HQs, India, Aug. 1916*, Military Department War Diary, NAI, speaks of the shortage of personnel and defective transport. In the 6th Cavalry Brigade Ammunition Column, for instance, in May 1916 out of 92 wheels 40 were instantly condemned and a further 23 were found fit for condemnation in a few weeks. Wagon bodies were in a bad state with their wood being split and broken. There was deficient forage for cavalry and motor ambulances were being demanded because wounded men were being carried on stretchers for miles before receiving proper medical attention. For detailed accounts of the hard-fought Mesopotamia campaign, see C.C. Trench, *The Indian Army and the King's Enemies*, pp. 75-90. Byron Farwell, *Armies of the Raj*, pp. 253-66. Reginald Hennell, *A Famous Indian Regiment: Kali Panchwin*, pp. 174-214, is an old-style campaign account of the Marathas in Mesopotamia based on contemporary war despatches.
23. *ECR*, p. 38.
24. Ibid., p. 39.
25. Ibid., Part V, p. 55.
26. Ibid., p. 53. That the fears and predictions of the Esher Committee regarding the consequences of discontent in the armed forces were not baseless becomes clear in the nature of correspondence contained in the Montagu Papers. For instance, a letter from Chas. E. Yate to Montagu, dated 24 Nov. 1921, Acc. No. 1934, Montagu Papers (Microfilm), NAI, mentions the fact that Kachin and other troops were requisitioned during the Moplah risings because troops at hand could not be trusted.
27. *ECR*, p. 56.
28. Royal Message to Rawlinson, 25/1/1920, quoted in the *ECR*, p. 56.
29. *ECR*, p. 57.

30. Ibid., p. 58.
31. Ibid., p. 58.
32. Ibid., pp. 58-9.
33. Ibid., p. 59; *The Army in India Committee Table of Meetings, Names of Witnesses* . . . , op. cit., offers the following list of Indian VCOs consulted as witnesses: Sub. Maj. Lachman Singh 15th Jats, Ris. Maj. Fazil Hussain 13th Lancers, Sub. Maj. Hari Ram 12th Pioneers, Ris. Maj. Prem Singh 20th Deccan Horse, Ris. Maj. Muhammad Akram Khan, 1st Lancers, Sub. Maj. Pertab Singh 36th Sikhs, Subadar Umrao Singh 1/10th Jats, Sub. Maj. Arjun Powar Sappers & Miners and Ris. Maj. Lakput Singh 26 Cavalry. Many of these VCOs submitted papers and memoranda on the amelioration of their service conditions influencing the *ECR's* view of the matter.
34. *ECR*, p. 59; D.C. Ellinwood, 'Ethnicity in a Colonial Asian Army: British Policy, War and the Indian Army, 1914-1918', in D.C. Ellinwood and Cynthia H. Enloe, *Ethnicity and the Military in Asia*, London, 1981 mentions that experiences in Europe, especially France, enhanced the 'ethnic pride' and self-esteem of Indian soldiers but curiously enough does not credit the VCOs with the ability to protest. In this 'ethnic' perspective the VCOs are described as 'in house elders' who 'having come from a relatively simple society . . . generally accepted their inferior status without quibble, as far as we can determine'. On the other hand, S.D. Pradhan, 'The Sikh Soldier in the First World War', in D.C. Ellinwood and S.D. Pradhan (eds.), *India and World War I*, New Delhi, 1978, after looking closely at Sikh recruitment and experiences during the War concludes that the War heightened the notion of equality amongst the soldiers bringing to the fore their grievances against the British who denied them their just dues and rights after the War. T.A. Heathcote, *The Indian Army: The Garrison of British Imperial India, 1822-1922*, London, 1974, p. 103, surveys Sikh unrest under political influence in the Army during the period of the Great War. Restrictions on Indian migration to Canada had led to noticeable discontent amongst Sikh troops as early as 1914.
35. Birkenhead Collection (Microfilm), NAI, Acc. No. 1949, 7/9/1927, General Staff Note on Army deficiencies—letter from Irwin to Birkenhead.
36. *ECR*, p. 59.
37. Ibid., p. 59. This was most unfortunate and became the ground for great discord between the British Raj and Indian nationalists in the inter-War period. The shortage of officers was stressed by Lt. Gen. Sir H.V. Cox in the Appendix: *Minutes of Second Meeting, 29th July 1919 in the Army in India Committee, Table of Meetings*, op. cit. Before the War the Indian Army Reserve of officers numbered 40 officers and there was no scheme of training or expansion. During the War the

British Army could hardly supply the rapidly expanding Indian Army with officers. This led to a severe crisis in field command because within the first few months of the war, as casualties mounted, the shortage of officers became acute.

38. *ECR*, p. 65. From Anil Seal, *The Emergence of Indian Nationalism*, New Delhi, 1971, p. 122, we know that in 1882 headmasters in Bombay government high schools earned on an average Rs. 462 per month and assistant masters got Rs. 90. In government middle schools the pay was about Rs. 87 and Rs. 45 respectively.
39. *ECR*, p. 66: 'The adoption of these proposals would provide, *inter alia*, for the elementary education of the sons of Indian soldiers, who would be sufficiently well grounded to proceed, with the help perhaps of military scholarships, to higher educational institutions.'
40. *ECR*, pp. 59-60.
41. Ibid., p. 60.
42. Ibid., p. 62.
43. Ibid., p. 62. The Committee wrongly calculated this as Rs. 7.8.
44. Ibid., p. 62. Such expectations were to arise, with strident political over tones, in vast sections of the armed forces even in 1945-6.
45. The implications of this competition have been studied by Anirudh Deshpande, 'Hopes and disillusionment: Recruitment, demobilisation and the emergence of discontent in the Indian armed forces after the Second World War', *IESHR*, Vol. XXXIII, No. 2, April-June 1996.
46. *ECR*, p. 62.
47. Ibid., p. 63.
48. Ibid., p. 63.
49. Ibid., pp. 63-6.
50. Hardinge to Morley, 16/3/1911 in Morley Collection (Microfilm) Acc. No. 1614, NAI.
51. *ECR*, p. 79. *Marine Regulations, India, Vol. I, Part I: Discipline, Part II: Finance*, Calcutta, NAI, 1886, *Marine Regulations India, Vol. I, Pay and Allowances and Non-Effective Pay, GOI, Finance Department*, Calcutta, NAI, 1918 and the *Marine Regulations, GOI, Marine Department, 1931*, Calcutta, NAI, 1931, failed to note substantial changes. The Jellicoe proposals appear in Appendix 1 of this book. Significant aspects of the Bombay Marine's history, including the politics of marine survey, are presented in Anirudh Deshpande, 'The Bombay Marine: Aspects of maritime history, 1650-1850', *Studies in History*, Vol. XI, No. 2, 1995.
52. *ECR*, p. 79.
53. Ibid., pp. 79-80. The reduction in military expenditure with special emphasis on the Navy of the East India Company launched by Bentinck and Macaulay was largely responsible for making Indian naval matters completely subservient to the Admiralty much before 1857. Our

generalization on this topic is based on the following: C.R. Low, *History of the Indian Navy (1613-1863)*, London, 1877, reprint, New Delhi, 1983, Vols. I & II; *Gazetteer of Bombay City and Island*, Vol. II, Bombay, 1909; Report of the Calcutta Civil Finance Committee dated 14 June 1830, in *Parliamentary Papers,* Vol. 5, Shannon, 1970; Anirudh Deshpande, 'The Bombay Marine . . .', op. cit. At the time Sir John Malcolm had opposed the abolition of the Indian Navy, saying that the Navy, managed by Bombay, was crucial in maintaining British domination over the Persian Gulf. He also stressed the point, made later by the *ECR*, that the Royal Navy would prove expensive to deploy in the Arabian Sea; *Parliamentary Papers,* Vol. 5, pp. 223-5, Extract from Sir John Malcolm's General Minute of 30/11/1830, and Malcolm's letter to Villiers, 26/3/1832, in *Parliamentary Papers,* Vol. II, Shannon, 1970.

54. *Marine Regulations, India, Vol. I, Part I: Discipline; Part II: Finance,* Calcutta, 1886, p. 120. *Gazetteer of Bombay City and Island,* Vol. II, Bombay, 1909, Marine section, points out that after 1863 legally only Indian sailors generally from the Ratnagiri District were employed by the RIM. Army in India Committee Table of Meetings, op. cit.: Captain N.F.J. Wilson, Director of the RIM, deposing before the Esher Committee in its 24th Meeting on 19 Nov. 1919 argued against Army control over the service. He also stressed the importance of educating Indians in modern seamanship, improvements in recruitment and service conditions, and the desirability of placing the service under the Admiralty in the interest of greater direction and efficiency.
55. *Marine Regulations, India, Pay and Allowances, Leave, Passage, Pension and Medical Rules of the Royal Indian Marine, Vol. I: All Orders issued upto 31 December 1931, GOI Marine Department,* Calcutta, 1931, pp. 15-17 for syrangs, tindals and lascars, Section I, table showing complement of enrolled ratings in 1930. Section I, pp. 19-22, on ship rates of pay. All ratings received an outfit allowance of Re. 1 annas 8 per month which was denied to topasses and bhandaries employed as menials.
56. *Marine Regulations, India, Volume I, Pay and Allowances and Non Effective Pay.* All orders issued up to 1.7.1917, GOI, Finance Department, Calcutta, 1918 (NAI), pp. 10-11. In the afloat establishments, p. 17, the situation in 1917 was as follows: Chief syrangs of lascars 2nd class—Rs. 45 per month, sukhanies Rs. 30 per month, tindals of lascars Rs. 25 per month, lascars 1st class Rs. 20 per month, 2nd class Rs. 16 per month, 3rd class Rs. 14 per month, 4th class Rs. 12 per month, and lascar boys Rs. 8 per month.
57. *ECR,* pp. 56-81. However, this was not the unanimous opinion of the Committee, for Maj. Gen. Sir A. Bingley during the 33rd Meeting of the *ECR, Army in India Committee, Table of Meetings* . . . , op. cit., tersely

dismissed Indian maritime traditions in the following words: 'The idea of an Indian Navy is impracticable. The people have no sea traditions or aptitude.'

58. *ECR*, pp. 99-100.
59. Ibid., p. 101: Minute by Sir Umar Hayat Khan. The Bengali Battalion was raised with great problems towards the end of the War and sent to Mesopotamia where in 1918 it cracked under pressure. This helped the advocates of the 'martial races' theory.
60. Keith Jeffery, 'An English Barrack in the Oriental Seas'? India in the Aftermath of the First World War', *Modern Asian Studies*, Vol. 15, No. 3, 1981, pp. 369-86, asserts that the *ECR* was guided by War Office ambitions of assuming direct control over the Indian Army. Edwin Montagu considered these aspirations 'idiotic' and the GOI, led by Chelmsford, firmly held that since India paid for it 'India must control its own Army'.
61. *India in 1921-22, A statement prepared for presentation to the Parliament*. . ., p. 14.
62. Ibid.
63. This sub-section is based on the following: GOI Army Department General Staff Branch. Organization Proceedings, February 1921, Nos. 2810-2831—Views of the GOI on Parts I and II of the Report (hereafter ADP, February 1921), HS.
64. *India in 1920, A statement prepared for presentation to the Parliament* . . ., p. 17.
65. Ibid., p. 18.
66. Criticisms by His Excellency the Viceroy on the Secretary of State's control over Military Expenditure in India, 1908 in the Morley Collection (Microfilm), Acc. No. 615. At the time the Secretary of State was accused of 'excessive rigidity' because a sentence in his despatch said that the restrictions on the GOI's power to begin buildings applied also to 'sanctioned measures'. In his reply the Viceroy stated the following: 'The same despatch makes it impossible for us even to build quarters for a subordinate without reference to you if the necessity for quarters arises out of redistribution.'
67. According to the information available from the Army Department Organization Proceedings, December 1923, Nos. 85-112, the Army consumed 50 per cent of the Central Revenues in 1921-2. India in 1924-5, *A statement prepared for presentation to Parliament*. . ., tells us that in the mid-1920s Indian military spending amounted to more than 20 per cent of the net central *and* provincial revenues (about Rs. 600 million out of Rs. 2,200 million). K.N. Reddy, 'Indian Defence Expenditure: 1872-1967', *IESHR*, Vol. VII, No. 4, 1970, points out that between 1900-45 the ratio of Indian defence expenditure to national income remained generally constant, and in our terms, on the higher

side. The situation did not change in the 1930s and the Chatfield Committee (referred to in Section 3 of Chapter 3) found that in 1938-9 the defence expenditure of India accounted for half the total revenue collected by the GOI. Lanka Sundaram, *India's Armies and their Costs*, Bombay, 1946, p. 145, tells us that as late as 1929 the Indian defence budget consumed 45.29 per cent of the total budget of the GOI.

68. *India in 1921-22, A statement prepared for presentation to the Parliament* . . ., pp. 12-13.
69. ADP, February 1921, W.M. Hailey's observations as a member of the Viceroy's Council, 15/3/1920, p. 4.
70. Hailey's observations, op. cit.
71. ADP, February 1921, p. 7, Telegram from the Secretary of State for India, No. 2185, 24/6/1920, Proceeding No. 2813.
72. ADP, February 1921, p. 7.
73. Ibid., p. 8.
74. Ibid., p. 9. The manufacturing capacity of Indian ordnance in 1918 was little short of pathetic; K.M.L. Saxena, *A history of the departments of the Indian Army*, New Delhi, 1974, p. 21, points out that in 1878 there were 10 factories and 1 manufacturing depot in India comprising 3 gun-powder factories, 3 gun carriage factories, 2 small arms ammunition factories, 1 foundry and shell factory, 1 harness and saddlery factory, and 1 small manufacturing depot; S.D. Pradhan, 'The Indian Army and the First World War', in Ellinwood and Pradhan (eds.), *India and World War I*, op. cit., mentions 7 ordnance factories in India in 1914.
75. ADP, February 1921, Munro's observations, p. 11.
76. Munro's observations, op. cit.
77. ADP, February 1921, W.H. Vincent's minute of 10/8/1920, pp. 17-18.
78. Vincent's minute, op. cit.
79. ADP, February1921, Hailey's minute, 16/8/1920, p. 19.
80. Hailey, 16/8/1920.
81. Ibid.
82. Ibid. Army Department Separate, Delhi, 1921, 3/2/1921—Despatch to the Secretary of State for India from the GOI.
83. Ibid.
84. Despatch to the Secretary of State, 3/2/1921.
85. Ibid.
86. Mowatt Committee Reduction of Military Expenditure MSS. Eur D.573/38, Report of Committee on Special Military Expenditure, 1907 in Morley Collection (Microfilm), Acc. No. 1615, NAI.
87. *Report of the Indian Retrenchment Committee, 1922-23*, Delhi, 1923 (*IRC*), CSL.
88. Ibid., p. 7.
89. In the immediate post-War years it was not possible to say that the GOI was certainly going to abandon its 'forward' policy on the frontier

in a hurry. The new policy of holding Waziristan was announced by Lord Chelmsford in 1920 after the conclusion of the Third Afghan War in the following words: 'It is not possible to set any limits to the period of our occupation, our main care being that we shall not lose the advantage gained during the past nine months at the cost of valuable lives and of much money'; Ref. *India in 1920, A statement prepared for presentation to the Parliament*. . ., p. 10.

90. *IRC*, pp. 9-10.
91. In fact, before the *IRC* the Innes Committee had recommended a reduction from 153 officers to 108 at the Army HQ to save 813,000 rupees. The C-in-C had agreed to most of this reduction but, according to the *IRC*, p. 12, even greater reductions were possible.
92. *IRC*, p. 37.
93. According to K.N. Reddy, 'Indian Defence Expenditure: 1872-1967', *IESHR*, Vol. VII, No. 4, 1970, per capita defence expenditure in money terms remained roughly constant between 1872 and 1900. Between 1900 and 1967 it increased, with the periods of large money-term increases being 1911-20, 1941-50, and 1961-7. On the whole, between 1900-45 even as wars pushed up the per capita defence expenditure, the percentage of defence expenditure to total state expenditure and the ratio of defence expenditure to national income remained generally constant.
94. *IRC*, p. 50.
95. Bisheshwar Prasad (ed.), *Official History of the Indian Armed Forces in the Second World War: Volume on the Royal Indian Navy*, New Delhi, 1956, p. 7. This volume was compiled by Lt. D.J.E. Collins of the Indian Navy.
96. Appendix, Case No. 9796: Organization. Attached to the report of the despatch of 3/2/1921, No. 10 (Prepared by General Munro, C-in-C), actually a position paper prepared by Munro before he left India in ADP, February 1921.
97. Munro's paper, ADP, February 1921.
98. Ibid.
99. Ibid.
100. Military Council, 15th meeting, 6/8/1921, MC Proceedings, 1921, File No. 601/10453/H, HS; *Army in India Committee, Table of Meetings* . . ., op. cit.: The fact that the MC was purely an advisory and not an executive body was stressed by its makers during the 33rd meeting of the EC d/4/12/1919 though it was understood that decentralizing staff functions in India would soon raise the question of employing more Indians in important positions.
101. MC Proceedings, 1921, 16th meeting 22/8/1921; 17th meeting 29/8/1921 and 19th meeting 12/9/1921.
102. Ibid., 20th meeting 19/9/1921; and 21st meeting 26/9/1921.

103. Ibid., 24/10/1921.
104. Ibid., 24/10/1921; and 28th meeting 19/12/1921.
105. Ibid., 1922, File No. 601/10454/H, 46th meeting-48th meeting 31/7/1922.
106. Michael Howard, *The Continental Commitment: The dilemma of British defence policy in the era of the two world wars*, London, 1972, pp. 11-16, 26: Imperial defence policy evolved in a tension between Britain, her dominions, and the colonies. London wanted to centralize defence by canalizing the contributions of the colonies and the dominions, whereas the latter desired the maximum permissible autonomy. The problem of paying for defence, however, always remained.
107. The Viceroy to the Secretary of State for India, Telegram No. 113 (Secret) 23/1/1922, File No. 601/10798/H, GOI, Army Department Organization Proceedings, December 1923, Nos. 85-112, Subject: Indianization of the Army, HS.

APPENDIX 1

Report on the Naval Mission to India: Admiral of the Fleet Earl Jellicoe's report to Lord Chelmsford from Bombay dated 30/4/1919

GENERAL OVERVIEW

The naval defence of India was insufficient for modern times for she lacked ships and her harbours were undefended against submarine attack. India had no minesweeping organization and the general and anti-aircraft defence of her ports was very outmoded. India's naval defence, despite the annual subvention of sterling 100,000 paid to the Admiralty by the GOI and the sterling 300,000 spent on the RIM, was the responsibility of the Royal Navy. However, in future India would have to become more responsible for her naval defence and would begin the process with harbour defence. The formation of a Royal Indian Navy equipped with a squadron of light cruisers and assigned the task of also defending the Persian Gulf in the near future was feasible. It was also desirable to have a Naval Board like the Board of Admiralty in England in India with the head of the Naval Board being a member of the Executive Council of the Governor General in Council.

RECOMMENDATIONS

1. The development of naval bases and dockyards.
2. The formation of the RIN as part of the Royal Navy (RN) 'in the strategic sense' but involving Indians and Indian revenues. It was important to enlist the 'considerable population of India which has been accustomed to the sea for generations' in the RIN. Before people who said that Indian seamen could not fight Jellicoe placed three factors requiring remedy: (a) Training and discipline (b) The absence of a long-service system and (c) Low wages. After weighing evidence carefully the following conclusion was reached regarding Indians. 'Generally it may be confidently stated that the balance of opinion is in favour of the capabilities of the Indian native seaman as a fighting asset when well trained and well led.'
3. The service conditions and pay offered by the RIN had to be made attractive to officers of the RN volunteering to serve in the Indian service. Suggested service strength was as follows:

   7 light cruisers with a combat aeroplane each, 3 sloops for the Persian Gulf, 2 or more special river gunboats for Mesopotamia, 6 submarines and a submarine parent ship, 1 Aircraft carrier and 20 armed escort ships for convoys mounting 6-inch AA guns and possibly carrying a fighting aeroplane on board.

PERSONNEL

The RIN would comprise the British, Anglo Indians and Indians for involving Indians in a naval service, considering the tradition of British seafaring, was not, 'by any means an innovation'. Initially the service would be officered by RN volunteers acting as RIN officers but later the transition would take place to an independent corps of officers trained in England. The RIN officers, conversant in Indian languages, would hold the King's Commission and maintain a constant link with the RN and England. Special attention had to be paid to the caste of recruited ratings for whom a long service of 12 years was recommended.

Appendix 1 is based on the following sources: A. Temple Patterson (ed.), *Publications of the Navy Records Society, Vol. III; The Jellicoe Papers, Vol. II; The Jellicoe Papers: Selections from the private and official correspondence of Admiral of the Fleet Earl Jellicoe, Volume II, 1916-1935*, London, 1968, pp. 298-312, Churchill Archives Centre, Churchill College, Cambridge.

TWO

Military Reform Revisited: Indianization in Colonial India (1900-1939)

INTRODUCTION

Indianization meant the commissioning of Indians in the British Indian Armed Forces as King's Commissioned Officers (KCOs). Although some views on Indianization go back to the early nineteenth century genuine Indianization, specially after the Great War (1914-18), implied the recruitment of Indian officers as KCOs in the Indian Army and the *accelerated replacement* of costly British officers with Indian officers. It may also be pointed out at the outset that the Great War created the historical potential for real Indianization which remained unexploited for reasons outlined below.

In the 1920s the colonial military discourse in India found its most systematic and resolute opponent in the vehement nationalist demand for Indianization. British schemes of Indianization before the Great War, like the Imperial Cadet Corps (ICC) created by Lord Curzon, had been designed for ceremonial and symbolic purposes. In the omnipresent colonial quest for loyalty, and in accordance with what the British considered martial in India, these schemes served a limited number of Anglicized Indian aristocrats who were fond of, and obviously impressed by, a lifestyle involving uniforms, parades, polo, and shikar.[1]

After the Great War the British seriously considered the possibility of developing commissioned officers (COs) from the ranks of the Viceroy's Commissioned Officers (VCOs), most of whom belonged to the agrarian 'martial races'. This contrasted with the earlier attempts to recruit a limited number of aristocratic

Indians as officers. British thinking remained preoccupied with the 'martial races' throughout the Indianization debate in response to the issues raised by the politicized Indian middle class. After the Mutiny of 1857 the British had gradually evolved the theory of the 'martial races' hand in hand with the Punjabization of the Indian Army to pursue their military and political interests in India. At the turn of the century the theory of the 'martial races' had become an almost unshakeable orthodoxy in the higher ranks of the colonial military establishment. Since this theory was considered essential to the successful functioning of the professional and largely non-political Indian Army any attempt to undermine it was perceived by the British as an attack on the guarantee of their Indian Empire. Hence, the Indianization of the Indian Army appeared as the beginning of the end of British rule in India for the vast majority of British officials and public.

On the other hand, Indianizing the Indian Army, sustained by Indian revenues as it was, was an essential element of the discourse of self-government preferred by a significant number of prominent Indians after the Great War. On both sides of the debate, the question of national and social identities was considered important. The British resistance to Indianization was predicated upon the rigid colonial classification of Indians into martial and non-martial groups. This semi-historical classification had been slowly and carefully cultivated after the Mutiny of 1857.[2] In contrast, and in opposition to the psuedo-scientific colonial discourse on the subject, the Indian opinion on Indianization was a 'subaltern' attempt to fashion, and even historically reclaim, identities denied to most Indians by colonial ideology.

INDIANIZATION, 1905-1925

Many aspects of Indian military history between the two World Wars were influenced by Indian opinion. Articulate Indians began to pressurize the GOI on matters of military reform soon after 1918 primarily because they had supported Britain during the Great War. This demand for reform was predicated upon popular Indian hopes aroused by the colonial war effort. Furthermore, as part of a broader agenda, the Indians highlighted the role of military reform in a scheme of self-government promised to India during the War. But the Indianization issue was older. Commissioning selected Indians was discussed in Calcutta at a conference held immediately after the Imperial Durbar in 1911. In it Sir Horace Smith Dorrien, representing the War Office, had categorically stated that Indians had to be trained at Sandhurst to be granted the King's Commission (KC). By implication it was emphasized that training in India would produce inferior officers and thereby strengthen racial prejudice in the Army. A course at Sandhurst, in comparison, was held capable of ushering in some equality between Indian and British subalterns to begin with. It was the fond hope of paternalists like Smith that after training at Sandhurst Indian subalterns, like their counterparts in the Anglicized ICS, would start 'their regimental careers with the manners and ideals of English gentlemen'.[3]

This was easier said than done. To the War Office, House of Commons and the British Officers of the Indian Army Indianization was anathema for obvious reasons. The matter was considered so 'delicate and risky' that the War Office's opinion on granting commissions even to the sons of Indian Princes was described by Morley as 'hopelessly narrow'. Morley confessed to Hardinge that the War Office did not 'comprehend the nature and content of the demand for a career of useful activity in the Native Army' and, therefore, its suggestions on the matter were 'sure to be hopelessly wide of the mark'.[4] It was true that in 1905 a symbolic commission for Indian aristocrats and 'gentlemen' had been conceded in His Majesty's Native Indian Land Forces. This inferior commission, authorizing command only over Indian troops, was not fodder enough for an ambitious Indian middle class.[5] By 1911 the War Office, with great reluctance and the approval of the King and Viceroy, had agreed to grant a KC in special cases to a Sandhurst returned Indian of 'high rank' in the ceremonial Household Cavalry. However, as Hardinge pointed out to Morley, this was not what the Indians wanted.[6] The Viceroy knew that giving commissions in the Household Cavalry was 'no solution at all' to a serious problem which was becoming politicized: 'It is a question that will certainly become acute before very long unless something is done to satisfy the aspirations of these younger men, and I think that the nettle should be grasped at once and the movement held in check before it becomes too powerful.'[7]

Regarding the opposition to Indianization amongst British Officers Montagu expressed reformist views even before the Great War ended. British soldiers and officers disliked the idea of serving under Indians. This militated against the times. If Britons could be subordinated to Indians in the Civil Service, according to Montagu, 'it was ridiculous to think that soldiers could maintain out of date privileges'. Montagu was aware of the obstacles in the path to Indianization. But, in his considered view, reform had to prevail over racial prejudice in keeping with changing times. The Indianization experiment had to be 'inevitably tried' even in 'a certain atmosphere of prejudice' because soldiers were 'not the most liberal minded of men'. Moreover, there were other problems waiting to surface because added to the ideological burden of the previous century was the fear of ragging at Sandhurst. After all, if Indians were selected for commissions it was important to make them comfortable otherwise the British would be saddled with the charge of scuttling the scheme in the beginning. Hence, the Viceroy was asked to explore avenues of granting commissions to Indians in India.[8] This implied the eventual establishment of a military college in India fashioned after Sandhurst.

The wartime promise of Indianization justified the Indians who launched a strident campaign for it in the Legislative Assembly soon after 1918. Earlier, on 20 August 1917, while Indian regiments raised with the help of Gandhi and Tilak were fighting for Britain, the Secretary of State announced in the Commons that the 'gradual development of self governing institutions with a view to the progressive realisation of responsible Government in India' would be encouraged by all means after the War.[9] This reformism was also reflected in the Montagu-Chelmsford report which discerned in India 'an ever growing discontent with [administrative] measures which were resented as evidence of racial discrimination'. Prominent among these was the exclusion of Indians from the commissioned ranks in the Army: 'Indian officers form a separate establishment from the British officers, and the highest and the most experienced of the former rank lower than the most junior of the latter . . . . The services of the Indian Army in the war, and the great increase in its numbers make it necessary that a considerable number of commissions should now be given.'[10]

In 1918 the Royal Military College in Sandhurst was totally dominated by the British. Sandhurst training was necessary for acquiring the KC in the Indian Army. But the realization that setting up 'a military training school in India' might 'be desirable' in future to satisfy the Indians was growing. Due to the influence of the widely publicized Montagu-Chelmsford declarations ten vacancies per annum were reserved for Indians at Sandhurst. However, the sources admit, this was 'more a gesture than the inauguration of a policy'.[11] And this gesture predictably failed to satisfy the Indians who soon started demanding substantial concessions. In March 1921, under growing Indian pressure the Legislative Assembly adopted a crucial resolution on the matter moved actually by the government.[12] According to this resolution, all arms of the Indian services were to be opened to Indian Commissioned Officers *in the near future.* Further, unofficial Indians were to assist the authority which would nominate Indians to an entrance exam for admission to a training school producing Indian Commissioned Officers *in India.* In the beginning 25 per cent of all the commissions granted per year were to be given to Indians and the pay of *all commissioned ranks* was to be set on an Indian basis to counter the serious charge of racial discrimination. In addition, adequate facilities were to be created soon for the preliminary training of Indians selected for Sandhurst and steps would be taken to finally establish a military college in India on the lines of Sandhurst. The Indians were later supported by the 'far-reaching recommendations' of the Report of the Military Requirements Committee (1921), which advocated gradual Indianization based on the development of military education in India.[13] It held that since dominions like Australia and Canada had their own military colleges it was only fair that India, with a large standing army, should ultimately establish a college to produce officers economically. Furthermore, since middle-class Indians would, in all probability, be admitted to the Indian services Indianization appeared to their leaders the 'natural corollary' of self-government in India.[14]

It would have been extremely embarrassing for the GOI to ignore the Assembly Resolution of 1921. Hence, it was left with no choice but to frame provisional plans for Indianization. Evidence clearly proves that men like Montagu were rare and on their own the British would *never* have taken Indianization seriously. The credit for putting Indianization on the post-Great War reform agenda goes to those Indians who fought for it in the 1920s. After the resolution of 1921 was accepted by the GOI two Indianization plans were drafted by the Army whereas the third was produced by the Shea Committee appointed by the GOI for the purpose.[15] Let us first look at Gail Wigram's paper on Indianization placed before the GOI in 1921.

Wigram pointed out that Indianization was the most vital part of British policy in India after the Great War and the friendship between the GOI and influential Indians depended on it. Expressing the worries of the Indian armed forces he also assumed that military reform would enable the Indian tax payers to 'shoulder the burden of high military expenditure more cheerfully and willingly'.[16] Nonetheless, it was difficult to grant the KC to Indians in an army wedded to traditions and favoured classes. Indianization also raised the problem of finding suitable Indians for higher military training. The issue was serious because firstly the Indian politicians were demanding the establishment of an Indian Sandhurst in the *near future* and secondly they expected the rate of granting commissions to Indians to *accelerate*. Commissions were being demanded in all the services including the artillery which, following the policy dictated by the rebellion of 1857, was controlled by the British. The issue was delicate because the transformation of the Indian Army and substantial Indianization in the context of mass nationalism could have meant the end of British rule in India. Nonetheless it had to be undertaken with minimum damage to British interests in India in the given political context.[17]

The best way of doing so was to first rationalize theory on the basis of age old stereotypes. Keeping this in mind, Wigram repeated the assertion that during the Great War the *subedars* and *jamadars* had demonstrated their dependence on British officers for initiative and leadership. The British officer possessed important public school attributes. He knew how to 'play for the side' with a 'sense of duty'. Indians, in contrast, were found 'noticeably deficient' in this public spirit.[18] Thus, it was implied that large scale Indianization carried the risk of military inefficiency. The solution to this was to be found in the Unit Scheme. Under this Scheme the Army would be Indianized unit by unit with the Indianized units ultimately comprising a

Dominion Army. Indians would receive a Dominion Commission, instead of the KC, and gradually this Dominion Army would expand into a sort of national Army of India. Since Indianization 'would do more to drive India out of the Empire than anything else' slowing down the reform process was essential in the British interests.[19] The merits and demerits of this unrealistic proposal notwithstanding, the Indians, who wanted to eliminate British officers from the Indian Army as quickly and economically as possible, would have opposed this scheme.

In 1921 another scheme, based on the assumption that Indians were racially and socially inferior to the British, was proposed by Lt. Gen. Cobbe (Secretary, Military Department, India Office, Whitehall). Cobbe knew very well that British officers and men hated even the idea of taking orders from Indians and this, according to him, *could be interpreted* by Indians as racial discrimination. The British, however, were apparently justified in thinking so because in the Army, as elsewhere, they generally considered Indians inferior. Expanding upon the dangers of Indianization, Cobbe stated that it would diminish the supply of British officers to the Indian Army and thereby make it inefficient. Furthermore, the likelihood of friction arising between the Indian and British officers made their permanent co-existence in units a bad idea. These adventurous experiments would weaken the Army and undermine the security of British rule in India in the ultimate analysis. Instead, a defence of British politeness lay in devising a policy designed to satisfy Indian opinion without unduly disturbing British officers. And this could only be done by dividing the Indian Army into a Dominion and an Indian Army. In the beginning a brigade would be Indianized and the number of British officers in it would gradually decrease. Finally, somewhere in the not so near future, more Indianized brigades would form the Dominion Army to replace the Indian Army in a self-governing India.[20] Cobbe's plan, it is easy to see, was similar to the Unit Scheme suggested by Wigram.

While the Dominion Army plan was being examined by a Sub-Committee of the Imperial Defence Committee, the Shea Committee, appointed by the GOI, went about the business of examining Indianization.[21] Opposing the Dominion Army concept on economic and moral grounds it concluded in favour of a careful transition *within* the Indian Army. In its opinion,

Indianization had to start slowly but ultimately Indian officers would have to be appointed to units irrespective of their class composition. First, Indianization would begin in certain carefully selected infantry and cavalry regiments of the Army with the intention of subjecting the Indian subalterns to the toughest conditions prevalent in the Army. This, it was assumed, would satisfy the advocates of Indianization.[22] Later the ancillary services like supplies, etc., would be Indianized. In the interest of military and political stability, and the unmentioned British vested interests in the Indian Army, the number of Indians would increase very slowly in proportion to British officers. The carefully worded conclusion of the Shea scheme militated against the *acceleration* of Indianization desired by the Indians. It was also not free of the racist bias evident in the submissions of Wigram and Cobbe examined above. Indianization was conceived by the Shea Committee as the means for 'ensuring the steady organic growth of *units* in which capacity for *command by and of subordination to members of their own race* shall become inherent in Indian officers and soldiers'[23] (emphasis added).

Arguing along the lines taken by the Esher Committee, the Shea Committee recommended using the class of the largely rural VCOs as a potential source of Indian KCOs.[24] Since there was little to prove that middle class and educated Indians made good officers Indianization had to secure 'the good-will and interests' of the 'fine body of Indian officers of the existing type'. Hence, following the conservative approach favoured by British military policy in India, the Shea recommendations were 'framed with a view to securing to the Army a continuance of the services of Indian officers already serving and of ensuring an adequate future supply of officers from the same sources'.[25] The Shea scheme of complete Indianization envisaged a process spread over 42 years in three stages of 14 years each. The scheme also envisaged the establishment of an Indian military college to produce Indian commissioned officers. After 42 years, according to the Shea Committee, 21 Cavalary regiments, 4 Pioneer and 94 Infantry Battalions, 20 Artillery Batteries and 33 Engineering units would stand completely Indianized. This effort would require 5,464 officers at a wastage rate of 3.5 per cent per annum throughout the period. The scheme, beginning in 1925, was supposed to end in 1967! The annually desired output from the Indian military college would be 111 officers from 1925 to 1938. In the third stage the number of cadets enrolled at the Indian College, which would open and replace Sandhurst from 1925 onwards, would reach its peak. On reconsideration, probably because the year 1967 appeared distant even in the official visions of decolonization, a revised 30-year schedule was suggested by the Committee.[26] Despite all its faults, some credit must be given to the Shea Committee for suggesting a time frame and rate of Indianization for the first time. However, as we shall see, by clearly mentioning the setting up of an Indian Sandhurst it played into the hands of the Indians perhaps a trifle unwittingly.

While the Shea Committee thrashed out the details of Indianization the Viceroy sent a resume of its lines of inquiry to the Secretary of State stating that since the matter was of 'great importance and perplexity' he wanted the Sub-Committee of the Imperial Defence Committee to consider the direction which Shea was taking. Cobbe's plan, which would most probably have necessitated extra expenditure on a Dominion Army, was rejected by the GOI because of the problems the military budget was raising in India.[27] A revealing and highly discursive correspondence between the GOI and London followed.

Whitehall was unhappy with the GOI's objections to Cobbe and desired more knowledge of its position on the matter. Even the economic arguments failed to convince the British government. By November 1921, and obviously to accommodate the Home Government, General Rawlinson had, in fact, formulated a Unit Scheme on the basis of the Shea findings. Now the Secretary of State wanted to know why the Unit Scheme was considered economical by the GOI. The Viceroy, reiterating the bias inherent in Cobbe's plan, explained the Indian position further. Cobbe had sponsored an untrustworthy brigade which was 'useless' from a 'military point of view'. Moreover, Indian opinion and the budget inveighed against the measure. Compared with this Rawlinson's scheme appeared practical and would give Indians a chance to work under British officers without unduly harming their interests. Furthermore, the Viceroy assumed, the Unit Scheme would satisfy the Indians in a way by suggesting a time frame of Indianization desired by them.[28]

However, he forgot to add that Indian opinion was not necessarily reconciled to the Unit Scheme and ultimately his assumptions were challenged by the Indians. Events soon proved that merely suggesting a time frame was not enough to deter Indian opposition to the official schemes of Indianization.

The Viceroy failed to convince the Secretary of State who asserted, somewhat ironically, that the Dominion Army would engender *esprit de corps* among Indians due to the sense of *nationalism* and *patriotism* inherent in it. Furthermore, the rising efficiency in the Dominion Army would eliminate the risk of letting Indian officers command Britons. But the Viceroy remained categorical in pointing out that Indian pressures and the legislature did not favour increases in military spending. Simultaneously, the demand for Indianization was growing and the press was criticizing the GOI's excessive military spending. In such trying times a besieged satrap could only refer to the 'grave embarrassment' a deficit of Rs. 40 crore was causing to his government.[29] The post-Great War financial condition of the GOI was actually quite serious. Although British India had decided to maintain peace with Afghanistan, and some troops were being retrenched on the advice of the Military Requirements Committee, widespread civil disobedience in India put the brakes on large-scale retrenchment in 1921. The government, facing the largest civilian unrest in its history, nonetheless expressed the hope of 'seriously weakening' the 'pernicious agitation' to win some respite in future. But, it was understood, in the near future the Raj would be forced to deliver a 'severe blow' to a movement which was threatening the roots of British rule in India.[30] Indianization, as part of this counter nationalist strategy, had to be politically, socially and economically safe.

London responded with a terse and imperious definition of reform. The outpost was asked to remain vigilant because the announcement of reforms could not be interpreted to mean that the British were even remotely thinking of retreating from India: 'Such an idea, if it exists, is a complete fallacy and its continuous existence can only lead to intensified challenges to our authority and to a decline in morale among the services.' British authority had to prevail at all costs because only a peaceful, loyal and successful working of reforms would lead to self-government. Indianization could be promised, conceived of and put into practice keeping this in mind. Extreme caution in military matters and unwavering fidelity to tradition were the touch-stones of British military policy in India. The historical continuities governing the Indian services since the previous century could not be overlooked in a fit of enthusiasm for the cause of political India produced by the War. In sum, therefore, and at best, the Imperial Government was only willing to tolerate a compromise between the schemes of Indianization present before the GOI. In keeping with these imperatives of British rule in India only four battalions could be selected initially for an Indianization experiment.[31] Wartime promises made to the Indians were to be shelved for the time being.

The Viceroy did not accept this sermon happily. The British Government, he quickly rejoined, had misconstrued the intentions of his government which were based, in fact, on Imperial policy declarations. The Raj, as the experience of British rule in India showed, also had to be benevolent to survive: 'We find ourselves therefore entirely unable either to comprehend or subscribe to the position that the acceptance of a practicable programme, which has been prepared by our own military advisers, can be interpreted as implying a concession to a suggested policy of retreat from India.'[32] Indian opinion on Army reform had to be placated or else the GOI faced the danger of losing more allies in India. In March 1921 the Central Legislative Assembly had passed a resolution saying that in future 25 per cent of all officer recruits per year would be Indians. A year later the Indians were demanding substantial concessions and a miserly Four Unit Scheme would compromise British credibility at a moment when danger was pressing from below. Since the GOI needed collaborators in its effort to overcome the Gandhi led Non-Cooperation Movement, permission was sought to urgently proclaim a broader scheme as soon as possible. But these entreaties fell on deaf ears. In response Whitehall remained quiescent. 'If pressed, your argument would be that policy be dictated by dissent' answered the Secretary of State. The Imperial Government, the Secretary made it quite clear, was 'not prepared to commit' itself 'to a particular programme of Indianization' until the loyalty and efficiency of Indian officers was proven. Initiatives could be sanctioned but substantial Indianization would depend only on their results. New experiments were welcome and even the number of Indianizing units could be increased but Indians were not to be commissioned just because they were Indians: 'It is, we are convinced, just as wrong in the interests of Indian development to give inefficient Indians opportunities the results of use of which will discredit their country as it is to deny efficient Indians the opportunity of serving their country with credit.'[33]

For much of 1922 discussions continued between Delhi and London on features of the scheme to be finally announced. In the summer of 1922 the Viceroy dispatched the summary of the Eight Unit Scheme to India Office stating that Four Units would be 'nugatory' and even Eight Units was a 'narrow basis' to begin with. Permission was needed to announce the Eight Unit Scheme in the Assembly as the beginning of total Indianization of the Army.[34] The salient features of the Eight Unit Scheme were provided by Rawlinson the Commander-in-Chief in India and an avowed opponent of Indianization. From 1923 Indian KCOs would be appointed to the selected Eight Units as Squadron or Company Officers on par with British Officers of the same age and rank. From 1926 only Indian officers would be appointed to these units. It was thought that in the beginning of 1927 all squadron or company officers of these Eight Units would be Indians. After this, promotions would be based on tests after which the Indians would begin replacing the senior British Officers of these units. In the final stages the Indian KCOs would also start replacing the VCOs. The GOI planned to wait till the Eight Units were completely Indianized before assessing the scheme. But the scheme was obviously designed to safeguard British interests and Rawlinson made this much clear to the Shea Committee on 25 January 1922 in the following words: 'However the experiment must be made and all we can do is to give it every possible assistance whilst at the same time preserving the *vested interests* of the British officers in the Indian Army'[35] (emphasis added).

An extremely modest programme of Indianization would have discouraged Indians from preparing for an army career and ten vacancies at Sandhurst were not enough to satisfy them. The possibility that the VCOs in the Indianizing units would be threatened when Indian officers started replacing them could not be ruled out. This would also cause discontent both in the more or less loyal VCOs as well as the Indian KCOs being demoted in comparison with their British counterparts.[36] The Unit Scheme proved unpopular with the Indians although the units chosen represented a cross-section of the Indian Army. But that made no difference to the charge of 'segregation' levelled against the scheme by the Indians. The pace of Indianization calculated for these units was so slow that it would have taken them roughly 22 years to become totally Indianized and that too after the replacement of the VCOs by young Indian KCOs starting their careers lower down compared with British Officers posted in other units. The Scheme was not destined to last that long thanks to the Second World War. By 1926-7, as the supply and frustration of Indian officers grew, growing Indian allegations of 'segregation' and service discrimination necessitated a review of Indianization.[37] In the meantime the Unit Scheme inadvertently enhanced the reputation of Indian officers despite British intentions to the contrary.[38]

Indians had always maintained that Indianization would ultimately be decided by the development of military education in India. Hence, while the Eight Units were being tried, they began to focus on the creation of an Indian Sandhurst which had also been mentioned by the Shea Committee. In December 1924 the Assembly accepted a resolution proposing the establishment of an Indian Sandhurst moved by Mr. Venkatapatiraju.[39] Having conceded Eight Units the government on its part tried its best to slow down the reform process. Hence, it reasserted the shibboleth that since an Indian college would most certainly dampen Army efficiency it was better to train Indians at Sandhurst. Furthermore an Indian Commission would be unacceptable to British personnel who, the GOI stated, would continue to swear by the superiority of the KC. The government also opined that it would be 'monstrously uneconomical' to start a military college in India for only ten cadets. Here the C-in-C completely agreed with it. Rawlinson's opposition to an Indian College smacked of racism: 'If I wanted to ensure the failure of the scheme for Indianization I would create an Indian Sandhurst tomorrow.'[40] In fact, this military bluntness left some of the members of the Viceroy's Council 'rather disturbed'. Rawlinson also denounced Indianization in the Assembly in the following words: 'One of the first difficulties with which we are confronted is that it is no simple matter to create a national army in India, because India is not a nation.'[41] Coming from the C-in-C, such abrasiveness went a long way in fortifying Indian opposition to the official schemes of Indianization. In the event, the view that the British were obviously prejudiced against military reform in India gained ground. But Rawlinson's views exemplified the ideology of the establishment to which he and his predecessors like Field Marshal Roberts belonged. These ideas comprised the core of a military discourse fashioned in India by the British since the nineteenth century.

THE SKEEN COMMITTEE: A BORROWING OF PERCEPTIONS

However, nation or no nation, it did not take very long for the British to realize that the matter was 'quasi-political, quasi-military' and, as usual, some of them wanted a committee to be set up to examine the possibility of opening a Sandhurst type military college in India. Several officials also believed that it was the government's duty to remove the 'ignorance' and 'prejudice' about the subject. Since the GOI had never rejected the Assembly resolution of March 1921 retreating from it in 1925 would have lowered its credibility further. In the meantime the Auxiliary and Territorial Force Committee, formed on the advice of Indian members, demonstrated Indian initiative in military matters. But, as events proved, the government still had fight left in it. Afraid of substantial Indianization, it opposed the Indian stand on the subject in the Assembly in February 1925. Although all Indian non-official members were pressing for an Indian Sandhurst some of them desired more information on the matter before deciding the issue. This division amongst Indians reprieved the government which noted with pleasure that some of these men were forced 'to acknowledge, in their minds at any rate, that further enquiry and careful constructive work by an expert committee would be required' before an Indian military college was established.[42] For the moment, and to the GOI's relief, more Indianization appeared indefinitely postponed. However, the situation could hardly be misinterpreted to assume that the Indians were diluting their long held demand for accelerated Indianization. Leaders like Jinnah, for instance, believed that serious constitutional advance in India was impossible without complete Indianization of the Indian armed forces.

A crisis was precipitated on 3 March 1925 when Jinnah threatened a vote of censure because the GOI's Indianization policy in the past had been 'disingenuous, dilatory and inadequate'. This was enough to convince the authorities that an agitation was 'boiling up' on the issue. Though an Indian Sandhurst was a Cabinet affair the majority of the Viceroy's council supported the idea of at least forming a Committee to examine the possibility of establishing an Indian Sandhurst in the near or distant future. But pockets of resistence remained. Rawlinson, as usual, preferred a committee of 'limited scope' to collect 'evidence regarding the supply of young officers to the army and the best means of giving them their military education'. This worsened matters and finally Jinnah's 'guillotine' fell on the government. On 14 March he forced the Home Member to admit that the GOI would soon appoint a Committee of Inquiry to speed up the process of Indianization. Pushed into a corner, as Army Secretary E. Burdon noticed, it became necessary for the GOI 'to put the matter in train'. Consequently, the formation of the Skeen Committee was announced in July 1925. The way Jinnah, as a secular nationalist, attacked the C-in-C in the Assembly in February 1925 is worth remembering:

> You come here with one excuse or another, and you tell us that there is this difficulty and that, that there is this to be done and that to be done . . . . Has there ever been a proposal which we have suggested which was not rash . . . when have you Englishmen ever agreed with us and said that any proposal we make is not rash? You say, 'It is rash, be cautious'. We have been 150 years under this government. You have deprived the people of India of arms. What have you done?[43]

The Skeen Committee (also known as the Indian Sandhurst Committee) was formed to probe three main and related issues of Indianization. It had to recommend ways of improving the supply of Indians to the Commissioned ranks of the Indian Army. It had to decide whether establishing an Indian Sandhurst was a practicable idea. Finally, it had to say whether an Indian Military College, if opened in future, would replace Sandhurst as the source of Indian KCOs.

To begin with, and in keeping with nature of its membership, the Skeen Committee criticised the Eight Unit Scheme and the general condition of education in India. But the result of its submissions was not spectacular and the period of Indianization it suggested was not very different from the one mentioned by the Shea Committee's plan. The Skeen Committee opined that the Eight Unit Scheme had neither produced significant results nor generated enthusiasm for Indianization in India. Coming closer to the British position on the matter, it asserted that Indians educated in public schools could make excellent officers. Hence, in its scheme, an Indian Sandhurst would succeed in an education system formed by the spread of public schools presumably dominated by the Indian middle class. The Committee also wanted the GOI to shoulder the responsibility of developing military education in India as part of general education. This was held up as the primary responsibility of British rule. After all, asserted the Skeen Committee, the culpability of British policy in discouraging the growth of military traditions in many regions of India could hardly be ignored. Since a general 'disarmament of the people' under British rule had diminished the military impulse among the educated Indians it was the government's duty to develop a 'more comprehensive and widely diffused' military tradition in India. In fact, under Indian influence, the Committee ended up calling British policy the 'general root cause' of the ills which plagued military recruitment in India.[44]

The Skeen Committee found educational standards in India quite low compared with the system of elite dominated public schools prevalent in Britain. These privately owned and run public boarding schools, which catered to various needs of the British bourgeoisie, were widely believed to develop initiative and independence in young boys. Members of the Committee visited England to observe this system at close quarters. Some of these members had personal experience of such schools. Not surprisingly, they were extremely impressed with what they saw. Furthermore publicized European praise of these English schools was harnessed to the argument to make the case of developing public schools in India stronger. The low publicity of military affairs and opportunities in India and the prohibitive cost of training abroad added to the problems created by insignificant investment in Indian education. The selection of candidates for Sandhurst was so 'rigidly official' that it was found 'seriously objectionable' by many witnesses before the Skeen Committee. In England special arrangements had been made to promote NCOs to the Commissioned ranks but in India nothing of the sort had been done. The Committee ignored the fact that this may have been done because the British Army had, due to reasons stated by Barnett, become unpopular in the British middle classes in the 1920s. Since Indianization had to depend upon the 'co-operation and good will' of the VCOs of the Indian Army it was necessary to keep their interests in mind.[45] However, paying lip service to the VCO interests in keeping with stated British policy objectives was one thing and actually converting VCOs into KCOs quite another. The matter might have raised crucial questions of class and caste. How, we are tempted to ask, would the Westernized public school educated urban middle-class Indian co-exist with largely rural 'less' educated and more native VCO turned KCOs in the same Officer Cadre. This problem and its potential consequences were not discussed by the Official and Non-Official advocates of VCO interests. If the problem between Indian and British Officers was racial, the problem between Indian Officers and aspirant VCOs was bound to be that of class and its attendant upbringing.[46]

The Skeen Committee felt that the Eight Unit Scheme made Indianization unpopular by encouraging an 'invidious form of segregation'. It noted that a lecture given at Sandhurst in 1925, which actually claimed that the Eight Unit Scheme was a slow process favourable to British interests in the Indian Army, had been widely misinterpreted in some popular works on India. Many British officers openly expressed the fear of losing control over Indian troops in the event of effective Indianization. The Skeen Committee dismissed these apprehensions and recommended more Indianization. It recommended that the number of seats for Indians at Sandhurst be doubled in 1928 and *increased* thereafter. The artillery, air, engineer, signal, and armoured sections of the Indian Armed Forces had to be Indianized. As a step in this direction, seats were demanded at Woolwich for training in artillery and Cranwell for training in the air force. The Committee recommended the opening of an Indian Military College in 1933. However, to maintain the Sandhurst connection, twenty seats for Indians there would remain. Following all this, according to the Skeen Committee's estimates, 50 per cent of all officers in the Indian services would be Indian by the year 1952.[47]

The submission of the Skeen Committee Report in 1927 was followed by a policy declaration as usual. The Commander-in-Chief, Field Marshall Sir William Birdwood, announced the official policy of Indianization incorporating some of the Skeen recommendations in March 1928. Twenty vacancies were reserved at Sandhurst for educated Indians. And, to satisfy the Skeen Committee *and* long-held opinion of the military establishment, five seats were specially opened for selected VCOs at Sandhurst. Six seats were reserved at the artillery college in Woolwich and six at the RAF college in Cranwell for selected Indians. These were the only concessions the British were willing to make in response to recommendations made by an Official Committee. Further progress, the government repeated, would depend upon the results of these new concessions. Despite the opinion of the Skeen Committee, the GOI stated its unwillingness to abandon the Eight Unit Scheme which was, in fact, to be given a 'full and fair trial'.[48] In fact, it was maintained that upon supply outstripping demand in these Indianizing units, Indian officers would replace the VCOs as platoon commanders to form homogeneous units on the British model. In sum the government planned to intensify Indianization of selected units in opposition to the Indian demand for extensive Indianization. In practice this meant the formation of a Dominion Army because the Eight Units would in any case have formed a 'segregated' army alongside the British led Indian regiments. Why couldn't British subalterns join Indian regiments as VCOs to model them on the British Army pattern is a question the GOI did not answer while sermonizing to the Indian Officers on the issue.

DECEPTIVE POLICY AND THE NATIONALIST CRITIQUES OF INDIANIZATION

A decade after the Mont-Ford Report of 1918 the main issues of Indianization remained unaddressed by British policy. In the meantime the Eight Units, upon which the policy of Indianization hinged, raised more questions. Nobody knew what would happen when Indian KCOs reached higher positions of command in the Indianizing units? How would they be ranked along senior officers of other units? Would the Indianizing units be trusted during War? Would Indian officers relish the idea of replacing the VCOs in the event of British subalterns not doing so in other units of the Indian Army? Policy had no answer to these questions in 1928. The atmosphere was also vitiated by the senseless pronouncements made by the government which, for instance, suggested that there was no need to recruit VCOs in the Indianizing units. This insensitivity to Indian needs was based on the racist presumption that desperate Indian subalterns would not mind replacing their subordinates and, hence, start their careers at a level much lower than that of British subalterns. This would have directly influenced seniority in the Officer Cadre and thereby the issue of higher command.

But by far the biggest blow to Indian aspirations was the rejection of an Indian Sandhurst. This thwarted the acceleration of Indianization. However, the sorely disappointed Indians were left with no choice but protest. Jinnah's adjournment motion in the Assembly, carried by 70 to 41 votes, soon after Birdwood's announcement highlighted the longevity of Indian support for rapid Indianization.[49] Due to the decision to intensify the Eight Unit Scheme only one out of eight Indian officers could hope to command units in future whereas before 1928 approximately one out of three Indian officers could have expected commands. The possibility that increased competition, due to deliberate policy, would generate bitterness in the officers corps and undermine military efficiency could not be ruled out. Among *jawans* too, with promotion to the VCO rank closed in the Indianizing units, disaffection would grow.[50] This could only end up lending credibility to British opinion according to which Indians did not comprise officer material and Indianization was a threat to military efficiency.

Parts of the classified discussion and official thinking on Indianization in 1927 support the charge of dishonesty levelled against the British by Indians like Jinnah. For example, Lord Irwin, wrongly blaming Indianization for the reluctance of young Britons at Sandhurst to join the Indian Army, confided to Lord Birkenhead that the British policy on Indianization was guided more by helplessness than anything else: 'We are all moreover so limited by the pledges of our predecessors, definitely to concede a certain measure of Indianization, that it is not likely to be possible to give any absolute guarantees, which would bring reassurance in this way to the hesitating young men at Sandhurst.'[51] The Viceroy also emphasized the need for more propaganda to influence the British recruits who were hesitating because of the unattractive service conditions in the India. Furthermore, the effect of falling prices on the British Army was discouraging recruitment to the Indian Army amongst the limited number of recruits in Britain. Earlier a boy could join a good British regiment only if he could spare 300 pounds a year. In the 1920s falling prices in England 'inevitably' militated against a Briton voluntarily exiling himself to India. The impressionable British subalterns had to be given inducements and told that the British element in the Indian Army was bound to be great, or perhaps greater than in the Civil Services, and that Indian defence would be the *real* Imperial problem of the future.[52]

The decisions of 1928 can be placed in better perspective if we see how the Viceroy's Council reacted to the Skeen Committee Report in 1927. At the outset it had become clear that the GOI had to increase the number of commissions offered to Indians because of the specific conditions prevalent in India and the official commitments made during the Great War. While discussing the Skeen Report the Viceroy's Council could use three methods of posting Indian officers to the Indian Army. The first, as the Skeen Committee suggested, was to post them anywhere they liked. For obvious reasons guiding long-term British policy this was impossible. The second was to post a maximum of 23 Indian KCOs to more units. Third, it was thought desirable to give Indians a Dominion Commission within the Eight Unit Scheme making them replace the VCOs and the British Officers in gradual course of time. Great caution was required in doing so because Indians disliked even the idea of being given an inferior commission. But to a government, which had all along been biased against Indianization, other matters too were crucial. Irwin expressed the fear of inefficiency once again in the following words: 'The real point of principle and substance, as it seems to me, is that you should do nothing to impair the efficiency of other units than those in which you are already conducting your experiment.'[53]

Considering this the Viceroy's Council, despite the C-in-C's opposition, agreed, in Irwin's words, 'upon a formula which, while not specifically mentioning the eight units' meant 'substantially the same thing'. The compromise lay in the Indian KCOs replacing the British KCOs upwards and Indian VCOs downwards in the Eight Units. The demand for seats at Woolwich and Cranwell had been conceded but was dismissed contemptuously by Irwin: 'We also decided to ask for admissions to Woolwich and Cranwell. As regards the first, I don't think, if you accede to our request, it is the least likely that for years to come any Indians—or at least not more than an odd one—will succeed in qualifying.'[54] This meant that the GOI, instead of addressing the criticism of the Indian education system made by the Skeen Committee, saw India's educational backwardness as a buffer against Indianization. Left to British policy Indianization would have stagnated at the level of 1928. However, under considerable Indian pressure, some decisions were taken by the Sub-Committee of Defence (No. VII) at the Round Table Conference in 1931. This Committee involved Indian delegates to the Round Table like T.B. Sapru, M.R. Jayakar, B.S. Moonje, and M.A. Jinnah. Its 'definite resolutions' demanded steps 'to increase substantially the rate of Indianising the Indian Army'. But Jinnah found this resolution too general and wanted a clear picture of the *pace* of Indianization. This Committee also called for the urgent establishment of an Indian military college. The GOI was asked to form a Committee of British and Indian Experts to 'work out the details of the establishment of such a college'. The Committee was also 'unanimous' in its view 'that the declaration must not be taken as a mere pious expression of opinion' but immediately after the Conference 'steps should be taken to deal effectively with the recommendations made'.[55] Consequently, a Committee of Experts under the Commander-in-Chief, Gen. Sir Phillip Chetwode, was appointed in May 1931. But the Dominion Army concept remained influential. Indianization would now cover a *complete division* of all arms and a cavalry brigade with proportionate provisions for ancillary services, staff, etc., with an intake of 60 officers per year. Since the Eight Units 'were not popular with either the Indian public or the young Indian officer' ostensibly, for the first time, 'a real start with an Indian Army as a fighting proposition, and not merely an experiment' was being made. An Indian Sandhurst was evaded and policy was mentioned in familiar phrases:

> In dealing with the expansion of Indianisation, our object is to create a recognised combatant force on a purely Indian basis, which would in time replace a force of a similar size in the Imperial Army. For it is by the gradual replacement of Imperial fighting formations alone that India will be able eventually to assume responsibility for her own defence . . . Our first task is to create a steady flow of fine young officers.[56]

The disappointed Indians protested. Six Indian unofficial members of the Chetwode Committee submitted 'dissertations' of dissent summarizing the Indian position on Indianization.

According to Chotu Ram, S.N. Mukarji, and Abdur Rahim, the Chetwode Scheme contradicted the Round Table Resolutions which mentioned steps to 'increase substantially the *rate of Indianization*'. In contrast the plan to replace the VCOs with Indian KCOs made the 'apparent increase' in Indianization 'entirely illusory'. There was no point in slowing down Indianization because in the Indian Army 17,000 non-Indians were serving as officers at the cost of the Indian taxpayer. Furthermore the future Military College proposed by the Committee contained no provision for naval and air training. The Minute was critical of the 'experiment' referred to by the Chetwode Committee because it negated the spirit of the Round Table Resolutions; replacing the VCOs by Indian KCOs in the Indianizing Units would reduce efficiency by denying promotion to the jawans and thereby adding to their service grievances. In such circumstances enterprising young men would not join these units.[57]

B.S. Moonje, the Hindu nationalist, asserted that after the Round Table Conference, the GOI had forgotten that Indians 'wanted to be the architects of their own destiny'. The Conference had claimed, *inter alia*, that soon Indians would become responsible for their defence and governance. Quoting extensively from the Defence Sub-Committee resolutions, Moonje highlighted the difference between the theory and practice of reform. Fixing the annual intake to the future college at 60 was a 'sad though highly instructive disillusionment' because no one knew who actually had the authority to fix the intake? The GOI was being presumptuous in fixing the intake because the Sub-Committee had clearly spelt out the functions of the Expert Committee. In any case, compared with the number suggested by the Shea Committee, 60 appeared, at best, parsimonious. With 60 per cent of the candidates being nominated, this concession violated the Skeen Committee Recommendations which wanted nominations restricted to 20 per cent:

This system of nomination perpetuates the myth of the artificial distinction of martial and non-martial classes. It serves as a handle for the people to charge the Government with the policy of 'Divide and Rule'. It propagates the poison of communalism in the body politic of India. It emasculates large sections of the people and as a reaction serves to create what may be called swelled headed in those who are generally enlisted in the Army. It strikes at the very root of the conception of a national Army, and perpetuates the system of a mercenary Army which is the inevitable concomitant of a foreign government.[58]

A comprehensive critique was provided by Sir P.S. Sivaswamy Aiyer and Maj. Gen. Raja Ganpat Rao Raghunath Rao Rajwade. Both criticized the limits imposed upon the Chetwode Committee's scope of enquiry by the GOI. The fact that the C-in-C emphasized the details of an Indian Sandhurst before and not the *pace of Indianization* smacked of authoritarianism. Hence, it appeared that in deciding the terms of reference of the Committee the central issue of Indianization was ignored by the government. The GOI also failed to realize that Indians would reject cosmetic changes and refute the illogical arguments favouring them:

The validity of these arguments will be examined later on. They are considered by Indians to be more specious than sound, but they appeal to the average British layman. The British mind is essentially empirical and wishes to build upon the results of experience and is content to solve the problems of the day without looking forward beyond tomorrow. 'Sufficient unto the day is the evil thereof' is a maxim which more or less accurately expresses the mentality of the average Englishman . . . . If the Empire had to face the danger of another world war on the same scale as the Great War, there can be little doubt that England would be obliged to train India for her own defence within a much shorter period.[59]

Furthermore, the myth of martial and non-martial races could not withstand historical scrutiny. Undermining this myth suggested that British policy on the subject was responsible for diminishing military initiative in the Indians. Since the nineteenth century the British had considered it 'necessary to impress upon the mind of the Indian soldier a conviction of his permanent racial inferiority to the British soldier'. But a different reading of history suggested that military qualities were predicated upon suitable opportunities and training. Since the theory of the martial races had evolved to suit the 'policy of combining absolute political safety with the maximum of military efficiency' the government relied on reports like the one presented by the Simon Commission on military matters. This was unfortunate because the Simon Commission showed 'no intelligent analysis or appreciation of the various causes affecting recruitment' in India. Even the climatic theory, according to which cold and 'bracing climates produced martial people, explaining martial behaviour was baseless:

> If this were a valid argument the British and the Gurkha soldier should not be enlisted for service in India or in expeditions to other tropical countries. During the wars in foreign lands in which Indian troops were employed, nothing was heard of unadaptability of the Indian soldiers to the climatic conditions of other countries.[60]

British military thought, conditioned by the geographical location of Britain, did not appreciate the importance of a national army whereas historical experience showed that a national army was morally stronger than a 'merely professional army drawn from particular classes'. Since the Indian military situation, with India's long land and sea frontiers, was similar to that of the Continental powers only Indianization could develop a national Army in India. The argument for segregation, which blighted the prospects of a national Army, was based on untenable colonial myths, racial discrimination, and British arrogance. Even the fear that British subalterns would ignore the Indian Army if commissions were given to Indians was substantiated only in the case of the aristocratic, and exceptionally haughty, Britons. Considering this, the Indian position on military recruitment was categorical: even if all Britons disliked Indians getting the KC, India would have to be 'prepared to face the situation and learn to do without British recruitment'. No matter what the British said, the real cause of segregation, expressed in the Eight Unit Scheme, was the deep-rooted British apprehension that 'the Englishman's prestige with the native troops themselves would be gone, if they were ever placed under other than British command'. The policy of segregation treated Indian officers *as a class* but nothing proved the superiority of British officers *as a class.* In fact, both the evidence as well as the observations of none other than Lord Roberts after the Boer War revealed serious deficiencies in British Officers and training methods.[61]

The reference to the Boer War, which revealed several drawbacks of the British military model, was most apposite. Our study of the Boer War suggests that the *martial races* theory could only have been sustained by the relative isolation of the NWFP—the main battle cum training ground of the Indian Army. Criticizing the British system of training officers Maj. Gen. R.S.S. Baden Powell had said the following to the Royal Commission on the War in South Africa: 'Junior officers should be given responsibility from their first entry into the service. They should be made to really command their unit, however small, and be answerable for its efficiency and success . . . . The so-called chain of responsibility is too often one of irresponsibility.'[62] Other distinguished officers like Roberts, who was instrumental in keeping the focus of the Indian Army on the NWFP and the 'Punjab Classes', Kitchener and Hamilton were equally, or even more, critical of British field officers. Kitchener said the following about staff and regimental officers: 'There appears to be too often a want of serious study of their profession by officers who are, I think, rather inclined to deal too lightly with military questions of moment . . . . I should like to point out, further, that in the higher ranks also there seems to be a want of that professionalism which is essential to thorough efficiency.'[63]

A tendency to shirk responsibility was noticed in the entire officer corps. Routine over-subordination of juniors to the seniors, in the words of the report, 'blighted the development of their self-reliance and power of decision'. Maj. Gen. Sir Henry Colvile called the 'want of initiative' the greatest fault of the British officers. How much the British officers had actually learnt from skirmishing with tribesmen on the highly romanticized NWFP was mentioned by Sir Ian Hamilton (Military Secretary in South Africa). He also attacked the peace time training methods of the British Army: 'The previous practical peace training of Aldershot proved itself quite unsuited to the requirements of

South African warfare. This training was *calculated* to stunt rather than to develop the initiative of company officers, section leaders, and men'[64] (emphasis added).

The African Wars proved that success in modern warfare depended upon the discipline and individuality of troops. Hence, the Australians, Canadians, and New Zealanders did extremely well in the Boer War because, compared with the average British recruit, they had 'more individuality'.[65] But despite this criticism and the experience of a World War, the mentality of British Officers did not change. After the Great War senior officers of the Indian Army like Lt. Gen. Corbett blamed this mentality for the rising discontent in the Indian Army. In his opinion the racist attitude of most young British officers, who were 'apt to consider themselves infallible with little reason for doing so', alienated the Indians with serious consequences. For example, young British officers in the Indian Army regularly reprimanded the VCOs and NCOs in front of *jawans*. This was deeply resented because British subalterns, also new to the Army and, therefore, prone to making mistakes, were 'not treated in this way'.[66]

The government, as mentioned earlier, also wanted to abolish the VCO rank in the Indianizing units. This was disliked by the Indians. However, because such arguments emerged *after* Indianization started made the Indians suspect them even more. Indeed the Official concern for the VCOs appeared hypocritical: 'The military authorities are so full of tenderness for the Viceroy's commissioned officer that they wish to improve his class out of existence.'[67] But this criticism did not rub off on the British even after the IMA opened. At the third session of the Indian Round Table Conference in 1932 a specific time-frame for Indianization was yet again excluded from policy: 'The view was stated on behalf of His Majesty's Government that the pace of Indianisation must continue to be regulated by stages, while it was pointed out that a programme of Indianisation already exists which extends much further than the previous stage and looks forward to still greater developments in future.' Besides Indianization, the Indians also desired some legislative control over the deployment of the Indian Army but the British were categorical on this point. It was 'implicit in the reservation of Defence' that the Viceroy remained supreme in the decisions involving the deployment of Indian troops anywhere in the world.[68]

CONCLUSION

Among many Anglophile Indians, a certain fondness and nostalgia for the so-called British sense of fair play endures to this day. This chapter has exposed British justice in an important Indian matter for all its worth. This has been done by underscoring the colonial context of military Indianization in British India. The ideological underpinnings of the Indianization problem made sure that Indians, as colonial subjects, were denied their due share in the colonial Indian Armed Forces. Indian and British critics might argue that Indianization was, after all, a policy matter which only affected the English educated Indian middle classes.[69] However, in our opinion, that would amount to overlooking the racism of the British position on Indianization. The point would also undermine the importance of treating the vast *majority of Indians as social subalterns in relation to the British during the colonial period.*

Our story of Indianization asserts that the British disliked the idea of giving the power of command to Indians in the Indian Army for obvious reasons. The fear of losing control over a predominantly Indian Army, and the consequent descent into anarchy, had continuously stoked imperial insecurities and influenced military policy since 1857. This fear virtually dictated British military policy in India since the Mutiny. Conceding the power of command to Indians in the Army threatened the carefully cultivated 'natural' superiority of the British officers. These fears became heightened in the political context of the disturbed 1920s and sharpened some of the British positions on Indianization. But the British discourse on Indianization was predicated upon ideological mechanisms of colonial control which had evolved in the nineteenth century. The division and classification of Indians into social groups identifiable on the basis of certain characteristics—from the British viewpoint—was an important element of colonial rule in India. Hence, certain Indians were said to have criminal tendencies while others were upheld as non-criminal. Some Indians were martial, most were considered non-martial Many were decadent, some were mercifully not. The classification of what was martial in India informed colonial military thought till the very end of the British Empire and became the basis of an identitarian conflict between the excluded Indians and the British. A large number of Britons continued to believe that Indians could be classified into martial and non-martial groups even as empirical evidence accumulated against these beliefs. Hence, the Indianization schemes were suffused with a racism best summed up in General Auchinleck's words. 'In my opinion', he wrote to Amery in 1939, 'we have been playing a losing hand from the start in this matter of "Indianisation". The Indian has always thought, rightly or wrongly, that we never intended the scheme to succeed and expected it to fail. Colour was lent to this view by the way in which each new step forward had to be wrested from us, instead of being freely given. Now that we have given a lot we get no credit because there was little grace in our giving.'[70]

Non-symbolic Indianization began with the Great War. It was explicit in the promises made to Indians by the British in their hour of crisis. However, this magnanimity was short-lived. Indianization was barely touched upon by the powerful Esher Committee. London wanted to revert to token Indianization. Left to itself reform would have ended there. However, the Indians who launched a vigorous campaign for *accelerated Indianization* represented an influential political class. The consequence was the Eight Unit Scheme which segregated Indian officers in selected units which were officially considered inferior to the rest of the Army. The criticism of this scheme led to the appointment of the Skeen Committee whose recommendations, it is well known, were influenced by Indian opinion. Nonetheless, every step of Indianization had to be extracted from the Raj. In 1932, after the Round Table deliberations, the IMA opened but the Indians remained unhappy. This reservation was expressed in well-researched, revealing, and critical commentaries produced by Indians associated with the Chetwode Committee. These commentaries comprise a pursuasive counter-colonial discourse. The opening of the IMA has recently been called 'a very carefully worked out deception plan which did not deceive anyone'.[71] This is so because the Indian Commissioned Officers coming from the IMA began to replace the VCOs in the units selected by the Divisional Scheme. *This did not amount to the acceleration of Indianization and the replacement of British KCOs with Indian officers across the board.* The Divisional Scheme was an *avataar* of the Unit Scheme. This Scheme remained operational till 1939 and can be held responsible for the shortage of trained officers faced by the Indian armed forces in 1939-40. To overcome this shortage created primarily by British policy between the wars the government created the cadre of Emergency Commissioned Officers (ECOs) to tide over the Second World War.

NOTES

1. Some of the racial problems associated with later Indianization were anticipated in these token schemes. One of these was the difficulty of making British soldiers and subalterns salute and obey these Indian officers.
2. I call the theory of the 'martial races' a semi-historical classification simply because military traditions, like other traditions, change. They transform temporally when troops of a particular community or region are deployed *or not deployed* in combat zones. This means state policy, over time, can make 'martial' or 'non-martial' troops. Hence, in the 1880s and 1890s the advocates of the 'martial races' theory conveniently pointed towards the 'unmartial' Madras Army. The system of regional recruitment and deployment followed after 1857 consigned the Bombay and Madras Armies to non-combat zones. In contrast the Punjabized regiments of the Bengal Army were regularly deployed against the Afghans and Frontier Pathan tribesmen. This gave them a more or less recent martial 'history', i.e. the historical content of the 'martial races' classification. The fictional content was, of course, provided by the favoured notions of colonial anthropology which coloured the Indian Army's *Caste Handbooks*.
3. Confidential Simla Records-3, No. 601/10482/H.A.D. Case No. 29147, 1927, Nos. 333-341 & Appendix, Subject: Proposed formation of a well-equipped Military College in a suitable locality in India to train Indians for the Commissioned Ranks of the Indian Army and Appointment of Indian Sandhurst Committee (HS). Recent works covering Indianization comprise the following: Partha Sarathi Gupta (posth.) and Anirudh Deshpande (eds.), *The British Raj and its Indian Armed Forces, 1857-1939*, New Delhi; Lt. Col. Gautam Sharma, *Nationalisation of the Indian Army, 1885-1947*, New Delhi, 1996; and B.P.N. Sinha and Sunil Chandra, *Valour and wisdom: genesis and growth of the Indian Military Academy*, New Delhi, 1992. Indianization is discussed by almost all the standard histories of the Indian Army but a specific bibliography cannot miss Lt. Gen. S.L. Menezes, *Fidelity and Honour: The Indian Army from the Seventeenth to the Twenty-First Century*, New Delhi, 1993; T.A. Heathcote, *The Military in British India:*

The development of British land forces in South Asia, 1600-1947, Manchester, 1995; and David Omissi, *The Sepoy and the Raj: The Indian Army, 1860-1940*, London, 1994.

4. Morley to Hardinge, 19/5/1911, Morley Collection (Microfilm), Acc. No. 1614 (NAI).
5. Committee on the Indianization of the Officer Ranks of the Indian Army (Secret), 18/8/1939, Draft Report, File No. 601/1281/H, p. 2 (HS). Also known as the *Indianization Committee Report 1938-9*.
6. Hardinge to Morley, 23/3/1911, Morley Collection. The Viceroy understood the problem better than many of his contemporaries: '. . . what Indians want is that the sons of important people should be allowed to have commissions in the Native Army. They do not in the least want to be in the British Army, and I hope that this will be borne in mind and that you will be able to come to a solution of this much vexed question on that basis.'
7. Ibid. The cause of concern was also a Resolution of the All India Muslim League passed in its 1911 annual session urging the government to increase commissions for 'sons of Ruling Chiefs and scions of other noble houses' to which Hardinge referred.
8. Montagu to Viceroy, 3/8/1917, Montagu Papers (Microfilm), Acc. No. 1930 (NAI). Opposition to the Indians gaining commissions in the Indian Army continued despite the services rendered to the British cause by the Indians during the Great War. In his letters to Chelmsford dated 16 May and 3 July 1918 (Acc. No. 1930) Montagu touched upon the subject again, saying that while the War Office was opposed to the grant of commissions to Indians, the Military members of the Army Council also expressed their 'grave displeasure' on the issue. Taking the fear of racial discrimination into account, Montagu also advised posting Indian Commissioned Officers to units where they could find some of their own people. Later they could be transferred to other units. The matter had to be handled very carefully because early failures would retard the scheme for many years and British officers of at least one unit did not like the appointments.
9. 601/1079/H, 1923, GOI Army Dep. Org. Proceedings, Dec. 1923, Nos. 85-111, Sub: Indianization of the Indian Army. Gail Wilgram's Confidential Note (GS File 11795)—Indianization of the Indian Army separately inducted in these proceedings (HS).
10. Montagu-Chelmsford Report, cited by Wigram, op. cit.
11. Notes from Appendix, 601/10482/H. Army Dep. Progs. A., March 1927, Secretary of State to GOI, Telegram No. 28, 5 April 1918 (HS): *Indianization Committee Report 1938-9*, p. 4.
12. 601/10482/H, op. cit., Appendix; *Indianization Committee Report 1938-9*, pp. 5-6. The Prince of Wales Royal Military College was opened in

Dehra Dun in March 1922 to provide 70 cadets with public school education. A cogent nationalist position on military reform soon after the Great War was presented in the famous Sivaswamy Aiyer Resolutions accepted by the GOI in March 1921—Ref: *Legislative Assembly Debates*, 1, 11, Official Report, 1921, NMML, pp. 1683-1762—Debate (28.3.1921) on 15 seminal resolutions on the *Esher Committee Report.* Aiyer had formulated these resolutions in a 'critical but constructive' vein.

13. For a summary of these 'confidential' recommendations, see Sharma, *Nationalisation of the Indian Army*, pp. 64-6.
14. 601/10482/H and 12810/H, op. cit.
15. The Committee appointed by the Commander-in-Chief was headed by Lt. Gen. Shea, acting Chief of General Staff, and is referred to as the Shea Committee hereafter—Ref: SECRET Indianization of the Indian Army, Report of a Committee appointed by His Excellency the Commander-in-Chief in India, Delhi, 1922 in the Army Dep. Progs., 1923, Nos. 85-112, Sub: Indianization of the Army.
16. Our account of Wigram's paper is based on a printed copy of it in the Army Dep. Progs., 1923: General Rawlinson, cited by Wigram.
17. Wigram's paper, op. cit., p. 4.
18. Ibid., p. 10.
19. Ibid.
20. SECRET PAPER—Indianization of the Indian Army by A.S. Cobbe, sent to the Chamberlain Committee from Whitehall, 14/9/1921, Army Dep. Progs., 1923.
21. Telegram from the Secretary of State to Viceroy, No. 5960, 21/22 Nov. 1921, Army Dep. Progs., 1923.
22. The move could easily have been conceived with the intention of making it backfire. Had the Indian subalterns faltered in these hardened fighting formations, their failure would have been held up by the colonial authorities as an example of Indian military ineptitude to the advocates of Indianization.
23. *Shea Committee Report*, p. 4. On p. 11 the familiar moral argument of British superiority followed: 'In the absence of a conscious, mature and homogeneous national spirit in India the moral factor most essential to the creation of a "Dominion Army" does not exist, and only in units of the regular army are to be found those moral influences arising from a history of service and achievement in war which are a most valuable reinforcement to the national spirit.'
24. I have examined the Esher Committee Recommendations in detail in Gupta and Deshpande (eds.), *The British Raj and Its Indian Armed Forces, 1857-1939.*
25. *Shea Committee Report*, p. 9.

26. Ibid.
27. Viceroy to Secretary of State, 24/11/1921, Tele. No. 2005, Army Dep. Progs., 1923.
28. Secretary of State to Viceroy, 29/30 Nov. 1921, Tele. No. 6088 and Viceroy in reply, 8/12/1922, Tele. No. 48c, Army Dep. Progs., 1923.
29. Secretary of State to Viceroy, 8/10 Dec. 1921, Tele. No. 6219, Viceroy in reply, Tel. No. 43, 11/1/1921 and Viceroy to Secretary of State, 5/2/1922, Tel. No. 19, Army Dep. Progs., 1923.
30. Viceroy to Secretary of State, 5/12/1992, op. cit.
31. Secretary of State to Viceroy, 14/15 Feb. 1922, Tel. No. 674, Army Dep. Progs., 1923.
32. Viceroy to Secretary of State, 18/2/1922, Tel. No. 262, Army Dep. Progs., 1923.
33. Secretary of State to Viceroy, 22/23 Feb. 1922, Tel. No. 807 and Viceroy in reply, 25/2/1922, Tel. No. 300, Army Dep. Progs., 1923. On foreign policy and Indianization the reservations and advice of the Home Government were accepted by Delhi 'with great regret'. Even in Waziristan the Imperial Government very regretfully allowed the GOI to abandon the unfavourable forward policy.
34. Viceroy to Secretary of State, 16/3/1922, Tel. No. 835-F and Secretary of State in reply, 20/21/3/1922, Tel. No. 1213, Army Dep. Progs., 1923.
35. SECRET 1922 Simla Army Dep. Separate No. 45, 3/8/1922: Dispatch to His Majesty's Secretary of State for India, Sub: Indianization of the Indian Army. The Viceroy sent the summary of the Eight Unit Scheme to the Secretary of State on 28/7/1922 ref. Tel. No. 999 (Simla), Army Dep. Progs., 1923.
36. Army Dep. Separate 45, op. cit., p. 5, warned against a communal combination of Indian officers and men even though the nationalists had never raised the issue: 'It is conceivable that a demand might be made under any scheme of Indianization for officers to be distributed to units on a communal basis. We should, in anticipation, for reasons which it is hardly necessary to specify, definitely exclude this possibility.'
37. This aspect of Indianization was noticed by the Indianization Committee of 1938-9. The units chosen were: 7th Light Cavalry, 16th Light Cavalry, 2/1st Madras Pioneers, 4/19th Hyderabad Regiment, 5th Marathas (MLI), 1/7th Rajput Regiment, 1/14th Punjab Regiment, and the 2/1st Punjab Regiment. Byron Farwell, *Armies of the Raj*, Viking, 1989, p. 298, mentions that the scheme 'was not a success'; Cohen, *The Indian Army*, p. 84, draws attention to the fact that the scheme only temporarily satisfied the Indians; Longer, *Red Coats to Olive Green*, p. 199, points out the extremely limited benefits of the scheme.
38. As a breach in the commissioned ranks, the Eight Units opened visions of success besides providing India her first batch of post-Second World

War generals. By concentrating Indian officers in a few units, and not dispersing them into obscurity, the Scheme gave the *jawans* a chance to judge them. It is probably true, and also because the chosen Eight Units were mixed, that working within the Scheme exposed Indian officers to a cross-section of the Indian Army. Personal details of this experience are recorded in the following: H. Evans, *Thimayya of India: A Soldier's Life*, New York, 1960, pp. 102-3; Gen. J.N. Chaudhuri, *An Autobiography as Narrated to B.K. Narayan*, New Delhi, 1978, p. 54; and Lt. Gen. S.P.P. Thorat, *From Reveille to Retreat*, New Delhi, 1988, pp. 1-47.

39. Confidential Simla Records-3, No. 601/10482/H.A.D. Case No. 29147, 1927, GOI, Army Dep. Organization Proceedings A, March 1927, Nos. 333-341 and Appendix, Sub: Proposed formation of a well-equipped Military College in a suitable locality in India to train Indians for the Commissioned Ranks of the Indian Army and Appointment of the Indian Sandhurst Committee, 1925-6 (HS) (hereafter *ADP 1927*).
40. *ADP 1927*, section on *loci classici* of Indianization. These views were expressed in 1925 the year Rawlinson died.
41. Viceroy Reading to Lord Birkenhead, Secretary of State for India, 12/3/1925, Birkenhead Collection (Microfilm), Acc. No. 1948, NAI.
42. *ADP 1927*; M.M. Malviya and M.L. Nehru were among such men.
43. Ibid., *Skeen Committee Report* (Report of the Indian Sandhurst Committee, Simla, 1927), chapter on the background of Indianization; *Legislative Assembly Debates*, Vol. V, Part II, Official Report, Delhi, 6 March 1925 (NMML)—Debate on Indian Sandhurst, Resolution *RE* Establishment of a Military College, 19 Feb. 1925, pp. 1220-73. The participants in this debate were B. Venkatapatiraju, Sir Sivaswamy Aiyer, M.A. Jinnah, M.M. Malviya, E. Burdon (Army Secretary), Col. J.D. Crawford (European member from Bengal), Captain Ajab Khan (non-official member from Punjab) and M.L. Nehru.
44. *Skeen Committee Report*, pp. 12-13.
45. Ibid., pp. 14-16.
46. This contradiction was resolved in favour of the Indian middle class in the Indian Republic. Commissioned Officers receive their Commissions after being trained at the Indian Military Academy (IMA), Dehra Dun (the equivalent of Sandhurst). The cadet entrants to Dehra Dun come from the National Defence Academy (NDA), Khadakvasala (near Pune), where boys straight out of school train for the three services before finally being commissioned in a particular service. The admission to the NDA is based on an open entrance examination which is much easier for public school-educated boys to clear in comparison with boys educated at the ill-equipped and neglected government schools.
47. Extracts of the Sandhurst Lecture are present as Appendix III of the *Skeen Committee Report*. Apprehensions of British officers were

articulated by Valentine Chirol whose *The Modern World Series*, India, 1926 was quoted by the Committee; SECRET 1922 SIMLA, Army Dep. Progs. Separate No. 45, op. cit. See the KCO time scale/age as follows: Beginning as Lieutenant at 20, Captain at 29, Major at 38, and Lt. Colonel at 46. Even the complement of officers carried by an Infantry Battalion of the Army was not very high: it had 12 Officers comprising 1 Commandant (Lt. Col/Col), 1 Second in Command (Lt. Col/Maj.), 4 Company Officers (Lts/Caps), 1 Adjutant Officer (Lt/Cap), and 1 Qquartermaster Officer (Lt/Cap); The *Skeen Committee Report*, pp. 23-33, called for public schools, scholarships and special arrangements for the sons of the VCOs in India.

48. *Indianization Committee Report, 1938-9*, p. 22; *Legislative Assembly Debates*, Vol. 1, Official Report, Delhi, 1-27 March 1928, announcement of government policy and general military review by Commander-in-Chief, 8 March 1928, pp. 1175-87. Certain concessions in accordance with the Skeen Committee recommendations would be granted to India but with time, 'the scheme would have to be reconsidered and, if necessary, revised from the standpoint of efficiency'. This left M.L. Nehru 'cold' and 'completely shattered' Jinnah's 'faith in the bona fides of the British Government'.

49. *India in 1927-28, A statement prepared for presentation to the Parliament in accordance with the requirements of the 26th Section of the Government of India Act (5&6 Geo V (Chap. 61)*, Calcutta, 1928, p. 31[illegible]; Government policy on Indianization remained doubtful in this period. *India in 1930-31, A statement prepared for presentation to the Parliament*. . ., Calcutta, 1932, p. 43, referred clearly to 'extraordinary difficulty, indeed the impossibility, of establishing a coherent, efficient, and reliable army officered by Indians within the time desired by the critics of the Government'. The Storeman Scheme, as the same source, p. 28, pointed out, was a good example of minor Indianization attempted by the GOI. The Storeman Scheme was designed to replace British Other Ranks (BORs) by Indians as assistant storekeepers in the Indian Army Ordinance Corps and was 'financed' by reducing the number of Indian sepoys in the same department! According to the report, this made 'it appear as though little or no increase in the Indian establishment' was actually being made.

50. 1/5 Correspondence and notes about Sikh troubles in the Indian Army, The Papers of Lt. Gen. Thomas William Corbett, Churchill Archives Centre, Cambridge tell us that elements of British recruitment policy geared to achieve a favourable balance in the units also led to growth in intrigue and discontent. For instance, during the late 1920s the policy of balancing *manjha* and *malwa* recruits in the Sikh cavalry was linked to discontent among Sikh troops. During court martials, promotions and recruitment, British officers could also easily be accused of

favouritism. In fact, the situation was serious enough for a certain officer Reynolds to write to Corbett that the Sikh troops were well behaved in face but extremely hesitant to use force against religious leaders. Reynolds was asked to exercise caution in promoting men because in at least one cavalry squadron promotions were being considered at the last moment and names 'calculated to reduce the efficiency of the Sqn.' were being mentioned, presumably by the Indian VCOs.

51. Viceroy Irwin to Lord Birkenhead, 28 March 1927, Birkenhead Collection, op. cit., Acc. No. 1949.
52. Ibid.
53. Irwin to Birkenhead, 14 July 1927, Acc. No. 1949.
54. Ibid.
55. Indian Round Table Conference, 12 November 1930-19 January 1931, Proceedings, London, 1931 (Cmd. 3778), Sub-Committee No. VII, Whole Conference held on 16 January 1931, p. 395.
56. *Chetwode Committee Report*, p. 21; *Indianization Committee Report 1938-9*, p. 31; *Progress Report on the armed forces for 1929-30*, 601/10848/H, Secret, Delhi, 1930 (H) tells us that the long-awaited Kitchner College was opened in July 1929 to prepare NCOs for VCO rank and as platoon commanders; *India in 1931-32, A statement prepared for presentation to the Parliament...*, Calcutta, 1933, section on Indianization mentions that the Indian Military Academy opened in Dehra Dun in October 1932 with the aim of taking in 40 cadets every two years. Of these 12 were to be selected by open competition, 3 were to be nominated by the Commander-in-Chief from among the other qualifiers of the examination, 15 were to be serving soldiers of the Indian Army including the Auxiliary and the Territorial Forces, and 10 were to come from the Indian States Forces.
57. Minute by Chotu Ram, S.N. Mukarji, and Abdur Rahim appended to the *Chetwode Committee Report.*
58. Minute by Dr B.S. Moonje appended to the *Chetwode Committee Report.* Earlier Indians had vehemently opposed the *Simon Commission Report* on similar grounds. Even Nirad C. Chaudhuri, *Thy Hand Great Anarch: India 1921-1952*, London, 1987, p. 321, called the report 'a dishonest document'. Even before the Indian Military College Committee (Chetwode Committee) had concluded its report in July 1931, Chaudhuri wrote a series of well-informed articles criticizing the martial races theory in the *Modern Review* between 1930 and 1931. Later in an article in the same Review for October 1931 he examined the Chetwode Report, finding it 'an ungenerous and unintelligent sneer'. Earlier in a letter to Sir Sivaswamy he had warned against the British attempts to 'convert' Indian 'cadets into imitation polo-playing English subalterns, weaned away from their habits and tradition, which will make them as ineffective or offensive as the majority of the Indian members of the services'. In fact, Chaudhuri

emerged as a publicist because of his acclaimed articles on the martial races. A precise summary of his involvement in the Indianization issue is given in *Thy Hand Great Anarch*, pp. 319-28.

59. Minute by Sivaswamy Aiyer and Maj. Gen. Rajwade appended to the *Chetwode Committee Report*.
60. Ibid. The example of the Duke of Wellington doing with the 'scum of the earth' in the Peninsular War was given by Aiyer and Rajwade.
61. Minute by Sivaswamy Aiyer and Maj. Gen. Rajwade appended to the *Chetwode Committee Report*.
62. *Report of the Royal Commission on the War in South Africa*, Vol. III, 1904 (Cmd. 1791, CUL), Minutes of Evidence, pp. 424-5: Powell's view was very critical. Angered by the fact that very few of the British officers or men knew 'how to sharpen a sword or how to keep it sharp on service', he emphasized the educational reform of the officer corps and the promotion of battlefield resource and cunning as opposed to the existing overemphasis on barrack square drill, form and deadening routine.
63. *Report of His Majesty's Commissioners appointed to inquire into the military preparations and other matters connected with the War in South Africa, 1903* (Cmd. 1789, CUL), pp. 53-4.
64. Ibid., pp. 55-6.
65. Ibid., p. 79; this was the view of none other than Field Marshal Lord Roberts.
66. 1/5 Correspondence and notes about Sikh troubles in the Indian Army (1928), Corbett Papers, op. cit., Corbett's advise to young officers was simple: 'We cannot all be interpreters in the language. A far more important factor is knowledge of human nature and justice tempered by cool judgement and the milk of human kindness. If British officers consider themselves exempt from the standards of smartness in dress, punctiliousness and general military thoroughness demanded of them, slackness and inefficiency are bound to occur in the Regiment.'
67. Minute by Aiyer and Rajwade, op. cit.
68. *Report on the Indian Round Table Conference (Third Session), 17 November 1932–24 December 1932*, London, 1933 (Cmd. 4238, CUL), pp. 45-7.
69. In some sense, this 'creamy layer' syndrome argument is used against affirmative action (policy of reservations) these days. There is some merit in it although it is significant to note that affirmative action must begin somewhere for a 'creamy layer' to develop and emerge in the first place. In the colonial context, therefore, a policy of Indianization involving relatively small sections of the Indian middle class would have constituted a progressive development.
70. Auchinleck to Amery, quoted in Menezes, *Fidelity and Honour*, pp. 338-9.
71. Gautam Sharma, *Nationalisation of the Indian Army 1885-1947*, Preface.

THREE

Modernizing the Indian Armed Forces: The Inter-War Period

> Strategy is harnessed to the political chariot. Therefore it is important for soldiers to understand political bearings on strategy. In modern war, a great problem of social economies and psychology has superimposed itself on the strategical problem . . . . The Indian Empire rests largely on Indian opinion . . . . Briton and Indian must co-operate.
>
> —2/11, Staff College, Quetta, 1931, Lectures I & II Precis, Winter Term, *Corbett Papers*

During the Second World War, more due to circumstances than conscious British policy, the GOI granted 15,000 Emergency Commissions to the Indians in a bid to overcome the debilitating shortage of officers faced by the Indian services in 1939-40. On the basis of the generalizations made in the previous chapter, it can be asserted that this deficiency was caused, *inter alia*, by inadequate Indianization during the inter-War years. However, the acute shortage of officers and trained personnel in the Indian armed forces in 1939-40 was one of the many problems plaguing the Indian services at the time. Some of these problems are studied in this chapter which shows how the legacy of the 1920s, involving economic limitations and policy indecision, continued to blight the Indian services in the 1930s.

THE ECONOMIC CLIMATE OF THE 1920s AND 1930s: A RESUMÉ

In the 1920s a widespread modernization of the Indian armed forces in accordance with changing international demands could not be undertaken because retrenchment and a budgetary freeze prevailed over the Indian military establishment. Between the two World Wars the Indian military budget comprised two parts. The 'standing charges' were the ordinary maintenance charges whereas the 'new demands' constituted the difference between the total budget and the standing charges. Sources make it clear that by 1927-8 the GOI was trying to 'escape from a dilemma' which lay in its inability to acquire much needed capital expenditure for the armed forces. It was estimated that Rs. 100 million were needed to re-equip the obsolete Indian services in the coming years. In 1927-8 the military budget alone stood at Rs. 550 million and the GOI could not spare more for improvements. Since the post-Great War retrenchment had gone too far, it was decided to create a system to hold the budget for the 1930s for the benefit of the services. According to this scheme, it was decided not to let the annual military budget decline below Rs. 550 million during the four years beginning with the financial year 1928-9 to permit savings in any year to be carried over to a suspense account which would be drawn upon in the later years. Simultaneously an affordable programme of reorganization and re-equipment was approved. Despite all the limitations faced by the Indian services, these steps could have led to some improvement but from 1930-2 onwards 'a deterioration in the general finances of India' postponed reform. In 1930-1 the sanctioned stabilized figure was reduced to Rs. 542 million and next year it declined to Rs. 563.3 million. Furthermore, as a 'contribution in the national emergency' the armed forces had to accept a cut of Rs. 52.5 million in the 1931-2 budget. This brought down the projected estimate for 1932-3 to Rs. 466.5 million. This was obviously resented by the C-in-C and could hardly be accepted as the new level of standing charges because the normal cost of maintaining the armed forces was about Rs. 480 million despite depressed prices.[1]

As a result of falling revenues in 1931-2 only 519 million rupees were sanctioned and the hard-pressed services were denied the savings made with great difficulty by them. The 'abnormal financial situation' forced the Army member to give up Rs. 11.3 million which represented the savings effected within the forces due to a fall in prices and economies carried out. The recovery formally initiated in 1928 stopped when retrenchment was forced in ordnance factories, expenditures were slashed in most departments, and *capital expenditure* was minimized. This happened in a period when the need for mechanization in the services was growing keeping in mind futuristic battle scenarios. In 1929-30 the armed forces were not even partially mechanized whereas ordnance, signals, and transport stagnated at the levels attained during, and due to, the Great War. From 1934, as War drew closer, conditions worsened, and it was unhappily accepted in official circles that a shortage of technical manpower would hamper mobilization in the event of War. Even day-to-day maintenance, leave alone additions, became difficult as the depression made its presence felt. New machine guns, for instance, could not be produced till as late as 1938-9. A specific programme for mobilization also could not be formulated till then. In 1938 the GOI admitted to the Secretary of State that continued financial stringency over the years had made India's military position extremely vulnerable and general war reserves were running dangerously low. New equipment was not easy to come by, coastal defence remained neglected and the deficiency of officers was more than serious.[2] It was in these conditions that the Chatfield Committee visited India to suggest a plan for streamlining Indian defence.

Problems were exacerbated by policy indecision. The differences between the GOI's position on military expenditure and the direction the British government wanted it to take persisted into the 1930s. Even as the debate on Indianization took precedence over other military matters, the problem of viably financing the Indian armed forces remained unsolved in the mid-1920s and British demands worsened matters. For example, as late as 1925 the War Office made large claims against India. An 'amazing' sum of 40 million pounds was demanded from India ostensibly for the services rendered to India by Britain during the Great War although it was clear that this could never be recovered 'in view of the contributions India did in fact make in the War'. Furthermore, as far as military burdens outside were concerned after the War, as the Viceroy mentioned, 'it would now seem impossible for India to assume obligations that rested somewhat lightly upon her shoulders before the War, but might at any moment now become a heavy burden without the power in her of controlling the major policy that caused the increase'.[3] The War Office claims were also related to the deployment of

Indian troops outside India in the 1920s. For instance, the War Office claimed payment from Indian funds for the Indian troops sent to China in 1927. This caused considerable concern in India at a time when post-1918 retrenchment was in full swing. In such circumstances, Irwin trusted Birkenhead to be 'able to induce the War Office to withdraw' this claim. The Indian position was once again emphasized by Irwin in the following words: 'Apart from the merits of the question, it would be, as you appreciate, a source of considerable political embarrassment to us if our revenues were so charged, and would be likely to raise very awkward questions of more general principle.'[4] However, the British government was not willing to take Indian objections seriously, and to justify its arguments it had resolved in early 1927 that the Army in India could be deployed outside India for purely defensive purposes. In addition, the Cabinet had also resolved that the Indian Army could be employed outside India in a very grave emergency, with the previous consent of the Governor-General in Council, of course, for purposes which were 'not purely defensive'. Furthermore, and as an assertion of imperial discretion, it was clearly stated that as a principle of policy Indian troops could be used for *continuous* garrison duties outside India.[5] This meant that for practical purposes London saw no difference between the Indian and the British Armies either of which could be used to safeguard the British Empire.

While the War Office continued to demand money of the GOI, which the Imperial government could not muster for its imperialist ventures outside India, observations on the economies being effected in the Indian Army spoke of the problems of internal military finance faced by the GOI during the late 1920s. We have already surveyed the financial impotence of the Military Council in India in the early 1920s. However, demands from all military departments grew almost relentlessly in the following years. By the late 1920s deficiencies in the Indian Army were great enough to prompt the General Staff to apprise the government of them. On the other hand, the GOI, trusting 'the goodwill' of its generals, was trying its best to enforce more economies in the military establishment. In this context, savings in the Indian Army went back 'in toto' to the government, making the entire intra-services exercise fruitless. The trend being set was bad because obviously no officer was inclined to save money which merely reverted to 'a remote Government from which it (had) been with difficulty extracted'.[6] But savings were important in the Army because they were needed to finance fresh expenditure and the reluctant officers had to be convinced that these savings would not go to the government 'in toto'. The Public Accounts Committee of 1927 realized that only this could be the real incentive to 'secure internal economies' in the Army. The Public Accounts Committee also made it clear that if the Army did not get a free hand in using the savings made within it the demand for additional grants would continue to rise to the growing discomfiture of the GOI.[7]

These conditions made the Indian Army unattractive in the labour market. A serious shortage of officers, the reasons for which have been examined earlier, was already threatening military efficiency in the late 1920s. In 1927, for instance, the situation of British officers in the Indian Army was 'not at all satisfactory'. The Indian Army was apparently living off its own capital; and on the basis of figures for 1923-7 a deficiency of 35 officers was predicted for the end of 1927 and 100 officers at the end of 1928. The normal intake of British officers required for the Indian Army, also due to retarded Indianization we may add, was about 120 a year but for the years 1923-7 the Indian Army averaged between 55 and 60.[8] By the end of 1927 the GOI was facing a crisis in the recruitment of British officers to the Indian Army and Irwin spoke of the 'very serious problem of stimulating recruitment for the Indian Army'. According to him, the youthful and adverse impressions of the Great War were 'subconsciously' weaning away young Britons from the Army. Also noticeable among the young recruits was the desire to earn quick money; become independent, and get married. Moreover, the great temptations offered by business propaganda were not being challenged by the service conditions offered by the armed forces in the 1920s. Irwin, in passing, also referred to the British fear of serving under Indians and the insufficient 'pecuniary inducements' prevalent in the Indian Army.[9] These trends could only be effectively countered by making the armed forces more attractive to the youths at Sandhurst and elsewhere.

Several senior officers also felt that the Indian Army had to be modernized but the arrangement of Imperial defence militated against this. Everyone knew that the Indian Army had an 'important element of talented, efficient and highly trained leaders' and the best of these were found amongst the subalterns of the Great War. These were men like Corbett who emphasized the growing significance of mechanization and general modernization in the context of international developments. They also 'urged modernisation, organisation of defence on an Empire basis, younger command, liquidation of sick shows' often '*against the strongest opposition* of their seniors' (emphasis added). One of the defects in the Army organization pertinent to the whole empire was the lack of opportunities faced by the senior officers of the Indian Army to serve as seniors in the British Army. Moreover, the Indian Army also suffered because quite often its veterans were consigned to Frontier Defence and Watch and Ward services in India. This wasted precious military talent and contributed to the growing frustration especially among the younger and better officers.[10] It was also important to maintain the supply of regimental officers whose significance had been demonstrated by the Great War. In sum, therefore, the lessons of the Great War taught that a peacetime scaling down of the establishment of regular officers proved costly during War. The regular officer, in the words of the critic, was 'not a luxury, but an insurance, for which the premium' was worth paying.[11]

The Indian military conditions of the late 1920s and early 1930s necessitated a formal review, and possible retrieval, but the overstretch caught up with the British Empire in the 1930s. In this context, the Chatfield Committee only stated the obvious while admitting the military failure of the British in the East in 1939: 'The fact must be faced that Great Britain may not now be in a position to guarantee India's external security in the same measure as in the past.'[12] Furthermore, the prospects of military reform, which would have included important social changes in the Indian armed forces, appeared bleaker in 1939 because the Chatfield Committee, as late as 1938, opined that Indians could not be trusted with self-rule and that British troops were necessary in India to maintain peace between Hindus and Muslims. The Indian National Congress, despite being in government in several Indian provinces after the elections of 1937, was viewed with unnecessary suspicion by the high-powered Chatfield Committee. The Committee also seemed to have overlooked the fact that under the GOI Act of 1935 defence remained a central and 'reserved' subject over which the provinces had no power. Furthermore, by the 1930s British policy had made it clear that Indianization and the Cabinet approval of military reform in India *did not mean granting control* to Indians.[13]

This only proved the nationalist critique of British military policy right and created the conditions of political trouble in India during the Second World War. The basic tenet of British military policy, according to which educated Indians were militarily untrustworthy, held steadfast during the 1930s only to be expressed in the Chatfield Committee's observations. However, the views of veterans like Corbett clashed against much of the official perception in the late 1930s. He wanted to associate 'representative and responsible Indian opinion' with British and Imperial 'military confidence' to enhance it. According to Corbett, Army organization in India, in order to become sensitive to contemporary needs, had to shift away from the presumptions of the Cardwell System which exaggerated the role of the NWFP in Indian and Imperial defence. But above all, no profit would accrue to the British if they insisted on holding India 'by the throat' or gain its 'grudging support in an Empire emergency'.[14] Although Corbett favoured respecting Indian opinion even in military matters, British military policy, in general, remained unaffected by either Indian opinion or the actual Indian military situation in the 1930s.

This also becomes clear by the way the Garran Tribunal surveyed Indian defence in 1933. In 1932 the Ten Year Rule was revoked and the process of British rearmament began. This obviously raised the question of Indian military preparedness and financial viability. However, the deployment of British troops in India and their burden on the Indian exchequer had been discussed at the Round Table Conference of 1931. Following this, in 1933, a Capitation Rate Tribunal was set up in London to assess the respective share of India and Britain in mutual defence and the subsidy India deserved. According to this 'Garran Tribunal', in future India would be responsible for managing the *minor* danger and England the *major* danger in the event of a full-blown threat to the Empire. Consequently, the 'Garran Award' relieved the Indian taxpayer of the cost of only ten British infantry battalions placed in India and in 1933 it was decided not to reduce further the number of British troops in India.[15] At the time these small steps could and did not generate a substantial sum of money for the much needed modernization of the Indian armed forces.

The Garran Tribunal Report reiterated the primary principle of British military policy in India. The Tribunal overruled the demand for 'generosity' voiced by the GOI which was desperate for more money to meet its military obligations. According to the Tribunal, the question of expecting Britain to be generous towards India did not arise because the latter was felt to be an 'independent bargainer' in its relationship with Britain. The Tribunal also remained impervious to the political sentiment regarding defence prevalent in India: 'Political sentiment considered apart from the question whether it has a sound basis in reason is irrelevant to the question of what is fair and right. Right is not made wrong merely by being thought wrong by a large number of people.'[16] Even India's economic condition and the poverty of the majority of her inhabitants were not considered causes real enough to determine her capacity to pay for defence. It was held that the ratio of Indian military expenditure to revenue was high (50 per cent of Central *and* 20 per cent of Central and Provincial revenues as indicated in Section 2 of Chapter 1 earlier) because of her geographical nature and internal strife and not because of British rule in India. The Tribunal, presumably forgetting that British rule *per se* was responsible for Indian problems, asserted that India, her government and people, had to learn that defence was not a luxury 'but a necessary protection that has to be paid for'. The security of the Imperial interest was foremost in British policy calculations and even if it was true that a decline in defence expenditure would release revenue for 'beneficial social expenditure' in India this was 'no reason' for the Tribunal 'to advise that India should be relieved of and Great Britain burdened with expenditure determined to be vital for the preservation of India's existence'.[17] On the other hand, the GOI claimed, on the basis of statistical evidence, that under the Imperial arrangements prevalent in 1933 the Indian revenues were being disproportionately taxed to the benefit of Imperial defence. After all, the GOI asserted, Indian defence *was* Imperial defence. The precedent of Hong Kong and the Straits Settlement, where a fixed proportion of the total revenue was fixed as a *maximum* of defence expenditure, supported the Indian demand for financial relief. But these realities of political economy, reflecting the financial problems of the British Raj, were tersely dismissed by the Garran Tribunal: 'We think that the answer to the question, whether a contribution should be made from Imperial revenues towards military expenditure from Indian revenue, is: Yes, but in respect of certain limited matters only.'[18]

The two Indians on the Tribunal disagreed with these conclusions. According to Sir Shadi Lal, India had a strong case for claiming more Imperial support especially with reference to certain colonies where British troops were present and where the Imperial government had adopted the rule of restricting defence expenditure to one-fifth of the total assessable revenue. Due to the heavy burden imposed upon India's revenues by the GOI's military expenditure enough money was not available to promote 'nation-building' activities in India. Furthermore, because the British Army gained valuable experience in India and since Indian frontiers were *de facto* Imperial frontiers it would be fair if Britain paid more for her army and defence in India. Unfortunately, the fact that the British Army in India defended British interests had been ignored by the Garran Tribunal. Britain could hardly relinquish its military responsibility towards India because for all practical purposes, in Lord Salisbury's words, India was 'an English barrack in the Oriental Seas'.[19] The minute by Sir Shah Muhammad Sulaiman said something interesting about the concepts of *major* and *minor* danger upon which most of the Tribunal's observations were based. He pointed out that after the Mutiny of 1857 the history of the Indian Army proved how important it was to the maintenance of the Empire. Since the Indian Army had always been available 'for averting to some extent the major as well as the minor, or purely local, danger' confronting the British Empire it deserved more financial support from Britain.[20] Furthermore, since in the 1930s the major danger had shifted eastwards it could be presumed that in future in an eastern theatre of War the troops placed in India would play the most crucial part. This alone was cause enough for Britain to shoulder a large proportion in the East.

Even in the early 1930s Imperial needs appeared overwhelming but the British Empire lacked the means to satisfy them despite the growing realization that the crisis in India *was* the crisis of the British Empire. The condition of naval preparedness was a testimony to this fact:

> It has not been possible, on account of financial stringency and the application of the 'ten-year' rule to build up the reserves of equipment required for the naval services in war, and serious deficiencies exist in regard to reserves of ammunition, torpedoes, mines, anti-submarine weapons and craft.[21]

In 1935 economies ruled because the 'financial and economic risks of the time were even more serious than the existing military risks'. Well-informed contemporaries probably expected British policy to be innovative and resourceful in such strained circumstances but surprisingly even during the mid-1930s official thought on Indian defence continued to concentrate on the increasingly improbable Soviet attacks from the north-west. Russophobia lingered despite the fact that in 1932 the Committee on Imperial Defence had concluded that in the event of strains Japan could 'without warning, inflict crushing blows' on Britain, making recovery difficult.[22] However, occasional insights could not overcome the general confusion which remained because later the same Committee wrongly and complacently concluded that none of the Axis powers was capable of waging a prolonged war against the British Empire.[23] Perhaps the best summary of British strategy in the 1930s was provided by Field Marshal Sir George F. Milne in his address to the Imperial General Staff in 1933:

> You are faced with a world crumbling economically, geographically, and militarily. The situation is going gradually from bad to worse. In the last few years I have advocated in every way I can that there is only one policy for the British Empire—its traditional policy. That policy is to sit on the fence, pull up the drawbridge, and pick up all the crumbs from the rich, or rather the poor, man's table. I am told I am morally wicked. I may be but I think of my country first and last.[24]

THE PRELUDE TO THE CHATFIELD RECOMMENDATIONS

The cost of developing Indian defence to a respectable standard was Rs. 180 million capital and Rs. 20 million recurring in January 1938. This 'staggering amount' was beyond the capability of the British at a time when even in England 'the ideal from the defence point of view' was simply 'not attainable'. The realization that the British Empire was unfit to meet the challenge of the imminent conflict slowly dawned upon the policy makers and the view that England neither had the money nor the manpower under a voluntary system to provide an army for continental warfare was 'tacitly accepted' in high circles. In fact, England's position was so precarious that the Chancellor of the Exchequer had warned that Britain was 'running up bills which even with the borrowings contemplated' in 1938 she would not be able to pay. Such was the general scenario in which Hore-Belisha at the head of the War Office was proposing a set of long-awaited military reforms. He wanted to make the British Army more attractive and was suggesting expensive moves towards modernization. In the beginning of 1938 the cost of defence presented by the three British services was described as 'staggering' by Zetland to the Viceroy. The proposed Hore-Belisha reforms were causing tremendous concern and policy could only concentrate on selected patches with possibly disastrous consequences: 'In other words, the policy is likely to be to concentrate on the Navy, the Air Force and on essential industry and not to attempt to make provision for an army greater than is required to secure the protection of the actual territory of the Empire and its outposts.'[25]

In January 1938, even as the demand for improvement in the service conditions of the unattractive British Army rose to a peak, the Exchequer appeared unmoved. Hore-Belisha wanted to raise Army pay first of all but under the conditions of rearmament in 1938 this was not acceptable to the Treasury. Pressures for reform were, however, mounting with the submission of the *Willingdon Committee Report* which had examined the causes of the shortage of Army officers in the British Army.[26] The Willingdon Committee found Army service in Britain unremunerative and this explained and strengthened Hore-Belisha's insistence on raising the pay in the Army. By February 1938 the War Office seemed to have gained a lead over the Treasury and despite his warning John Simon, the Chancellor of the Exchequer, was found retreating before Hore-Belisha. The demand for an increase in Army pay was now being considered and this alone had grave implications for India with her large garrisons of the British Army operating within the Cardwell System. A raise in the pay of the British soldier would burden India with more expense and re-emphasize the question of either an Imperial grant to India or the reduction in the number of British troops stationed there. Military opinion in India would oppose this and the nationalists would certainly oppose an increase in defence expenditure on account of British troops. Quite predictably, in the beginning of 1938, Zetland could see 'no satisfactory solution of this problem'.[27]

Although the Garran Tribunal had looked at the question of India's role in Imperial defence in 1933 it was in the beginning of 1938, rather belatedly, that this question assumed the importance it deserved. Obviously the Garran arrangement had been superseded by new demands. What role, it was being asked, would India play in the maintenance of the British Army stationed in India on the Cardwell principle? For Hore-Belisha the answer simply lay in the reduction of British troops in India after an improvement in their pay. The idea of retaining a Reserve Division in India by the Imperial government, normally at the service of the GOI but to be used by the Imperial government if circumstances so dictated, also began to be floated by the War Office at the same time.[28] It became very clear that India's opposition to these Imperial schemes would be brushed aside very soon. After all, the British Army faced the objections of the GOI and in February 1938 the Cabinet finally approved Hore-Belisha's proposals to make the British Army more attractive. Faced with this Zetland could do nothing but place on record his view that 'further burdens' upon the revenues of India in 1938 were impossible to place. He also pointed out to the Cabinet that the Cardwell System had become obsolete.[29]

The summer of 1938 made it clear again that finance is the crux of military affairs. In Britain, following the approval of the Hore-Belisha reforms, an agreement was reached between the War Office, the India Office, and the Air Ministry, according to which the GOI first of all would release four British battalions for duty in Palestine and Malta. Furthermore, the agreement stated that India would furnish an up to date Air Force and 'a considerable programme of reorganisation and re-equipment . . . including the establishment of factories for the production of munitions'. A rough estimate of the cost of all this was in the proximity of 30 million pound sterling capital and 2 million pound sterling recurring. India could not find this money except at the risk of a constitutional crisis, as Patel indicated.[30] In Britain the government had decided to ration the finances available for the services whose plans were rapidly outstripping available money and the Chiefs of Staff made it clear that money could not be found in these rations for the Indian services.[31] But finance was not the only difficulty faced by the Indian services. Problems were bound to arise because of the attitude with which the Air Ministry surveyed Indian air defence. The Air Ministry actually wanted a specified sum in return for which it was prepared to provide India with an Air Force.[32] This meant accepting the fact that the Royal Indian Air Force (RIAF) created in 1932 was a token service. Furthermore, the Air Ministry's offer would not have gone down very well with the GOI and the Congress both. The condition of reserves, on the other hand, was deplorable in 1938. The European officer wing of Class A reserves which carried out periodic training for the cavalry, engineers, signals, infantry, and the RIASC had an authorized strength of 685 in 1937 but the actual strength on 1 July 1937 was only 296. Class B reserves which did not train because their civil and military duties were similar were authorized an establishment of 227 but on 1 July 1937 the actual number of officers was only 163. Significantly, the European wing was 'seriously under establishment in the combatant categories' though applications for reserve commissions in the Indian wing were 'far in excess of the number of vacancies available'. Furthermore, in 1937 about 400 candidates had applied for the 15 open vacancies at the Military College in Dehra Dun showing how popular the idea of military service and Indianization was becoming in India and how insufficient the facilities for the advancement of Indianization really were.[33]

By July 1938 the Cabinet and the Treasury both had made it clear that the British taxpayer could find no money for the starved and obsolete Indian services. Furthermore, as Simon put it, the Cabinet, ignoring possible Indian opposition, resolved to charge Indian revenues for the Imperial Reserve Division's *maintenance*. The Cabinet Committee which reviewed Indian matters also decided to set up an expert committee to suggest further economies in the Indian military budget. This unwittingly proved the biggest charge levelled by the Indian nationalists against the GOI—that the British spent too much on the Army in India normally—at a time when actually the services required more money for modernization. Zetland at this point warned the Cabinet Committee that sending out such an expert committee to India would 'give great impetus' to the Indian nationalist demand for a much more rapid programme of Indianization.[34] The Congress would certainly have liked to press the issue of Indianization because the Indian was much cheaper to employ than the Briton.

As the Second World War drew closer, it became evident to the GOI and the India Office that an increase in India's defence expenditure, without adequate concessions to Indians, would precipitate a constitutional crisis in India. For obvious reasons the Congress governments in the Indian provinces working under the GOI Act of 1935 would not easily accept take arbitrary increases in military spending. Finally, the resignation or dismissal of these governments could easily lead to another round of mass protests. Perhaps these were the considerations which forced Zetland into a last stand before the Cabinet Committee in August 1938. Zetland told the Cabinet Committee on military reorganization that political objections to the Imperial Reserve Division in India were real and that the British could not ignore the fact that in India, and especially the Punjab, propaganda against India's participation in a future war was sufficiently widespread. The Indian legislature and Indian public opinion could hardly be ignored and it was unproductive to maintain that Defence was a reserved subject about which the Indian Legislatures could do precious little. Unfortunately for British policy Indian realities had changed between the Wars:

> Whatever the legal position might be, we were under a moral obligation to consult the Legislature whenever that was possible; in the event of a situation arising which rendered desirable the despatch of troops from India to some other theatre of operations, and anyone who thought otherwise was living in a wholly unreal world.[35]

This had a sobering effect on the Treasury and John Simon agreed to find five million pound sterling for equipping the Imperial Reserve Division which, to bypass Indian criticism, was not to be 'described as being at the unfettered disposal of the Home Government'. Zetland wanted the Imperial Reserve

Division to be called the First Field Division. Three and a half million pound sterling were also to be found for the re-equipment of four bomber squadrons with up to date aircraft. The Treasury also agreed to increase the British contribution to current Indian military expenditure calculated by the Garran Tribunal but only after an expert committee on Indian Defence had submitted its report.[36] In fact, the Imperial government decided that no financial assistance would be forthcoming for India until and unless an expert committee reviewed Indian defence expenditure in the light of new conditions.[37]

THE CHATFIELD RECOMMENDATIONS

The Chatfield Committee recommendations followed the proposals made by the Indian General Staff on the basis of assessed requirements in 1938. The following is a brief, though critical, review of the Chatfield recommendations according to which the Indian Army had to be uniformly *and* economically modernized. And despite the serious shortage of officers the Indianization process was to be reviewed as late as 1945. On the whole, the Chatfield Committee tried its best to evade a substantial social reform of the Indian services while advocating greater defence *without* laying down proper provisions for substantial additions. This was understandable because the aim of the Chatfield Committee was to recommend economy but also paradoxical because without extra expenditure and social reform of the services modernization was impossible in 1939. Hence, air defence, for instance, was reckoned *vis-a-vis* the Afghan Air Force and the Committee, with misplaced confidence, opined that the RAF could defend the Indian skies adequately with only 142 assorted aircraft.[38]

The picture of naval defence painted by the Committee was equally disheartening. The naval subvention, a drain instituted in the nineteenth century amounting to some 120,000 pound sterling, paid annually by the GOI to the British government for the naval defence of India, ended finally in April 1938. Following this, and in the hope of a better future, the Flag Officer Commanding RIN (FOCRIN) prepared a nine-year expansion plan for the RIN in May 1938. The short-sighted Chatfield Committee poured cold water over this by recommending a small navy concentrating on escort duties and minesweeping. Finally, while highly probable Axis submarine attacks on the Indian coasts were overlooked, the RIN was entrusted with the coastal defence of India with the services of 14 assorted ships which would be available only in 1947.[39]

The Chatfield Committee suggested a five-year plan with a new total capital cost of Rs. 451.9 million presumably at 1939 prices. Of this the Army was provided Rs. 363.6 million, the Air Forces 62.1 million, and the RIN 26.2 million. The Committee also assumed, for incomprehensible reasons, that the war would not begin before 1944. The defence expenditure of India amounted to some Rs. 461.5 million in 1938-9 which was half of the total revenue collected by the GOI. The provinces had been promised more after 1935 and the Indian political parties were emphatically demanding a reduction in military expenditure in the interest of socio-economic development. Everything pointed to the fact that the weaknesses of British colonialism in India were becoming transparent by the day and general confidence in the ability of the British to ensure a viable military alternative for India was becoming seriously undermined. The Chatfield Committee realized that theory could no longer be put into action even if a belated turn around in the consciousness of British policy occurred in 1938-9: 'It does not appear to us that the large funds required to meet this expenditure can be found out of resources at present available in India.'[40]

However, despite this gloomy outlook, Imperial demands upon India continued even after the *Chatfield Committee Report* had been submitted. In August 1939 the Committee of Imperial Defence placed several 'embarrassing' demands upon Indian resources. A mountain battery was demanded for Kenya and signallers and medical men for Singapore and East Africa. Skilled men for anti-aircraft defence were required for a battery in Aden even as Zetland made it clear that these were re-enforcements demanded over and above those stipulated by the Chatfield Committee. There was also talk of adding four bomber squadrons to India for 'external duty' and two for its 'local defence'. With regard to this Zetland pointed out that the four demanded were 'as a matter of fact' required for strictly Imperial purposes and might not even be quartered in India: 'This, therefore, must be the responsibility of the Imperial Government and not of the

Government of India.' Also, there was no money for the two additional bomber squadrons proposed for India.[41] Sources also show that the new Indian services, i.e. the RIAF and the RIN, were suffering particularly as a result of the paucity of funds. Indeed, in the light of British policy followed towards the modernization of the Indian services in the 1930s the creation of the RIAF (1932) and the RIN (1934) appear more symbolic than anything else. The naval defence of India in 1939 was encountering considerable 'financial difficulty' and although some officials wanted the RIN interests to be promoted Indians were usually found ignorant of the service and its future.[42]

The results of the submission of the *Chatfield Committee Report* were predictable and failed to dissuade the Imperial government, which knew the dilemma of the GOI very well, from placing more claims on Indian resources. The Report went down rather well with Zetland although there were points in it which Indian opinion would have disliked. However, the Chiefs of Staff felt that the Air Force proposed by the Chatfield Report was 'markedly inadequate' and John Simon at the Treasury compared the 'lack of lucidity' of the Chatfield Report to 'the utterances of the Pythian priestess which made famous the Temple of Apollo at Delphi'.[43]

CONCLUSION

Before the Chatfield Committee submitted its report, the Modernization Committee, appointed by the C-in-C in India and led by Maj. Gen. Auchinleck, had stated that the Indian armed forces in 1938 were stagnating at the technological levels of 1918. In fact, the services would have been even more obsolete but for the Great War. It was calculated that this state of affairs would jeopardize Indian participation in the imminent World War and would hinder coordination between the colonial and the metropolitan armed forces. Cavalry, it is easy to imagine, could hardly be expected to work with tanks in a modern war. Colonial India had only six outdated munitions factories and most of them dated back to the Company days. India could supply primary produce, leather, and clothes to the War effort but her transport and communications were primitive. Imports were crucial to any Indian War effort and uneven development within the colonial empire dictated their importance and nature. Automobiles, tanks, artillery, and aircraft were neither manufactured in India nor could they be serviced satisfactorily to begin with. Almost all essential items for peace and war such as scientific instruments, machine tools, high explosives, tinned foodstuffs, special glass, surgical equipment, rubber, artillery equipment including large guns, petrol and allied oil products, ships, and modern weapons of all sorts were imported mainly from England where even they were becoming scarce over time.[44] Furthermore, Indian storage systems were deficient in terms of available space and technology to handle the vast quantities of material generated by the demands of modern war. Considering all this, it is not surprising that the War Department History accurately summed up the military scenario of India and the British Empire in 1939 in the following words:

> Here, then, were the seeds that were to give rise to all the major problems in the coming years of war. The armed forces under-equipped and unready to take the field against enemies more fully armed, India unable to make up the deficiencies from her own resources, the unreadiness for war of the whole Empire, and the absence of any Imperial plan envisaging the comprehensive expansion of the Indian forces were also factors destined to retard progress when speedy preparation became of vital import.[45]

This arrested development gave rise to many problems during the Second World War. Some of them are discussed in the next chapter.

NOTES

1. A retrenchment had taken place in the armed forces during the early 1930s; *Report (Final) of the Army Sub-Committee of the Central Retrenchment Advisory Committee, 1932*, pp. 8-10 (CSL); *India in 1928-29, A statement prepared for presentation to Parliament . . .*, Calcutta, 1932, pp. 194-5 mentions the official attempt to stabilize the military budget; *India in 1931-32, A statement prepared for presentation to Parliament . . .*, p. 82 provides the figures quoted above and *India in 1932-3. A statement prepared for presentation to Parliament . . .*, Delhi, 1934, p. 62 tells us how the reduction of 5.25 (5.50?) mentioned above was carried out in 1932-3. Retrenchment accounted for Rs. 3.10 crore,

postponement of the programme of re-equipment Rs. 1 crore and the emergency cuts in pay totalled Rs. 1.40 crore.

2. In fact, the Sub-Committee of the Central Retrenchment Advisory Committee, op. cit., specifically advised reductions of capital expenditure to a minimum. *Progress Reports* for 1929-30, 1930-31, 1933-34, 1935-36, 1936-37, and 1937-38. *On the distribution of the Army and RAF in India, their preparedness for war and for the maintenance of law and order within India*, No. 601/10848/H, Secret, Delhi, 1930/31 (HS) also reveal similar trends. By 1937-8 the shortage of British officers and technical personnel had become very acute. The 1930s were also characterized by the downward revision of the military budget estimates even though the ratio of military expenditure to overall government expenditure did not change, *India in 1933-34, A statement prepared for presentation to Parliament* . . ., Delhi, 1935, p. 73 and *India in 1934-35, A statement* . . ., Delhi, 1937, section on budget, tell us that the military budget for 1933-4 was fixed at Rs. 46.12 crore but was reduced to Rs. 44.34 crore during the course of the year. The military budget was fixed at Rs. 44.30 crore for 1934-5 but slid to the lower estimate of Rs. 44.26 crore during the same year as conditions in India, as elsewhere, failed to improve.
3. Viceroy Reading to Secretary of State Birkenhead, 26/2/1925, Birkenhead Collection (Microfilm), Acc. No. 1948.
4. Viceroy Irwin to Birkenhead, 24/2/1927, Birkenhead Collection, Acc. No. 1949.
5. Irwin to Birkenhead, 16/3/1927, Acc. No. 1949, op. cit.
6. Ibid., 7/9/1927.
7. Ibid., 8/12/1927.
8. Ibid., 20/1/1927.
9. Ibid., 16/11/1927.
10. Document No. 1/6, Letter to a Dear Crost mentioning important facts regarding the modernization of the Indian Army between the two World Wars, Corbett Papers. In fact, during the early stages of the Second World War Corbett urged that senior and experienced officers of the Indian Army be given a chance to serve in the expanding British Army.
11. Document No. 2/16, Notes on Certain Lessons of the Great War, Corbett Papers. These notes are extracts from the Report of a Committee (Kirke Committee) which considered this subject. By command of the Army Council. The War Office, 30 April 1934 these notes were issued down to the headquarters of squadrons, batteries, and companies of the Regular Army to serve as a basis for thought, study, and discussion by officers. The Kirke Committee endorsed the idea of mobile war as the method of war for the coming years and called for full support to mechanization, air cover, and reserves. It also wanted the authorities to learn from the surprises offered by the Great War to produce leaders,

'versatile, mentally robust and full of common sense and self reliance'.

12. SECRET Report of the Expert Committee on the Defence of India *(Chatfield Committee Report)*, File No. 601/1280/H, 1938-39 (HS).
13. Defence of India under the new constitution, File No. 601/10636/H, Army Department, 1935 (HS): A lecture prepared in the Army Department; Secret 1112-B, Committee of Imperial Defence, papers prepared for the use of the Chiefs of Staff in their Annual Review of Imperial Defence (1933), Whitehall, 1933, Copy 52, F-460, 45816/MOI, Committee of Imperial Defence Papers 1933-37, General Staff Branch (HS): Letter from the Permanent Under-Secretary of State for India to the War Office and memorandum by the India Office on the preparedness of the Army and the RAF in the India.
14. Document No. 1/15, Evidence of Brigadier Corbett to the Expert Committee on the Defence of India 1938-39, New Delhi (Dec. 1938), Corbett Papers. Corbett wholeheartedly favoured the mechanization of the Indian Army and wanted the problem of India to be approached from a wider perspective and as part of the 'mosaic of imperial defence as a whole'. He also wanted the British to deny a handle to Indian politicians by drawing no distinctions between Indian and Imperial reserves in practice.
15. Simla Record 10970, 601/10790/H, Secret File No. 31908 II M.O.I., 1935, GOI, Army Dep. General Staff Branch, Progs. B, Feb. 1935, Nos. 848-867, Sub-Expert investigation of the strength, composition and functions of the Army in India; Ref. Progs B, July 1932, Nos. 1979-1986 in the same file. The Garran Award was not of much help because already the re-equipment plan begun in 1928 could not be completed in 1932 because of severe financial problems: Ref. Memorandum by India Office/Committee of Imperial Defence Papers, op. cit.
16. *Report of the Tribunal on Certain Questions in regard to Defence expenditure in dispute between the Government of India. The War Office and the Air Ministry*, London, 1933 *(Report of the Indian Defence Expenditure Tribunal 1933)*, Cmd. 4473 (CUL), p. 9.
17. Ibid., pp. 10-11.
18. Ibid., p. 15.
19. Ibid., p. 34, Note 1—Brief summary of Sir Shadi Lal's Note on a Contribution from Imperial Revenues.
20. Ibid., p. 36, Note 2—Brief summary of Sir Shah Muhammad Sulaiman's Note on a Contribution from Imperial Revenues.
21. SECRET 1113-B CID Policy, Previous Paper No. COS 307, Annual Review (1933) by the Chiefs of Staff Sub-Committee, Copy 72, Oct. 1933, 45816/MOI (HS).
22. SECRET 1181 CID Policy, Annual Review by the Chiefs of Staff Sub-Committee, 1935 (Prepared in connection with discussions with Dominion Prime Ministers, 29 April 1935 Whitehall), CID Papers 1933-

37 45816/MOI 1112-B conclusions, 1932, p. 98: Since 1921 the Royal Navy had shifted to the *one-power standard.*

23. SECRET 1311-B CID Papers Copy 51 Preparedness for War of Great Britain in relation to certain other powers by May, 1937, Annexure A, COS 552, CID Chiefs of Staff Sub-Committee, comparison of the strength of Great Britain with that of certain other Nations as at May, Report, Whitehall, 9 Feb. 1937.
24. Document No. 2/15 CONFIDENTIAL: Report on the Staff Conference held at the Staff College, Camberley, 9-11 January 1933, Under the Orders and Direction of The Chief of the Imperial General Staff, Corbett Papers. At the conference it was also observed that the Dominions had neither men nor the money to contribute to Imperial defence but the time would soon come when each of them would have to defend an area of the globe separately as 'their share of Empire defence'.
25. Secretary of State Zetland to Viceroy Linlithgow, 17/1/1938, Acc. No. 1969, Zetland Collection (Microfilm), NAI.
26. Ibid., Zetland to Linlithgow, 24/1/1938.
27. Ibid., 7/2/1938.
28. Ibid., 14/2/1938
29. Ibid., 20/2/1938. In a letter of 15/3/1938 Zetland also mentioned that he was the only one opposing Hore-Belisha at the time in the Cabinet meetings. He made it very clear that India could not, and could not be expected to, shoulder the burden implied in the reforms of Hore-Belisha designed to make the British Army more attractive to recruits. Another letter of 22/3/1938 refers to Zetland playing a 'lone hand' against a united Cabinet. The Hore-Belisha reforms were raising fears in Indian circles of the War Office making more claims upon Indian revenues.
30. Zetland to Lord Brabourne, 28/6/1938, Acc. No. 1969.
31. Ibid., 28/6/1938. Such were the conditions which made protagonists of mechanization like Corbett a desperate lot. In 1939 Corbett (3/1, Corbett's correspondence on the purpose of the Army in India, including his worry at the lack of progress in the equipping and training of the Indian Army, Sept. 1939, Corbett Papers) described the economic conditions as a 'ghastly break' on all efforts to materially improve the Indian Army. Modernization was held up due to finance and looking at this Corbett suggested involving Indian workshops, railways, and even the Tatas in developing armour for the Indian Army.
32. Zetland to Brabourne, 5/7/1938, Acc. No. 1969.
33. Document No. 2/23, Corbett Papers. Papers for Senior and Junior Divisions Comprising Conference Notes, Lectures and Data 1936-38, Subject: Organization, Spring Term, Staff College, Quetta, 1938. Junior Division Lecture: Organization of the Army in India. In 1932 the cavalry regiment and seven infantry battalions were added to the Eight Units

for Indianization. In 1934 Artillery and Divisional troops of the 4th Indian Division and No. 1 Squadron RIAF were added. From 1938 the Indian KCOs started acting as the platoon commanders replacing the old VCOs in the new units they entered.

34. Zetland to Brabourne, 19/7/1938, Acc. No. 1969.
35. Ibid., Zetland to Brabourne, 2/8/1938.
36. Ibid.
37. Ibid., Zetland to Brabourne, 8/8/1938. In August Zetland spoke to Chatfield who agreed to go to India in November 1938 at the head of the Expert Committee.
38. *Chatfield Committee Report*, pp. 22-41, 43-7. Brigadier Corbett (Corbett Papers, 1/5) found the strength of the RAF inadequate in India for the purposes of taking the counter-offensive against an enemy. Even anti-aircraft defence, which had to pay regard to the 'extreme moral effect' an air raid would have on an Indian city, was woefully deficient in 1938-9.
39. *Chatfield Committee Report*, pp. 48-9; The FOCRINs nine-year scheme with an estimated capital cost of Rs. 733.30 lakh and the recurring cost of Rs. 64.1 lakh had been re-examined by the military authorities with an eye to 'minimum insurance' and several items in it had been found too expensive for Indian finances. Official attempts to reorganize the Indian Marine into the RIN usually ended in committee reports as the following suggests: Reorganization of the RIM: *Report of a Departmental Committee*, GOI publication, 1927 (CSL). Early naval failures are noted in the RIN Memorandum on the general state of the service at the outbreak of War in 1939, OSD/CLO/ii, H.S., OSD/D in 601/7/169/H (HS).
40. *Chatfield Committee Report*, p. 58.
41. Zetland to Linlithgow, 4/8/1939, Acc. No. 1969.
42. Zetland in conversation with Fitz Herbert reported to Linlithgow, 4/8/1939, Acc. No. 1969.
43. Zetland to Linlithgow, 16-17/5/1939, Acc. No. 1969.
44. Secret War Department History 1939-45, Head I, General State and Role of the Armed Forces of India prior to September 1939, 601/7/169/H (HS). Till 1935 defence continued to concentrate on the perceived threat from the north-west as the following shows: SECRET, 1183-B, CID, Imperial Defence Policy, summary of decisions prepared by the Secretary, C.I.D., period 2 June 1934-1 June 1935, Whitehall, 1935, copy 54, *C.I.D. Papers* (HS). Information about India's War potential was relayed by Gen. K.M. Loch's 'Note on India's productive capacity', 6/4/1944, OSD/B18/iv, General HQ, 601/7/169/H (HS).
45. War Department History 1939-45, op. cit., p. 27a.

FOUR

Recruitment, Demobilization, and Disaffection, 1939-1946

The armed forces of a country, like other institutions of a social formation, exist in continuous interaction with its society and polity. The preceding chapters of this book have made this clear in the framework of 'war and society'. It is our contention that the armed forces cannot be politically, militarily, or academically abstracted from the society to which they belong even for the purpose of social analysis. Hence, military questions, like other histories in general, are essentially *contextual, social,* and *political.* This chapter elucidates the connection between military recruitment and demobilization and the prevalence of widespread discontent in the Indian armed forces in 1945-6 with reference to the failures of British military policy in India surveyed critically in the earlier chapters of this book.[1] Part I introduces the chapter and briefly examines the obsolescence of the Indian armed forces before 1939 in order to place their Second World War experience in context. Part II studies the social transformation of the Indian services during the Second World War and its implications for the Indian political scenario of 1945-6. Part III compares demobilization after the two World Wars before describing its pronounced failures in the 1940s, and Part IV concludes the chapter.

INTRODUCTION

The existing historiography has concentrated more on the political origins of the post-Second World War situation in India despite the fact that large-scale popular protest in the Indian armed forces was also important to Indian politics during the winter of 1945-6. This protest was linked to the problems faced by the Raj in expanding and contracting the Indian services during, and after, the Second World War and was largely predicated upon the failure of British policy to ideologically, socially, and technologically modernize India and its armed forces between 1919 and 1939. The imperatives of a large-scale modern war raised unprecedented problems of military organization, recruitment, and demobilization for the British in India. These problems remained unsolved because the Second World War neither freed British military policy nor the Indian War effort from the financial and ideological trappings of the Raj between the Wars. The British opposition to an Indian consensus on the War, and settlement for unpopular autocratic rule, continued well into 1945. This was nothing new. Earlier, though the GOI had enjoyed Indian support during the Great War, throughout the political and economic crisis of the 1920s its survival had been difficult.[2]

Between 1919 and 1939, while excessive retrenchment, budgetary constraints, and British inability to innovate made the Indian armed forces stagnate, only the accelerated Indianization of the officers' corps and great modernization could have significantly changed their social composition.[3] The orthodoxy of British policy on Indian military matters was also exemplified in the response of the Raj to the recruitment and combat lessons of the Great War. During the Great War several Indian communities, earlier not classified as martial, like the Mahars and the Mazhabi Sikhs, served in the Indian Army in large numbers and, contrary to the myth of the martial races, fought well in France and the Middle East.[4] But the Mazhabis and the Mahars were the first to be retrenched after it.[5] In the problem-ridden decade of the 1920s the experience of war only expanded the 'martial races' classification without in any way diminishing its sway over recruitment.

As late as 1932, officially the most important 'ethnic types' represented in the Indian Army were the Punjabi Musalmans, Gurkhas, Sikhs, Dogras, Rajputs, Pathans, Marathas, Garhwalis, and Kumaonis.[6] And, underlining the political basis of the 'martial races' theory, one government report claimed that 'reasonable men' would not support 'far-reaching experiments or alterations of policy' in the Indian armed forces. It was also made explicit that the British had to remain in India, which was threatened by internal strife, so as to maintain peace between the 'martial' and 'non-martial' Indians. Speaking confidently of the 'natural military aptitude' possessed by different Indians, the report also added that India could provide the 'most formidable fighting forces in the world' and others 'which alike by their physique and traditions are rendered practicably incapable of resisting military aggression of any kind'.[7] Such assertions either ignored, or were oblivious to, the historical nature of the myth and the failure of the British military model as early as the Boer War.[8]

Popular and recruitment literature reflected this bias. It was widely believed that only the regimental officer understood the sepoy and 'as a rule' one only knew the 'particular type' he commanded.[9] This informed the colonial ethnography of the 'martial races' which, despite the professed experience of officers, could not define the abstract military virtues of particular types. For instance, the Punjabi Musalman—either Gakkar, Khoreshi, Bhatti, Jangua, Khetwal, or Manj—was not physiologically different from the other Punjabis and the 'class' of Punjabi Musalmans, a British favourite, had nothing special *vis-a-vis* other Punjabi groups. No doubt writers often ran out of adjectives while describing groups from the same region and ultimately to Candler the Punjabi Musalman appeared simply more human compared to others.[10]

The *Caste Handbooks* legitimized the myth and impressed it on the mind of the khaki-clad, sunburnt senior officer and the young subaltern. The Jats, Gujars and Ahirs, for example, were described by them as thick headed and manly . . . yeomen cultivators . . . eminently adapted to the profession of arms', albeit the Gujars were 'surly in disposition'. Furthermore, the purity of these Scythian warriors was established by the rare occurrence of venereal diseases among them.[11] Similarly, the Punjabi Musalmans appeared Aryan but the mental equipment of these 'heavy thickset men with good chests' was poor. The converted Jats, with no 'pride of race', were suitably docile and obedient. Eastwards were found certain 'fighting' classes, including the Pathans, Moghuls, Shekhs, Sayads, Khanzadas, Muslim Jats, and Mewatis. However, because the 'martial races' were necessarily rural, the experts inveighed against the town Muslim who, as the 'possessor of all sorts of vices', was militarily unfit.[12]

The bracing climate of the Himalayas yielded non-Aryan, but

suitable, material and, six years before the most modern war in the history of the British Empire, the Gurkha was perceived as 'phlegmatic, and slow in intellect and feeling, but goodhumoured, cheerful, and tractable . . . amiable'. Compared to other 'orientals', they were found to be 'bold, enduring, faithful, frank, very independent and self reliant'. Jealous of foreigners, they *despised the natives of India* but respected Europeans because of the latter's superior knowledge, strength, courage, dress and habits.[13] The Kumaonis were found to be 'sober, frugal and usually good tempered'. But again, like the urban Hindustanis, the 'types' found dissipating themselves in the bazaars of Almora and Ranikhet were to be definitely rejected. Thus, the 'long lanky lad' was unfit but the certified rural, short, stocky lad, 5 feet 3 inches tall with a 'fair complexion', was the best.[14]

It was this abstract notion of a community's military virtues, neither justified in practice nor academic portrayal, which determined military recruitment in India before 1939.[15] Beside this the shortcomings of the Indian armed forces in the inter-War period were too many to be discussed here. However, a brief description would be in place. First, before the 1940s the official definition of the role of the Indian armed forces in Imperial and Indian defence did not change much.[16] As a consequence, British policy and Imperial strategy kept the Indian Army tied to the concerns of the North-West Frontier of India and civil order within the colony. Second, the orthodoxy of recruitment and technological stagnation made the mentality and material of the Indian armed forces unsuitable for a modern war in 1939. Third, the new services, the Royal Indian Navy (RIN) and the Air Force (RIAF), formed in the early 1930s, remained on paper till the early 1940s only to expand suddenly, with drastic consequences for the British, during the War. And finally, due to British fears of losing control which retarded Indianization, the Indian armed forces were inadequately officered, and, in addition, lacked effective recruitment, medical, and organizational infrastructure before the Second World War. Sources make it clear that motorization, mechanization, and the money to augment, or the willingness to innovate with, existing resources were absent from them when war was declared on Germany:

> Here, then, were the seeds that were to give rise to all the major problems in the coming years of war. The armed forces under-equipped

and unready to take the field against enemies more fully armed, India unable to make up the deficiencies from her own resources, the unreadiness for war of the whole Empire, and the absence of any Imperial plan envisaging the comprehensive expansion of the Indian forces were also factors destined to retard progress when speedy preparation became of vital import.[17]

RECRUITMENT DURING THE SECOND WORLD WAR

In September 1945 the Indian armed forces comprised a total of 2,581,726 men. During the War, while 302,732 south Indians, 112,378 Sikhs, 100,235 Christians, 73,121 Rajputs, 58,421 Marathas, 10,059 Mahars, and 143,199 men of the so-called miscellaneous classes, including Bihari tribals, served their fighting arms, the percentage of the 'martial races' in the services declined considerably.[18] Clearly the overwhelming, and varied, need to save the Empire dictated wartime recruitment in India. Let us first examine the role the GOI played in this process. Since the conservation of manpower became a top priority in 1939 extraordinary power was wielded in India by the state during the War. This was also necessitated by the opposition of the Congress, India's largest and most influential political party, to India's unconditional participation in the War. This made coercion necessary to preserve the armed forces from subversion and to keep India in the War. That Britain would hold India down by force became known as soon as the Congress provincial ministries resigned in 1939.

A series of military Ordinances, designed to circumscribe voluntary recruitment, soon followed. For instance, the Ordinance No. XI of 1940 called the National Service (Technical Personnel) Ordinance empowered the National Service Labour Tribunals to *conscript* certain kinds of technical personnel for service such as civilians in factories catering to War. The Indian Forces (Transfer Ordinance), No. X of 1940, provided for the compulsory transfer of persons, enrolled under the Indian Army Act, from one corps or department to another within the Army. The Active Service Ordinance, No. X of 1940, subjected all civilians serving in the Army to military law. The Essential Services (Maintenance) Ordinance, No. XI of 1941, sanctioned the compulsory retention of civilians employed in specified employment. The Ordinance No. LVIII of 1942 called the Army and Air Force (Enrolment) Ordinance could prevent anyone on the rolls for that period, from claiming his discharge on the grounds of any irregularity in his enrolment. The RIN (Extension of Service) Act of 1940 made for the compulsory retention of persons in the RIN for five years from the date on which their services would otherwise have terminated.[19] But, as events studied in this paper show, ordinances neither detracted from the mercenary nature of Indian recruitment nor lowered desertion rates.

Limitations were also imposed upon recruitment by the Quit India Movement of 1942 and towards the end of 1942 desertion was causing the military authorities serious alarm. Although homesickness, loneliness, discontent and harsh discipline certainly caused desertion the influence of politics on the process cannot be ruled out. It was also true that older units were often diluted with fresh entrants and this probably created problems of social and service adjustment. Though officially several measures to show kindness and lenience to newcomers were adopted the British suspected that in the disturbed conditions of 1942 subversive influence was most probably working in the armed forces. Desertion declined gradually but remained endemic till the end of the War. The problem was especially serious in the Navy and the Air Force, which faced severe administrative, organizational and recruitment-related problems throughout the War.[20]

The recruitment drives of the 1940s also revealed that military recruitment in India was dependent upon agricultural activity and seasonal epidemics. Plague, malaria, and cholera decreased recruitment and often prohibited the movement of people between different areas. While disease made potential recruits unfit for duty, during festivals or *melas* (rural fairs) men resisted enlistment in large numbers even though such social assemblies witnessed extensive recruitment propaganda. During Ramzan the recruitment of Muslims dropped only to pick up after Id and during the largely Hindu marriage season often even special efforts proved futile. Good monsoons and greater agricultural activity pushed up the demand for agricultural labour and restricted the mobility of men while drought helped recruitment. In the cities, as the recruiting officers searching for technical personnel found out, the best recruiting time was just after the annual examinations held by schools and colleges when youths were most anxious for a job.[21]

Since recruitment had to contend with, and possibly overcome, the rythms of agricultural activity, strong nationalist sentiment and other peculiarities of a volunteer system several rewards were announced to encourage enlistment. From September 1941, with recruitment, the number of stimulatory rewards also increased. Among the several measures announced were the grant of sanads, presentation of gifts barring lethal weapons, and the remission of land revenue in special cases. Monetary awards to entire communities for the purpose of welfare schemes were also given. In 1943 a Recruiting Badge was introduced. Typical gifts comprised watches, fountain pens, walking sticks, swords, and *pagris* (turbans). As an incentive 'Bringing in money' was paid to the recruiter at the rate of Rs. 3 for a non-technical recruit and Rs. 5 for a technical one. By 1941 due to the paucity of dhobis and sweepers Rs. 3 was sanctioned per head for bringing them in. The mercenary nature of recruitment was underlined by the officially admitted fact that without these steps 'demands at the time could not have been met'.[22] Recruitment also produced its own moments of speculation and fraud due to the demand for labour it generated. The following case illustrates the point. At the peak of recruitment several men began trading in recruiting 'Receipt Tickets' issued to recruiting agents. Traders in these tickets toured the recruiting areas with bands of professional deserters. After enrolment the 'recruit' deserted and the same performance was repeated elsewhere. The tickets, thus, acquired were sold to speculators aiming to claim a reward for their 'services' at the end of the War. In a way the British, by announcing rewards for wartime services, encouraged such practices. To counter this the practice of entering the 'sponsor's' name and address on the enrolment form was begun and greater security for the receipt books was provided. This ended the fraud in a year or so.[23]

The inter-War economic limitations of the armed forces, referred to earlier, continued to influence recruitment during the Second World War with unhappy consequences for the Raj and its services. Thus, a bonus was not usually granted to the new recruits and throughout the War the basic pay of soldiers compared unfavourably with the pay for civilian labour while prices in the domestic market rose. Recruits could not remit much to their families and this was cause enough for engendering rebellion in the long run. However, the simultaneous rise in agricultural prices, which must have compensated the families of many rural recruits, probably checked discontent during the War. It was also known that civilian pay for comparable activity was always higher than military pay in any branch and that this fuelled continuous desertion.[24]

In the beginning, like the Great War, the expansion of the services was based on the established pattern but soon demands rose to unprecedented levels forcing open the ranks to everyone. Initially, the favoured groups were subjected to excessive demands which, despite intensified drives, they could not meet. Ironically, and as the sources clearly point out, the response from most of these peasant groups also began decline as the War progressed because of the well-known rise in agricultural prices. As the War-driven demand for agricultural produce grew the cost of even casual field labour rose. And in this context the 'farmers' and 'landlords' began dissuading their sons and sometimes even tenants from joining military service.[25]

In such transformed circumstances new castes and tribes entered the armed forces forcing some change even upon the cramped official view of the 'martial races'. Bihari tribals made satisfactory infantrymen in large numbers. Hos, Oraons, Mundas and Santals, once deliberately kept out of the Army, now made excellent soldiers. Chamars, neglected untouchables for long, were found making 'excellent' soldiers and due to numbers and effect a Chamar Regiment was also formed temporarily. Dotials of Nepal, earlier shunned, proved 'excellent stretcher bearers, particularly in rough country'. Gilgits handled mountain artillery and mixed well with Punjabi Muslims. The Kabirpanthis of the Dogra region did well and by the end of the War a complete garrison battalion of the Lingayats was included in the Maratha Light infantry. The Mahars once again flocked to arms in large numbers and finally got their regiment in 1941. The Oriyas, Assamese, and Bengalis were reported satisfactory in several branches of the armed forces. Once again experience proved the 'martial races' theory wrong. On the whole, the shifts in recruitment were considerable and as early as 1943, south Indians comprised the second largest regional group in the armed forces and Madras reported the second highest Military Participation Ratio.[26]

Wartime recruitment propaganda was an important cause of this shift. Recruitment advertising assumed unprecedented importance during the War because, to begin with, the 'martial races' could not supply the number and type of men required by the Indian services in their first modern war. Second, the active nationalist opposition to the War and the easy availability of enemy radio broadcasts necessitated counter-measures. At the outset it became clear that, unlike the Great War, the Second World War would not become easily popular amongst Indians when as early as 1939 senior and experienced officers like Corbett found recruitment enthusiasm 'evaporating' in Punjab, the primary military province of India. Corbett also realized the danger posed to the troops' fidelity by the widely used enemy radio broadcasts. The British also knew that it was not easy to hide the truth from the better informed Indian *jawans* of the 1940s.[27]

For its part, the War by stimulating the economy, employment, and urban centres created new opportunities in civilian life. By 1942, when the Quit India Movement was launched by the Congress, all these factors were already competing with, and often besting, military recruitment. Civilian industry by offering more attractive terms to applicants made it clear that mere classified advertisements in the papers were not enough to meet the needs of the armed forces. Considering this grants were sanctioned for an intensified ideological campaign. A recruiting Advertising Section and a Creative Publicity Unit were created to adapt advertisement to local conditions. The choice of media was based upon the circulation and popularity of the periodical concerned. Advertisements were planned according to the periodical chosen and the class of reader being addressed. For the upper-class urban reader well versed in English a call for officer categories was designed. In the 'B' class vernacular media large lists of advertisements for enlisting clerks, matriculates, and some technical personnel were brought out. In the 'C' class vernacular media comprising some ten lesser known Indian language papers advertisements to attract matriculation zone and semi-educated men were inserted.[28] Since recruitment was a recognized political task its propagation had to counteract enemy propaganda by creating a 'healthy war atmosphere' in India. Its main aim was to enhance the public appeal of the services.[29] As P.J. Griffiths, Member of the Legislative Assembly and the GOI's representative in the conference on recruitment, pointed out with great acuity, recruitment would have to account for the 'emotional resistance' of the crowd being addressed. The political nature of the Indian groups being informed had to be understood to doctor propaganda:

> In the politically advanced areas the propagandist should be very circumspect in his use of emotional appeal. Any emotional appeal to the love of country might in such areas, produce precisely the wrong effect—particularly if Congress influences were at work. The safest emotional appeal in such areas was to the desire to defend women and children but probably it was safer still to rely on the solid practical advantage of joining the army.[30]

Thus, for the 'martial races' the appeal could play up traditions and the love of adventure. To the 'less adventurous people of certain parts of India' a good job and pension had to be offered. Recruitment drives were to like election campaigns and short-term intensive drives would obviously exaggerate the benefits of military service. The pre-Second World War Eurocentric bias in recruitment propaganda had to give way to a projection of the recruit's perspective. In the new propaganda designed from 1942 onwards government orders and demands were to be played down. A positive sex appeal had to replace negative images like the one showing a failed recruit being rejected by a girl. More appeals to valour and honour and more slogans in the vernaculars were necessary and recruiting officers had be good salesmen. As Griffith observed:

> . . . If a shopkeeper could not sell his goods, it was no use saying what a hopeless and useless lot his customers were. It was far wiser to put the blame on himself and realities that his methods were wrong. In the same way, if recruiting officers could get no recruits in a particular area or from a particular class of people they should not be too ready to throw the blame on the people but they should at any rate begin by assuming that there was something wrong with their methods. The customer was always right.[31]

Press campaigns were carried out through 10 inch/2 inch-column-sized advertisements. For the Indian language dailies carefully designed 12 inch/3 inch powerful displays were prepared. In 1942-3 a large number of posters were made. In a size of 20 inches/30 inches they were coloured and provided information about the background of the service being advertized. Posters near the recruiting offices helped tremendously by becoming an 'unmistakable means of identification'. Broadsheets or 'reader posters' were also printed to great effect during this period. Coloured booklets in 8 inches/7 inches size were generally meant for the groups with higher education and apparently contained full details of terms and conditions of the service being described. Life in the services was painted in attractive terms. About 30 to 40 such booklets were produced during the War of which the most popular were three commissioned rank publications called 'How to become a Naval Officer', 'How to become an Army Officer', and 'How to become an Officer in the RIAF'. A booklet titled 'Mutu joins up', published in 1943, became a unique success. It depicted a pictorial record of the life of a soldier in the 3rd Madras Regiment following his transformation from a young recruit into a trained *jawan*. Copies of it were sent to the Madras Regimental Centre for distribution to fresh recruits. Several recruits sent copies to their relatives and friends and, as the demand for it grew, orders for a new edition were soon placed. It was an acknowledged fact that this booklet positively influenced the intake of the Madras Regiment.[32]

Leaflets and folders printed in large numbers addressed the matriculates and the under-matriculates. Handbills were distributed in large numbers and cinema slides were found quite successful. Display models of equipment and clothing stimulated popular interest and the exhibition of model rupees representing various scales of pay were a hit with the crowds. Influential images were thus created and tours exhibiting the use of arms were carefully followed by the rural audience. Propaganda films were produced from 1942 onwards but popular response to them varied. The peasants were culturally unaccustomed to films and had difficulty in following the sequence or intentions of the films being shown. However, in certain *mofussil* areas, where theatres were known before the War, films were better received.[33]

The objective of this propaganda, involving press conferences as well, was to make Indians accept a reified, honourable, image of the armed forces. As Air Vice Marshal M. Thomas of the RIAF put it candidly, the objective of conferences and films was to make the public 'air force minded'. Films had to depict the valour of the service and the individuals comprising it. They also had to include romance and the impressive 'feminine touch' with references to the pride of ladies in their men's abilities.[34] These films as forerunners of modern military propaganda expounded stock themes and myths and their heroes were stereotypes. But simultaneously recruiting officers were briefed with care: myths had to be credible because as late as 1944 it was noticed that optimistic prophesies, unjustified by following events, often caused visible embarrassment.[35]

Recruitment propaganda would have been unsuccessful without allies in a pliant press, willing theatre owners and promoting agents at various levels. In several places the local bourgeoisie actively patronized the armed forces possibly because of the war related profits. So in 1944 when the Royal Indian Air Force (RIAF) magazine *Sentinel* was brought out in the frontier town of Kohat it carried advertisements of the 'Dew Drop Inn', master tailors, the local press, watchmakers and repairers, a dental surgeon, shoe stores, canteen contractors, wine merchants, the London Book Company, local hotels, sports manufacturing units and some stores offering goods and provisions.[36]

The *Sentinel*, edited by Flt. Lt. C.E. Stevens and Petty Officer G. Rangachari, was designed for the middle-class drawing rooms and had articles on palmistry and penicillin, a couple of short stories written by officers, a poem, sports news, a quiz corner, some book reviews, jokes and light 'frontier funlets'. It was introduced by Wing Com. S. Mukherjee, Officer Commanding, RAF Station, Kohat. To forge a sense of comraderie among all and sundry the magazine carried a column dedicated to Kohat gossip, condescendingly humorous rhymes about *chaprasis*, night guards and orderlies and an extremely sympathetic article praising the planning system of the Soviet Union called 'Facts about Russia' which exaggerated the level of British aid to it. The *Sentinel* did not comment on the War and was printed with the feeling that war, like Kohat, was quiet and remote. The armed forces, especially the RIAF, were described as a gentlemanly lot and, on the whole, a mythical harmony of classes with underlinings in their allotted space prevailed in the *Sentinel*.[37]

Recruitment propaganda, aided by Indian agents and designed

by the British, was successful in establishing hopes of a satisfactory career among the male population in general. However, as the naval case indicated, promises made to young naval recruits were generally 'falsified by facts' and did rebound on the British. In fact, Admiral Godfrey later observed before the RIN Mutiny Commission of Enquiry that 'The average rating firmly believed that he was going to be found a post-war job by the services' because much of the recruitment advertisement was literally run on the lines of 'join the Navy and secure yourself a post-war job'.[38] Among ratings it was a common belief that the recruiting agencies had misled them into believing a 'rosy picture' of naval service. This is understandable because unemployed youths, facing rising inflation, were strongly attracted to posters promising permanent careers and the facility of earning while learning. The pay mentioned in some of the posters was exaggerated and the additional perks mentioned were usually not sanctioned. Similarly, on the basis of some posters, etc., college students began to expect promotions too quickly.[39]

A typical poster showed a sailor on guard with the following words on the margin: 'Many hundreds of young men are today building their careers in the Navy. . . . Be proud of your son, let him join the RIN if he wishes to. Give him your blessings.' The Navy would offer the recruit a healthy life with smart clothes in the process of making him a 'real man'. History was falsely appropriated in the suggestion that the RIN had a great tradition and a glorious future. The appeal to machismo was not wasted and even to men like B.C. Dutt, initially the brutality of instructors appeared impressive. Such posters ultimately led to widespread disillusionment for no youth in his teens could become a 'real man' in about four to five years of 'a temporary service'.[40]

Posters promised a happy life with pictorial representations of free rations. 'Many allowances' were also mentioned. In fact, the recruitment booklet published in 1938 called forth educated men and stressed the point about India having a long coastline and a great naval future. Pamphlets designed for a questioning reader struck up a debate because objections to official assertions had to be overruled. A typical pamphlet of 1943, emphasizing the spirit of adventure and its clash with the doubts raised by an older generation, narrates the story of Kishore and Khalil, representatives of the two biggest Indian religious groups.

Kishore, a lawyer's son, runs away from home to join the RIN at a pay of Rs. 80 per month. On returning home he advises Khalil, shown in civilian clothes, to join the RIN at the artificer rate of Rs. 100 a month. Then both go to Khalil's father who voices doubts saying that the youths would be asked to leave after the War. Khalil answers this emphatically: 'No, sir, the contract is for ten years and it is believed that after the period is over a great majority would be retained in the permanent service. I have seen an article in a newspaper saying that India has a coastline of 4,000 miles and it must have an adequate navy.' To a question about pay Khalil responds that he believes it goes up to Rs. 460 per month.[41]

The booklets continued to misguide. *The Navy and its Job* claimed that the RIN was based on the Royal Navy and would grow rapidly, requiring men of intelligence and singleness of purpose. It was left unexplained how in the RIN the standards of the Royal Navy would be followed. 'India's Navy' set out terms and conditions of service for seamen, stockers, artificers, shipwrights, and ratings of other branches without mentioning the menial work which many of them were forced to do. In fact, in HMIS *Shivaji*, the artificer training establishment near Pune, mutinies occurred several times when young recruits insisted on following caste taboos regarding work. Cooking arrangements in the Navy, not made public, were insensitive to the pollution taboos of recruits and, in fact, common galleys, where beef was also cooked, created considerable social friction in the service.[42]

To attract educated men to the communications branch lucrative propositions were made and advertisements stated that naval training would benefit men after the War. Appeals were made to the intelligence, education, and smartness of recruits. This propaganda of half-truths drew large numbers of men to the Navy but, according to one recruiting officer, had the recruits known the truth not a single man would have joined the technical branches of the RIN because conditions were better in the Army and the RIAF. In the event, and given the uneven distribution of economic resources among the Indian services, exaggerated propaganda was politically indispensable:

> Soon after the war began and during the duration the government had to encounter the opposition or apathy of certain leading political parties in the country and large sections of people who sympathised with them.

The government, therefore, found it necessary to organise intensive propaganda for war effort of which recruitment was the most important and vital part. In the course of such propaganda it was undoubtedly brought home to all people that the men who were recruited would participate in the fruits of victory and the Government would take care of them, their families and their future.[43]

Naval recruitment posed several problems because the British were not experienced in raising technical and modern services in India.[44] As early as 1939 the RIN was fighting a battle of rates with the mercantile marine which left only 'the beach rats for the navy'. It was also difficult to find Hindu seamen willing to work with the predominantly Muslim crews which dominated the Royal Indian Marine from which the RIN evolved. Rates of pay were not uniform, accommodation, kitting and rationing were big problems which made the Navy prone to discontent, desertion and even mutiny.[45] Education posed more problems because matriculation levels varied in India, with the highest standard prevailing in Bombay and the lowest in the NWFP. Furthermore, the senior school leaving certificate of Bengal, Madras, Assam, and Orissa was considered above some matriculate standards. This was fodder for service discontent because while an educated south Indian became a seaman at the rate of Rs. 40 per month the matriculate from the NWFP became a writer at Rs. 60 a month 'to the despair of the wretched accountant officer whose office he' encumbered. In sum, the unevenness of educational standards in India resulted in 'much trouble and waste of effort' in the initial years of the War.[46]

Since educated men were not to be found among the traditional seafaring communities of coastal India, the RIN tried to enrol the 'proper material' of the upper provinces. However, north Indians and the middle classes in general were usually ignorant of naval service though from 1938 efforts were made to attract middle-class youths to the RIN.[47] Education and habit inculcated by colonial under-development also hindered recruiting for the RIAF. Air service demanded high standards and, initially, suitable men also feared the risks involved. The peace time prospects for civil aviation in India were poor and, thus, the supply of pilots was low. To top it all, the government did not assure permanent jobs to volunteers risking their lives in a new and relatively unknown service like the RIAF. Hence, the few elite Indians, trained at considerable private cost, were not enamoured of the RIAF.[48]

In September 1939 the ordinary seaman in the RIN and the merchant service received the same pay (Rs. 20 per month) with some allowances. On 4 September the shipping companies declared a war bonus of 25 per cent and the RIN followed suit on 11 September. In December 1939 the companies revised rates again but this time the Navy could not compete. This naturally moved the best talent towards the merchant companies despite the fact that this 'parsimony and lack of understanding' towards naval pay had been discussed by the Establishment Committee set up on the advice of the Financial Advisor, Military Finance Department in 1938.[49] Throughout the War desertion rose whenever the merchant rates were revised and later even the C-in-C described pay as the factor leading to discontent, disaffection, indiscipline, unsuitable recruitment, and desertion in the RIN. Later this was also the opinion of Admiral Godfrey (FOCFIN 1943-6) in his *Naval Memoirs*.[50] In February 1942, at the height of the War, the Director of Recruiting warned that without improvement in pay entry to most rating branches would stop. Soon an increase was granted but again previous rates were not upgraded and as a result new recruits began getting better pay than more experienced sailors employed at older rates. This only meant employing the 'sergeant and the private at the same rate of pay!' and 'providing a very fertile ground for fifth column activity'.[51]

Generally speaking, throughout the War the demand for men exceeded the supply and requirements were never satisfactory. Due to vigorous publicity the number of applicants undoubtedly rose but standards usually declined, and 'the response from well-educated young men of the potential officer type remained poor'. The majority of the applicants were men who had not been successful in finding employment elsewhere and who were attracted to the services by the seemingly high economic benefits offered. The best university students were not attracted to the emergency commissions offered by the services and 'preferred to seek a career in which a reasonable tenure of security could be expected'. The rate of rejection also remained high during the War probably because of the Indian education system. A study of recruits pointed out that colonial education over-stressed academic results to the detriment of the development of character or the ability of leadership needed in the new and rapidly expanding armed forces. The high rate of rejection during the recruitment of officers made for the similarity in the official conclusions of 1946 and 1927:

> In a future war it is assumed that officers for all the three Services will be predominantly Indian, and that large numbers will have to be obtained from the civil population. To provide these, it is essential that the educational system throughout the country be reformed in peace-time, and that pre-cadet training schools be opened on a large scale immediately a grave emergency is imminent [*sic*].[52]

The RIAF illustrated this further because all recruitment to it was considered technical. On an average wastage in it remained just under 10 per cent of the intake but peaked at 60 per cent in the middle of 1944. The demand for and supply of recruits was small compared to the Army but the standards desired were very high and recruits conforming to official guidelines were usually rare. Experienced, qualified, and mature men were not excited by the prospects of the RIAF and colonial India had not created enough pilots.[53]

Let us now briefly sum up the end of recruitment before turning to the themes of demobilization. From June 1945 recruiting offices began to close down and recruiting officers were asked to undertake post-War resettlement work instead. The closure of recruitment and the growing social uncertainties sparked off a wave of desertions in some areas. In Punjab, where *jangi inaams* were common, discontent over the insufficiency of land grants after the Second World War was clearly visible. Around Delhi recruitment dwindled as civilian pay began to attract more men. In many areas popular scepticism about the future of the armed forces was being expressed more openly. In the Agra region responses declined sharply in 1945 due to the remuneration and the short service being offered by the armed forces. Response was also very poor in highly fertile areas because agricultural prices were rising and, as a consequence, in several localities even Jats and Ahirs refused to come forward. In Lucknow and Calcutta enrolment declined considerably because it was popularly believed that military recruitment would result in a sudden release since the War was about to end. In the Poona zone as wages outside the services rose recruitment nosedived because several wartime contracts were reaching completion in 1945, raising the price of labour outside the services. The end of hostilities also dampened the enthusiasm of the recruiting agencies who had made money during the War by handling the public relations of the services. Now killings were to be made elsewhere as the military reduced the commissions paid for recruitment.[54]

As demand fell the services began to raise standards to the detriment of mass recruitment. From early 1945 other factors also militated against recruitment. Opposition from INA sympathizers was successful in the Rohtak and Hissar districts of Punjab. In the Bombay region, as late as 1946, the influence of the Prati Sarkar worked against the services. In several parts of India communal troubles were threatening domestic security and post-War discontent was adversely affecting fresh recruitment as dissatisfied demobilized men made the armed forces unpopular. Even castes like the Mahars and the Lingayats, which had gained from wartime recruitment, were seen dithering in their attitude towards the armed forces. It was reported that in the rural areas of Punjab, an anti-recruitment propaganda was fairly active and showed no sign of abating even when the all-India recruitment for the post-War Indian armed forces was opened in March 1946. In these changed conditions the failure of the authorities to promulgate new scales of pay only made the armed services more unpopular.[55]

DEMOBILIZATION

It is important to bear in mind that soon after the Great War 420,000 acres of land were distributed among 5,902 Viceroy's Commissioned Officers (VCOs) and Indian Other Ranks (IORs). In the Punjab the scale of allotment was 2 squares (unspecified measure of land) to a VCO, 1 square to an IOR, and 1/2 a square to a follower. In the provinces where land was less fertile than in Punjab proportionately a larger unit of land, with the same annual income, was granted to the demobilized soldiers. Another kind of reward called the *jangi inaam* was also given.[56] It was granted to 14,100 men for two lives with the following details. The VCOs received Rs. 10 per month, IORs got Rs. 5 per month, and the followers were given Rs. 2-Annas 8 per month. Two hundred *jagirs* were awarded to especially selected VCOs for distinguished services. These *jagirs* comprised grants of land with full proprietary rights yielding a net annual income of Rs. 400 or an assignment of land revenue for three lives in the following order. For the first life Rs. 600 per month, second life Rs. 300 per month and third life Rs. 150 per month. Two hundred honorary commissions as King's Commissioned Officers (KCO) were granted to selected VCOs, the majority of whom were Risaldar/ Subedar Majors about to be discharged from service! These men drew the pay of KCOs while still on the active list and double the normal pension of the VCOs on retirement.[57] By all means, and compared to the number of men enlisted during the Great War and the promises made to them, these rewards were at best extremely modest in scale and almost certainly gave rise to resentment in the thousands who felt excluded from the process. The same story was repeated after the Second World War but with graver repercussions.[58]

During the Second World War, to begin with, a proposal that central land grants should be made had to be dropped due to the large amount of land required for colonizing the demobilized soldiers. So it was decided that the main rewards were to be *jangi inaams* and honorary commissions and the total cost of both was estimated to be Rs. 2.5 crore, most probably in 1945. *Jangi inaams* sanctioned for the RIN, the Indian Army, and the RIAF totalled 12,500 only when about 100,000 men were enrolled in the RIN and the RIAF. Furthermore, the distribution of these rewards was heavily skewed in favour of the Army. Of these *inaams* 12,024 were allotted to the Indian Army, 191 to the RIN, and 285 to the RIAF. It is surprising that 275 *jangi inaams* were also granted to Indian States Forces personnel who had served the Crown when the Indian services like the RIAF and the RIN could have been better rewarded. The distribution of *inaams* worked out to a scale of one award per 144 troops, the ratio between VCOs, IORs, and Non Combatants being in the proportion of 4:10:1. The Indian Commissioned Officers were ineligible for these rewards. The *jangi inaam* was worth Rs. 20 per month for the VCOs and Rs. 10 per month for IORs and the Non-Combatants and this time was granted for only one life. The heirs of deceased personnel were also eligible to receive a *jangi inaam* which became admissible from 1 April 1946 onwards.

Two hundred honorary commissions as Lieutenants were granted to senior VCOs with effect from 1 April 1946 for especially distinguished service with a pay of Rs. 400 per month and double the normal pension on retirement. Furthermore, the gallantry decorations also carried modest monetary payments with them. As far as land grants were concerned only the Punjab government formulated an extremely modest scheme in 1943 according to which gifts of land at the scale of two squares each were earmarked for Victoria Cross and George Cross winners. One square each was to be given to those who won the Distinguished Service Order, Indian Order of Merit, Military Cross, Distinguished Service Cross, and Distinguished Flying Cross. These were described as 'Punjab gifts to Punjabi servicemen who had gained distinction in the field'.[59] But these grants left out the winners of the Indian Distinguished Service Medal owing to the limited amount of land available for the purpose. All other provinces decided to give monetary awards.[60]

In 1945 the limitations of demobilization were apparent even though the process was initiated quite early during the War. In 1941 a Demobilization section comprising one Assistant Adjutant General, one Lieutenant Colonel, and two Clerks was formed by the General HQ. Skeleton regulations were also drawn up before July 1942 when the section began to be called the Directorate of Demobilization and Reconstruction. In 1942 though more staff was added to the Directorate it became clear that forming an organization to carry out demobilization soon after the War was much easier than controlling and executing the process itself. In India the practice of voluntary recruitment, the prevalence of surplus manpower, and the illiteracy of a large number of recruits to be demobilized were identified early as the major problems confronting demobilization at the end of the Second World War. The process of demobilization had to overcome these hurdles to become successful. The officials were aware that demobilization after the Great War had led to 'great discontent' among the Indian Other Ranks because often they were discharged without their accounts having been settled. The majority of recruits did not know English and this brought home the lesson that after a future war every man would have to pass through a demobilization centre where his records and accounts would be kept. The military authorities knew that in spite of the drawn up and published regulations in many cases the individual's credit could not be quickly and accurately assessed and this gave rise to discontent. The emphasis was on the efficiency of the demobilization machinery: 'Correct documentation is also the only means by which a soldier can be assured that his interests are given the attention they require, and without complete confidence in this aspect of his army service a soldier can have little faith in his officers.'[61] Obviously a great deal of cooperation between several departments of the Army and the Air and Naval HQs was necessary for successful demobilization. But this was not forthcoming in the event: 'If a satisfactory solution is to be found to the problem of resettling large numbers of men in civil life at the end of a war, the outstanding need is for early planning and preparedness. All through the period under review, plans were too slow in being translated into action.'[62]

The question of resettlement also could not be answered easily primarily because of the immense size and nature of the armed forces raised during the War.[63] In 1945 millions had to be demobilized and the number of skilled, urban, and trained personnel in the three Indian services had grown considerably between 1939 and 1945. The aspirations of these men were quite different from those entertained by the peasants of 1918 and this change of mentality in the armed services was faced by the British for the first time in India. Thus, officially, 'it was considered that post-War development schemes and *post-war industrialisation would be the principal channels* through which it might be possible to absorb those who did not want to return to their previous occupations'[64] (emphasis added).

The deliberations of the Reconstruction Committee set up by the GOI in 1942 to win the peace after the War led to the realization that unemployment had to be contained at all costs. Provincial governments were expected to play an important role in the reconstruction process by utilizing surplus military stores and hardware in the direct interest of ex-servicemen and their proposed cooperatives. A fund for resettling demobilized men was necessary and it was suggested that each serving man pay two rupees a month to raise a huge fund roughly at the rate of two million rupees per month. Men had to be convinced into not demanding rapid demobilization, and 'extravagant hopes' in the Emergency Commissioned Officers (ECOs) had to be curbed by circulating approximate figures of the number of government appointments likely to be available to such officers after the War.[65]

In the 1940s land grants on a significant scale were impossible because most provinces could not afford them. Almost 50 per cent of the new men were urban or semi-urban 'tradesmen' who wanted to 'make use of their skill', and after the War would 'crowd to swell the unemployed in the cities'. This nightmare had to, and could possibly have been, averted by making the villages attractive to the returning soldier by the use of 'imagination and financial assistance'.[66] The extent of change in the armed forces became clear in July 1945 when a simple questionnaire was given to 100,000 servicemen in one thousand units of all arms of the Indian services with the aim of finding out the kind of employment the average serviceman desired after the War. The replies revealed the following:

Men	%
Who had assured jobs other than agriculture	8.74
Who desired agricultural employment	35.26
Who desired employment as teachers	1.05
Who desired industrial employment	31.30
Who wanted to become domestic servants	3.84
Desiring work as mechanical transport drivers	7.14
Desiring clerical or other non-technical jobs	7.35
Matriculates desiring non-clerical work	1.01

Source: Se. No. 365, *Demobilization of the Indian Army*.

The survey also stated that 85 per cent of respondents desiring employment expressed a preference for government schemes.[67] Against 82 per cent agriculturists and village artisans, as shown in the release roll, there were now only 35 per cent who wanted to return to agriculture. Almost an equal proportion of men were looking for industrial employment. In sum, 51.69 per cent of the respondents desired employment *outside agriculture*. These expectations would put tremendous pressure on the GOI in 1945-6 precisely at a time when it faced the challenge of Partition and the growing threat of civil war.

The future employment of officers posed a more complex problem because of the anticipated scarcity of jobs in military and civil departments. It was known that the officer's implicit trust in the Raj to give them jobs, if inculcated during demobilization, would lead to 'disappointment and discontent'.[68] The demobilization plan noticed the contradiction between the wartime experience of young men and the 'uncompromising medievalism' of their rural homes. Thus, it was thought better to spend some money on resettlement to save demobilized men from 'every kind of theorist, agitator, grumbler and grievances hunter' than to hold down a 'disgruntled soldiery by force'. Simultaneously, the military connection and spirit of obedience to the state had to be maintained among the ex-soldiers through the medium of apolitical ex-servicemen's reunions, societies and welfare activities.[69] However, all this was easier contemplated than done because while conscripts would be happy returning to their civilian jobs in Britain many Indians would have preferred permanent employment in the services. Departmental surveys indicated that during the War 33 per cent of the cavalry and infantry units were trained to a trade. Good tradesmen had joined the transport and other technical units in large numbers with dangerous implications for the British: 'The younger of these men know little of the land and will, unless inducements are given, tend to crowd to the cities to seek the opportunity to make use of their technical skill. Many will *inevitably swell the ranks of the unemployed.* Disgruntled they may turn to the only other trade they know, fighting, and become dacoits' (emphasis added).[70] The quality of men demobilized would prove important for post-War politics. While the VCOs and NCOs would eye promotion, most technicians in all the services would clamour for quick demobilization because of large scale unemployment in India. It was foreseen that even for those released early jobs would be scarce. In these circumstances, most probably some men would prefer *delayed demobilization*, with leave, to explore alternatives before final discharge. Matters were more delicate in India where individual demobilization, due to industrial backwardness, and despite an over-ambitious military card index proposed for the Labour Department, was impossible. In Great Britain, the Trades Union Organization, the smallness of the country, the comparatively large proportion of the population which was were engaged in industrial work pre-War, among other factors makes it possible to devise an elaborate system of individual demobilization to attempt to deal with the problem.[71]

Furthermore, it was feared that peace would actually contract industry and the demand for technicians would fall at the very moment when they would be demobilized in large numbers. Massive unemployment, thus, incurred would fuel political disturbances which an exhausted government could ill afford. As early as 1942, as the growing demand for vocational training and propaganda to ensure tranquillity among the men suggested, anxiety was manifest within the armed forces.[72]

Finally demobilization was influenced by the principles outlined in the Imperial White Paper on release placed before the Cabinet in September 1944. The Imperial plan assumed that conscription would continue in England and resettlement in the intervening years between the armistice and final peace would depend upon post-War military requirements and the arrangements for release acceptable to the armed forces.[73] Influenced by the Paper, which was accepted by the Cabinet, the War Committee of the Commander-in-Chief in India began taking up demobilization seriously in its periodic deliberations. It was anticipated that Indian demobilization would depend upon the assessed responsibility of the Indian armed forces after the War, a post-War defence budget and the rapidly rising need to resettle demobilized men. Infrastructural factors further conditioning, and most probably slowing down, Indian demobilization would be shipping and the capacity of ports, rail and road transport to handle the large-scale discharge of men, the ability of a colonial bureaucracy and military red tape to process paper work related to release and the capacity of the medical services to complete examinations, etc., on time.[74]

The GOI, as usual, was dragging its feet over the matter. It had set up a Reorganization Committee to draft a plan for the post-War reorganization of the Indian economy. Till October 1944 neither had the Committee met nor had a preliminary plan emerged, making it impossible for the military leaders to 'plan too perfectly'. Though the General Staff had estimated the strength of a post-War interim force keeping in mind the 'futuristic' lines apparent in 1944-5, the Financial Advisor 'wished to reconcile the expenditure required for those forces with the financial resources likely to be available'.[75] In September 1944 the Military Finance Department had surveyed the overall military expenditure likely to be incurred in India in the immediate post-War years. This general survey calculated needs based on the assumed availability of normal reserves and budgetary allocations for three years after the War. Demobilization, on the lines of the 1920s, would take eighteen months and the 1944 levels of pay and allowances, with British control intact, would continue after the War. Post-War inflation, expansion in key areas and technological development was ignored by the survey and nothing crucial emerged even when an extraordinary meeting of the C-in-C's Secretariat took up these issues in November 1944.[76]

In December 1944 specific questions pertinent to the future of the new services remained unsettled and Auchinleck could only ask the Military Finance Department to prepare a new budget forecast for the services' consideration.[77] His terms of reference were based on the long-standing official assumption that political and constitutional changes in India *would not* affect the services and in future India would once again manage the minor danger threatening the Empire.[78] This indicated that demobilization would be chalked out within the policy framework of the early 1930s. Though political factors specific to India were recognized, no 'retrogression' from the levels of trade, port development, naval defence, and industry attained during the War was advisable after it. But solutions, in India, could only be general:

> Modern war is synonymous with total war. Every country which is to survive in the future must have the ability to expand its forces rapidly as soon as war threatens and must be able to direct its industries quickly into war channels. It will be the responsibility of the armed forces to ensure that their own expansion can be rapidly implemented.[79]

In April 1945 the services submitted their financial estimates for the upper and lower requirements for the immediate post-War years in keeping with the 'minor danger' and the War Committee asked the old question whether Britain would be willing to share defence spending with India if the latter gained 'an autonomous constitution' after the War. Naval estimates came in for more criticism because of the overwhelming need to assess the 'financial lower limits' before an attempted post-War reorganization could even be contemplated. The Financial Advisor dealt another blow by reporting that the price index in the immediate post-War years was likely to be higher than pre-War by 50 to a 100 per cent leaving only Rs. 70 to 75 crore for the armed forces.[80] This financial forecast made Auchinleck realize that despite plans the services would soon have to be slashed to the minimum. Hence, from the 'minor danger' the emphasis retreated to 'the smallest number of purely local defence forces' necessary for India. In his directive to the Chiefs of Staff in May 1945 the C-in-C demanded recommendations detailing the 'lowest limits' permissible in the event of the GOI not even being able to maintain the 'lower limits'.[81]

In July 1945 the services prepared fresh estimates on the 'lowest limit' principle which were accepted by the government and in August demobilization, envisaged over two years, began in stages. Throughout 1945 estimates kept changing because of government views and the economic climate. On their own while the services, especially the new ones with mass discontent threatening them, may have tried to salvage the maximum from retrenchment but the government relentlessly drove down the estimates. The result of effecting such stringent economies during demobilization belied several promises made to the recruits earlier during the War.[82] The consequence, as the following naval case illustrates, was the rise of popular protest in the post-War Indian armed forces.

The official history of the RIN informs us that in 1945 'within a few months . . . considerable progress' was made in solving the 'outstanding problems' of demobilization by the post-War Planning Directorate under a Captain in the Naval HQ. Discontent is not only perfunctorily brushed aside but the recruits are blamed for it:

> Unfortunately there was a strong tendency, amongst officers and ratings alike, to believe that a man was only to sit back and wait for the Government to find a job. Steps were taken to inculcate into all ranks the correct outlook on resettlement, which was that every man was expected to do everything possible himself to resettle, and that the function of the Government was to advise and assist.[83]

This is a travesty of the facts because discontent originated in the failures of demobilization. On 16 November 1945 the Naval HQ received an anonymous letter narrating the problems faced by the ratings in HMIS *Kakauri*, the RIN release centre. Describing the 'most horrifying' conditions prevalent in *Kakauri* the author made it clear that this experience had 'poisoned' the minds of young men. Accounts of the men had not been settled as late as

November 1945 and some ratings were in fact drafted into a General (Labour) Pool which was used for menial work. This was obviously resented by the men who expected something much better after the Second World War. Official hamhandedness and tactlessness was also evident elsewhere. Often when ratings refused to sign the pay receipts without being paid they were threatened with punishment. Many of them had served till 1945 without having been punished even once and did not relish attaching punishment to their leaving certificates just before discharge when a clean chit would have helped their civilian career. On the spot such men obeyed but remained discontented and later made their 'suffering' known to the RIN Mutiny Commission of Enquiry.[84]

Contrary to official claims made after the Second World War, demobilization in the RIN was totally 'unplanned' and 'clueless' and the insensitivity of the Military authorities to the issue was demonstrated soon after the victory day when the Hostilities Only (HO) men were discharged without gratuities or even railway fares. To make matters worse they were made to refund the cost of kit which, in most cases, had never been issued. Overcrowding of establishments, with drastic consequences, was common. For example, Castle Barracks, designed for 500 men, was packed with more than 1,000 in 1945. Fort Barracks, meant for 600, had 1,400 men in it. Smaller ships and establishments, unsuited to tropical climate, carried twice the number of ratings normally allowed on board.[85] It was futile to overcrowd the release centres because the administrative machinery necessary for satisfactory demobilization was never created. The Morale Reports criticized the RIN establishments for their bad quarters, food, and hard manual labour. In several instances the ratings were also retained for weeks against the officially allowed twelve days. Even Godfrey, no sympathiser of the rebels of 1946, admitted that demobilization caused confusion, controversy, and dissatisfaction in the service. In fact, officers responsible for smooth demobilization were complacent and the Mutiny of February 1946 took them completely by surprise.[86]

Demobilization, which converted Bombay into a centre 'clogged' with eager men awaiting discharge, in the words of Godfrey, was a 'thankless' and 'never-ending' task. The British, for their part, wanted to go home with the Indians wanting them to make haste. The process was ponderous and ships could not be paid off and crews dispersed fast enough before the collective mentality of mutiny took hold of the ratings. The atmosphere was charged with rumour and the INA sentiment even though to Godfrey in the winter of 1945-6 Bombay appeared full of ratings about to be paid off, 'but [with] nothing to do but think up grievances'. Finally, the 'quite legitimate grievances' regarding pay, allowances, travelling, the colour bar, promotion, and the pay disparities between services which existed in the Navy were making their presence felt.[87] These circumstances, as many officers and men recorded later, left most Indians 'sadly disillusioned' and full of 'malice and bitterness towards the service'. And Godfrey later observed, rather thoughtfully, that the Navy was reflecting the general rebellious sentiment of the years. Indeed, the tinder had accumulated and only a spark was needed to touch things off because the denouement of war had made most ratings thoroughly 'Bolshi'.[88]

CONCLUSION

Prolonged, large-scale wars often produce mutinies and military history, contrary to the view expressed in official documents, shows that this does not happen because mass voluntary recruitment or conscription necessarily infuses militarily unsuitable men into the armed forces. Mutinies are usually caused by the inability of over-stretched governments to raise the material standards of their armed forces and sagaciously answer the political questions raised by their disenchanted troops. This chapter has made this point by demonstrating that the post-Second World War discontent in the Indian armed forces was caused by the contradictions inherent in the GOI's war effort and its termination. The inter-War theory and practice of military recruitment, despite the experiences of the Great War, was conditioned by the limitations of the Raj and remained predicated upon the 'martial races'. This is one reason why demobilization, as Tai Yong Tan's study of Punjab cited earlier suggests, was better managed after the Great War.[89] In the inter-War years some of the social realities of the Indian colony changed. In 1939 the Indian military establishment, lulled into complacence by the Punjab experience of the 1920s, neither anticipated nor was prepared for the changes in recruitment which the Second World War brought. And the sources admit that these changes cast their shadow on the entire Indian war effort.

The Second World War technologically and socially transformed the Indian armed forces substantially. But this transformation occurred in circumstances which were not always favourable to easy military recruitment. In the process, as this chapter has shown, the colonial recruitment drives had to contend with several Indian peculiarities before the volunteer-recruits were procured. Significantly enough, by the end of the War, a large majority of the new recruits belonged to the erstwhile 'non-martial' groups. Although the British managed to run a successful war effort in India between 1939 and 1945 several problems affecting the Indians in the process remained unaddressed for a variety of reasons. Throughout the War desertion, for instance, continued to threaten the recruitment drives. This happened largely because the terms and conditions of military recruitment compared unfavourably with the conditions obtained in the civilian labour market. Obviously there was a colonial limit to the incentives which were being offered to the recruits to distract them from the civilian labour market.

Recruitment problems were also exacerbated by rising agricultural prices and the Indian nationalist opposition to the war effort. Considering the mercenary nature of Indian recruitment the British could have overcome these problems only by raising the material standards of the Indian armed forces substantially. But given the legacy of the inter-War period, the priorities of imperial defence, and the economic resources available to the GOI in the 1940s, achieving this was extremely difficult beyond a certain point. This made for a near perfect case of chronic service dissatisfaction even before the War ended. The GOI did respond to these challenges by trying to sell recruitment better. In the event recruitment propaganda was overdone almost to the point of totally, and dangerously, justifying the excessive hopes it aroused in the recruits. Subsequent events proved that this was an important step in the creation of widespread disturbances in the Indian services after the War.

While the war effort severely overstrained the Raj, the demobilization process, an inevitable outcome of abnormal recruitment, further underlined its rapidly growing weakness.

Our brief comparison of demobilization after the two World Wars established the modesty of the process after the First World War and its extreme inadequacy after the Second. Quite early during the Second World War the GOI became aware of the immense challenge posed to its security by the prospect of ultimately demobilizing the large, and much transformed, wartime forces. The central question raised by demobilization was whether the GOI could retrieve the political and psychological ground lost to the volunteers during the war effort in an economically backward and politically troubled colony like India. But before demobilization dissolved into the popular protest of 1945-6 and the civil war of 1946-7 the GOI seemed to have betrayed the confidence of its main wartime allies—the Indian recruits. In consequence the causes implicit in wartime recruitment and explicit in the failures of demobilization prepared the ground for the emergence of large-scale social unrest in the Indian armed forces during the politically charged months following the defeat of the Axis powers.

NOTES

1. For details of popular protest in India in 1945-6 see: K.K. Ghosh, *The Indian National Army*, Meerut, 1969; Hugh Toye, *The Springing Tiger: Subhas Chandra Bose*, Bombay, 1993; N.R. Ray et al. (eds.), *Challenge: A Saga of India's Struggle for Freedom*, New Delhi, 1984; S. Banerjee, *The RIN Strike*, Delhi, 1954; B.C. Dutt, *Mutiny of the Innocents*, Bombay, 1971; S. Singh, *Under Two Ensigns*, Delhi, 1985; B. Farwell, *Armies of the Raj*, London, 1989; R. Kadian, *India and its Army*, New Delhi, 1990; A.I. Singh, *The Origins of the Partition of India 1936-1947*, Delhi, 1987; S. Sarkar, 'Popular Movements and National Leadership, 1945-47', *Economic and Political Weekly*, Annual Number, April 1982; A. Deshpande, 'Sailors and the Crowd: Popular Protest in Karachi, 1946', *Indian Economic and Social History Review* 26, 1, 1989; 'Hopes and Disillusionment: Recruitment, Demobilisation and the Emergence of Discontent in the Indian Armed Forces after the Second World War', *Indian Economic and Social History Review*, 33, 2, 1996; 'Crowd Intervention in Indian History: An Overview of popular resistance coterminous with the 1946 RIN Mutiny', *Mainstream*, 22.2.1992 and 'Remembering the RIN Revolt: Popular Celebration of Nationalism Fifty Years Ago', *Mainstream*, 24.2.1996.

2. A comprehensive study of demobilization after *both* the World Wars lies beyond the scope of this chapter. Demobilization after the First World War, highlighting the Indian attempt to subvert British authority and the British inability to satisfy a large number of volunteers, is examined in my thesis upon which this book is based. For details of service expansion during 1939-45 see B. Prasad (ed.), *Official History of the Indian Armed Forces in the Second World War: Expansion of the Armed Forces and Defence Organisation 1939-45*, New Delhi, 1956. Discontent after the First World War in the Indian Army is mentioned in D.C. Ellinwood and S.D. Pradhan (eds.), *India and World War I*, New Delhi, 1978; S.P. Cohen, *The Indian Army*, New Delhi, 1990 and 'The Untouchable Soldier: Caste, Politics and the Indian Army', *The Journal of Asian Studies* Vol. XXVIII (3), May 1969; T.A. Heathcote, *The Indian Army: The Garrison of British Imperial India 1822-1922*, London, 1974; V. Longer, *Red Coats to Olive Green*, New Delhi, 1974.
3. Chapters Two and Three of this book; *The Chatfield Committee Report*, 1939, Historical Section of the Ministry of Defence (hereafter HS), New Delhi, confirms the assertion; B. Bond, *British Military Policy*, pp. 105-6, finds the Indian Army in the 1920s a '. . . depressing backwater still living in the atmosphere of the Victorian era' to which the Great War had neither given new ideas nor much equipment.
4. Cohen, 'The Untouchable Soldier', op. cit.
5. Ibid., Cohen, *The Indian Army*, p. 56, points out that the 'martial esprit' of the Army became 'increasingly irrelevant' and even a 'hindrance' to the development of the Indian Army as a modern organization in the early twentieth century; V. Kiernan in B. Bond and I. Roy (eds.), *War and Society*, Vol. 2, London, 1977, pp. 20-40, shows that in the Great War African soldiers also demolished the unfavourable myths associated with them.
6. *India in 1930-31, A statement prepared for presentation to Parliament*, (GOI publication) Calcutta 1932, p. 26.
7. *India in 1929-30, A statement prepared for presentation to Parliament* (GOI publication), Calcutta, 1931, p. 61
8. *Report of the Royal Commission on the War in South Africa, Volume II, with Minutes of Evidence*, 1904 (Cd. 1791) and *Report of His Majesty's Commissioners appointed to inquire into the Military preparations and other matters connected with War in South Africa*, 1903 (Cd. 1789), Cambridge University Library, U.K. The cross-examination of witnesses, involving senior British Army officers, revealed that the British method of training and warfare were not conducive to the development of initiative and individuality in the troops and officers alike. Patrick Cadell, *History of the Bombay Army*, London, 1938; Reginald Hennel, *A Famous Indian Regiment: Kali Panchwin*, 1927, rpt New Delhi, 1985 and George MacMunn, *The Martial Races of India*, London, 1932, speak

of those 'martial races' which were degraded by the rigid paradigm fashioned by Field Marshal Roberts in the late nineteenth century. On the British perceptions and policy regarding the South Asian 'martial races' see the following recent works; Anirudh Deshpande, 'Contested Identities and Military Indianization in Colonial India (1900-1939), *Contemporary India*, Vol. 1, No. 1 (Jan.-March 2002; Gupta and Deshpande (eds.), *The British Raj and its Indian Armed Froces 1857-1939*, New Delhi, 2002 and Channa Wickremesekera, '*Best Black Troops in the World*': *British Perceptions and the Making of the Sepoy 1746-1805*, New Delhi, 2002.

9. E. Candler, *The Sepoy*, London, 1919, pp. vii, 2.
10. Ibid., pp. 57-9.
11. *Handbook for the Indian Army: Jats, Gujars and Ahirs*, first compiled under the orders of the GOI by Major A.H. Bingley, 7th Duke of Connaught's own Rajputs, 1904. Revised in the same language by Lt. Col. R.C. Christie, M.C., Recruiting Officer, Delhi, 1937, pp. 33, 71-2, 79.
12. *Handbook for the Indian Army: Punjabi Musalmans*, compiled for the GOI by Lt. Col. J.M. Wikely, seventh Cavalry, Late Recruiting Officer for Punjabi Musalmans. Revised 1927, 2nd edn. 1935, New Delhi, 1936, p. 5; *Handbook for the Indian Army: Hindustani Musalmans and Muselmans of the Eastern Punjab*, compiled under the orders of the GOI by Major W. Fritz G. Bourne, 10th Jats, Late Recruiting Officer for Hindustani Musalmans, Calcutta, 1914.
13. *Handbook for the Indian Army: Gurkhas*, compiled under the orders of the GOI by Lt. Col. Eden Vansittart, 2nd Bn., 10th Gurkha Rifles, Calcutta, 1906, pp. 3-9, 11, 60. The revised edition of 1933 by Captain Morris contains identical descriptions.
14. *Handbook for the Indian Army: Kumaonis*, by Lt. Col. A. Latham, late 18th Garwhal Rifles, 1933, rpt. New Delhi, 1941 without changes; also see *Handbook for the Indian Army: Garwhalis*, by Captain J. Evatt, 39th (The Garwhal Rifle) Regiment, 1894, revised by Lt. Col. Henderson, 18th Royal Garwhal Rifles, Calcutta, 1924 and *Handbook for the Indian Army: Dogras*, by Lt. Col. W.B. Cunningham, M.C., 2nd Bn., 17th Dogra Regiment, Calcutta, 1932.
15. P. Mason, *A Matter of Honour*, p. 529 presents a literal, and untenable, interpretation of the theoretical Hindu *varna* system favouring the myth; D.C. Ellinwood and C.H. Enloe, *Ethnicity and the Military in Asia*, London, 1981, p. 92, asserts that the interaction of 'British interest in racial differences' and Indian social distinctions was responsible for producing the 'theory' of the martial races; T.A. Heathcote, *The Indian Army*, p. 82, provides the corrective by stressing the historical specificity of the myth in the 'classic' period of the British Indian Army; A. Deshpande, 'Limitations of Military Technology: Naval Warfare on the

West Coast, 1650-1800', *Economic and Political Weekly*, 25 April 1992 does not discover any 'theory' of the martial races before the Mutiny.

16. *Report of the Army in India Committee, 1922-23*; *The Army in India and its Evolution* (1924); *Chatfield Committee Report* and Committee of Imperial Defence Papers 1933-35.
17. Secret War Department History 1939-45, Head I, General State and Role of the Armed Forces of India prior to Sept. 1939, p. 27a, 601/7169/H (HS). But against all available evidence Pradhan in Ellinwood and Pradhan (eds.), *India and World War I*, New Delhi, 1978, p. 65, claims that by 1939 the Indian Army, 'had become capable of fighting against European armies without the assistance of any of the services of the British Army'.
18. File No. 601/9074/H, No. 26 WDM, War Department History-2 (HS): Expansion of the armed forces, Statistical material supplied by AG's branch (statistical section) with previous references to (A) Summary of estimated strength evolved by 1940 expansion scheme, (B) Strengths of officers, (C) Recruitment tables 1939-43, (D) Army strength on 1.7.1945.
19. File No. 601/7832/H, Draft and Fair Copy, 1946 (HS): *Monograph on Recruitment for the Defence Services in India*, Colonel Day, 1946, 200 pages, maps, and figures for all services, Defence Department, p. 37.
20. Ibid., Appendix I, pp. 143-4: Instructions to effect reduction in desertion—No. 2833/A.G.-2(a-1), General HQ, India, Adjutant General's Branch, New Delhi, 16.11.1942; Anirudh Deshpande, unpublished M.Phil. thesis, 'The Royal Indian Navy Uprising and Popular Protest, 1946' (Centre for Historical Studies, JNU, 1987); MS *Naval Memoirs* of Admiral J.H. Godfrey, Flag Officer Commanding RIN (FOCRIN), 1943-46, Vol. VII, India, *passim*, Churchill Archives Centre, Churchill College, Cambridge (hereafter *Naval Memoirs*).
21. *Monograph on Recruitment* . . ., p. 39: The recruitment directorate and officers usually considered all these factors before launching any specific drive.
22. File No. 601/7016/H (HS) Proceedings of a conference to consider India's recruitment, 19, 20 and 21 March 1942, pp. 6-7; *Monograph on Recruitment* . . ., p 45: In certain cases civil and courtesy titles, honorary commissioned ranks, one month's pay to the recruit and communal awards of wells and hostels were given.
23. *Monograph on Recruitment* . . ., p. 38.
24. Ibid., p. 44.
25. Ibid., pp. 46-8.
26. Ibid., pp. 46-8; File 601/9074/H: War Department History-2. Also see Appendix A at the end of the paper.
27. The Papers of Lieutenant General Thomas William Corbett, Churchill

Archives Centre, Churchill College, Cambridge, File 1/16—Corbett's papers and letters while Brigadier in command of Sialkot Area on *inter-alia* cavalry organization, organization of Indian Armoured Brigade modernization of Indian Army and examination of officers for promotion, Sept. 1938-Jan. 1940 & File 3/1—Corbett's correspondence on the purpose of the Army in India, including his worry about the lack of progress in equipping and training the Indian Army during 1938-42.

28. *Monograph on Recruitment*. . ., pp. 89-91.
29. 601/7016/H: Proceedings of a Conference . . ., p. 7.
30. Ibid., p. 22.
31. Ibid., p. 23.
32. Ibid., pp. 93-5.
33. Ibid., p. 8: The representative of Madras pointed this out. A list of films produced during the War is given in Appendix B.
34. File No. 174, AOC/ADM/108, I.A.F. Public Relations, Air HQ Directive-3/11/74 and Air Vice Marshal's remarks on the synopsis of a film on the RIAF, 2/11/44, in the Air HQ in F.174 (HS).
35. Ibid., Notes for the guidance of IAF officers conducting Public Relations on behalf of the service.
36. Ibid., first copy of the *Sentinel*, size 6.3"/9.7", 30 pages with cartoons and illustrations.
37. Ibid.
38. The RIN Mutiny Commission of Enquiry Report (hereafter CER), July 1946, Se. No. 7, RIN Mutiny Papers, National Archives of India (NAI), New Delhi, pp. 119-22.
39. Se. No. 4—Karachi Statements, RIN Mutiny Papers, NAI comprising written and typed letters and petitions of ratings and officers to the Commission of Enquiry; *CER*, p. 125: views of RIN veterans Allah Ditta and Commander Gush.
40. Commission of Enquiry's observations, *CER*, pp. 128-9. Also see B.C. Dutt, *Mutiny of the Innocents*, Bombay, 1971.
41. *CER*, pp. 129-31; *Naval Memoirs*: Poor pay remained a cause of discontent in the RIN throughout the War and increases in 1943 were insufficient to offset the damage.
42. *CER*, p. 131. Most artificers were described as members of Hindu families of some 'social status'.
43. *CER*, pp. 150 and 134: One poster questioned the pride of the recruit. 'Are you young and smart? If you are young and smart and between 17½ and 24 years of age and have studied up to matriculation there are good opportunities and prospects for you in the RIN. Your job will be interesting. . . .' Unfortunately the official history of the RIN neither mentions the Mutiny nor looks at the CER nor the facts associated with recruitment.

44. File No. 601/7450/H(A), Head I, General State of the RIN on the outbreak of the War in 1939 and RIN Expansion Head 2 (HS).
45. Ibid., pp. 11-19: In 1939 the personnel totals of the RIN were: 109 Commissioned Officers, 63 Warrant Officers, 1,443 Ratings and 37 Reserve Officers. In 1943 the total number of officers was 2,219 and ratings 20,590. In a telling commentary on the new services the RIN officials concluded with some relief in 1943 that it was, 'perhaps as well that Japan did not enter the war until a later stage'. In comparison the merchant navy allowed its seamen time off between voyages to cultivate family land. Professional seamen, especially in the absence of monetary incentive, were also reluctant to accept the change from 'patriarchal discipline to impersonal naval discipline' implied by naval service. Shipping companies were also better placed because they did not require official permission to raise rates.
46. Ibid., pp. 41-5.
47. 601/7016/H: Proceedings of a Conference . . ., points made by the RIN representative Commander Streatfield James. The RIN began its recruitment propaganda in 1938 with the publication of a small booklet compiled by Commander P.A. Mare, foreworded by the FOCRIN and addressed to the English educated elite titled *How to become an officer in the RIN: Being a detailed account of how a young Indian may become an officer in His Majesty's Indian Navy*, Calcutta, 1938. The Navy was advertised as a service affording travel, a 'man's life' and honour. A candidate with considerable private finance, education, manners, common sense and self-discipline was demanded. But the first clause in this was missing from the recruitment propaganda of the 1940s.
48. Proceedings of a conference . . .: The RIAF representative pointed out that earlier in England too the right type of boys were often discouraged by school masters and parents from joining the RAF.
49. 601/7450/H, General State of the RIN . . ., p. 45.
50. *Naval Memoirs*, vol. 6, Churchill Archives Centre.
51. File No. 601/7188/H: RIN Manpower Review, 1939/1945, 3 Sept. 1939 to 30 Sept. 1945: Monograph approved by FOCRIN (HS) SECRET, p. 18. Wastage was serious and uneconomical for a service which could neither combat homesickness nor promise a bright future; 601/7450/H, General State of the RIN . . ., p. 46: This was said to the FOCRIN by a Commanding Officer of a RIN depot in 1942. A comparison of merchant and naval rates is presented in Appendix C at the end of the paper; *Monograph on Recruitment*. . ., p. 20, tells us that during the Wars regular commissions in the RIN were granted on a diminishing scale. Officer reserves were established in 1939 with all reserve officers being trained in India and most of the commissions granted during the War were temporary emergency commissions.

52. *Monograph on Recruitment* . . ., p. 36, section on Officer recruiting. This was the conclusion arrived at by the Indian Sandhurst Committee in 1927. The *Report of the Indian Sandhurst Committee*, Simla, 1927 (also called the *Skeen Committee Report*) was set up due to the Indian pressure to review Indianization and the Indian education system in the late 1920s. For more details regarding the Skeen Committee see P.S. Gupta's paper on Indianization in Gupta and Deshpande (eds.), *The British Raj and its Indian Armed Forces 1857-1939*, and Deshpande, 'Contested Identities', op. cit.
53. *Monograph on Recruitment* . . ., Section on RIAF recruiting; File No. F 182-AOC/ADM/116—Personnel Grievances in the RIAF (HS); Men in the RIAF considered their pension and allowances inadequate and this played an important role in the post-War RIAF 'Strikes' which haven't received due academic attention so far.
54. File No. 601/7640/H Annual Recruiting Report, 1945-46, Defence Dept. (HS).
55. 601/7640/H, Annual Recruiting Report for the year ending 31 March 1947, Defence Dept., File No. 2.
56. SIMLA RECORDS 1919 GOI Home Dept. Political Deposit Proceedings, July 1919, No. 37: Suggestions for allaying the feelings of disappointment prevalent among the rural population of the Punjab and elsewhere at the absence of any announcement of some general boon as a reward for their services during the War, Hom/Pol, NAI.
57. B Prasad (ed.), *Adjutant General's Branch, Monographs, Vol. III, War System of Accounting and Honours and Awards*, Combined Inter-Services Historical Section (India and Pakistan), HS, New Delhi, 1957, section on the First World War.
58. Tai Yong Tan, 'Maintaining the Military Districts: Civil-Military Integration and District Soldiers' Boards in the Punjab, 1919-1939, *Modern Asian Studies*, Vol. 28, No. 4, 1994 is an interesting narration of the demobilization process in the Punjab following the Great War. Tan draws our attention to the formation of the District Soldiers' Boards (DSB) and their socio-political ramifications in the Punjab during the crucial years following the end of the Great War. These DSBs represented the cooperation of civil and military authorities in an official attempt to form a 'cordon sanitaire' around the military districts which had become politically vulnerable in the charged atmosphere following the Great War. Although the DSBs could not prevent the emergence of discontent in large parts of Punjab in the military districts they seemed to have boosted the image the Raj as a benevolent *sarkar*. However, what could be achieved in the Punjab between the Wars *could not be* achieved on an Indian wide scale during the demobilization process following the Second World War. The Punjab case was predicated upon the fact that 60 per cent of the Indian Army in 1919 comprised the

Punjabis. This underlined the serious colonial attempt to preserve loyalty in the Punjabi martial classes examined by Tan.

59. Tan, 'Maintaining the Military Districts', op. cit.: The network of DSBs created in Punjab in the inter-War period and the official experience of dealing with a potentially disaffected demobilized soldiery most probably underlined these announcements.

60. Ibid. We also know that by the end of the War only 15,000 commissions had been given to the Indians and, in testimony to failed Indianization, most of these were temporary Emergency Commissions. This was a cause of considerable unrest among middle-class Indians in the armed forces.

61. Se. No. 365, *Demobilisation of the Indian Army*, Monograph in Adjutant General's Branch, Combined Inter-Services Historical Section (India and Pakistan), General Editor Bisheshwar Prasad, p. 10.

62. Se. No. 365, *Demobilisation of the Indian Army*, introduction.

63. Ibid., Resettlement, Section I, overstates demobilization after the Great War: 'Lands were offered to men, and the majority of ex-servicemen were thus settled. Elsewhere, too, land awards were made, and many ex-servicemen were absorbed in Government services of all kinds.'

64. Ibid., Resettlement, Section I.

65. File No. 601/7029/H (HS): Informal meeting of Official Members of the Reconstruction Committee (Labour and Demobilisation) Agenda, 1942; (ii) Revised notes on which to base the Demobilisation Scheme (1 June 1942); Principles governing the agenda. In 1919 the policy of auctioning off stores to profiteering contractors had proved unpopular. Hasty discharge and unremitting retrenchment with attendant discontent, as witnessed between 1919 and 1925, could also cost the government peace after the War.

66. Ibid., pp. 2-3, deliberations: Vocational training was seen as a good method to turn demobilized troops away from sedition.

67. Tan, 'Maintaining the Military Districts', op. cit., arrives at similar conclusions regarding demobilization responses following the Great War. Those ex-soldiers who were given jobs in private mercantile concerns by the DSBs took these jobs with great reluctance. The *kamin* castes who had given up tilling land in favour of military service did not want to return to the villages and a life of caste subjugation. Government service, even if it was not very remunerative, was preferred by almost everyone as a matter of *izzat*.

68. File No. 601/7029/H, p. 4.

69. Ibid., 'Winning the Peace', a note by Col. Brayne.

70. Secret 17502/A.G. (Demob), General HQ, AG Branch Simla, 1.6.1942, Appendix E: Reconstruction of Industry for the absorption of labour and Resettlement in Civil Life, HS.

71. Ibid.

72. Ibid.
73. File No. 601/10609/H (TOP SECRET), Demobilization when Germany out, 1944 (HS) containing correspondence between the Secretary of State and the Governor-General on the subject, an important letter dated 29/2/44 on demobilization by the Auditor-General to the Governor-General and the Draft government white paper vide Telegram No. 20756 (Secret) from the Secretary of State to the Governor-General.
74. File No. 601/10605/H, Demobilisation and Resettlement Planning, Vol. I 1944-45 (HS): In early 1945 it was decided that 63 infantry battalions and 23 garrison companies would be required for internal security in India after the War. 50 battalions forming a permanent garrison for the NWFP were needed besides 3 divisions for Burma, 1 for Malaya and Siam each and 2 for the Middle East. Per division (about 40,000 men) the British element would be represented by two artillery regiments and three infantry battalions.
75. Ibid., Minutes of a meeting held on 23.10.44 to consider demob. and post-War reorganization planning chaired by Lt. Gen. Lindsell (PAO) in the C-in-C's Secretariat (India) SECRET.
76. Ibid., SECRET PAPER, Military Finance Department, Sub: Reduction of Defence Expenditure during post-War years, No. 11401-C, D/12/9/44 with appendices; Reflections on the paper from [Secret, C-in-C's (India) Secretariat] Inter-Service meeting, Minutes of an extraordinary meeting held on 6 Nov. 1944 to consider paper No. 11401-C; Ref. Minutes of 203rd meeting of C-in-C's War Committee 7.11.44, Minutes of a meeting held on 13.11.44 to consider demob. in C-in-C's Secretariat. A Demob. Planning Staff in principle was set up as a result of these meetings. In the absence of a clear-cut government policy on India's post-War military standing the General Staff could only plan for an interim step keeping in mind the 'fluid' situation likely to emerge after the War.
77. Ibid., Minutes of the 217th meeting of the War Committee dated 14.12.44.
78. Ibid., File No. 2, Chiefs of Staff (44) 636 and COS (44) 642, Report on the size and composition of the post-War forces in India and Auchinleck's directive in Appendix A (TOP SECRET).
79. Ibid., File No. 2, Chiefs of Staff's Report on the size and composition of post-War forces. The Staff alerted the government by stating its fears openly: 'At the end of the war, therefore, there is likely to be a period of internal unrest coinciding with a weakening of the civil administration and decreased effectiveness of both British and Indian troops.'
80. Ibid., Vol. II, 288th meeting of the War Committee, 18-19/4/1945.
81. Ibid., TOP SECRET Draft directive to the Chiefs of Staff Committee by the C-in-C after 289th meeting, 20 April 1945; Minutes of 299th meeting of War Committee, 4 May 1945; Secret directive of C-in-C to Chiefs to Staff, 8 May 1945.

82. File No. 601/7180/H: Demobilization—Paper received from Demob. Planning, Head-14, 1945 (HS). The RIAF submitted a separate estimate vide File No. 601/9710/H–Outline Post-War Plan, Air Force Requirements (HS). Ref. 601/10605/H, Vol. II, pp. 344-52; Appendices submitted to the Governor-General by War Department on matters of priority in demobilization immediately after the War. In fact, demobilization continued well into 1947 even as the country and its Army was divided and the transfer of power was effected; Ref. Demob. Plan 287—March, May, July, Aug., Sept. and Nov. 1947, File No. 601/8018/H (HS).
83. B. Prasad (ed.), *Official History of the Indian Armed Forces: Volume on The Royal Indian Navy*, New Delhi, 1964, p. 330.
84. *CER*, pp. 394-7.
85. *CER*, p. 400; Lt. Commander Mukerjee's evidence. The ratings had advertised their discontent in a poster at Kakauri calling it 'the most glorious hell in Bombay'.
86. *CER*, pp. 401-2; Commodore Jefford's and Admiral Godfrey's views. Also Report of the Board of Enquiry into the causes of the Mutiny in HMIS Talwar, NL 9930, RIN Mutiny Papers, NAI; Flag Officer Bombay Rear Admiral Rattray's evidence.
87. *Naval Memoirs*; *CER*, pp. 402-4: Lt. McRae, closely associated with the RIN Benevolent Association, mentioned invalidated men staying up to ten months without receiving their disability pension. The case of Lal Din, an injured seaman of Jammu from HMIS Rajputana, who arrived in Delhi on discharge after spending eighteen months in hospital without a penny of his back pay, without service documents or pension, in a singlet and pants in December 1945, was typical. The files of the Benevolent Association contained an astonishing number of such 'pathetic cases'. Hundreds of ratings were discharged with a 'dirty slip of paper' as their service record which the civilian employers, facing a deluge of demobilized servicemen, flatly refused to believe.
88. *CER*, p. 407; Lt. Ghatak's view; p. 410, memoranda by A.G. Sigamany, A.J. Nayagam and T.A. Nathan. According to Sigamany demobilization was designed specifically to leave the 'aye aye sir' variety in the Navy. Lt. S.N. Kohli's view in the Report on the causes of the mutiny, Exhibit B-4, NL 9930. By the winter of 1945-6 morale of the officers had really sunk low. Karmakar, CO Talwar from 23/2/46 onwards, in his personal report on the mutiny (Exhibit 2), NL 9930, clarified that the Chief Petty Officers and the Petty Officers, most of whom were middle-class youths, had openly joined the rebels. During the mutiny as the men called Karmakar a bastard, for he had grey eyes, and a traitor most officers either looked on or even laughed, NL 9930 and Report of the Board of Enquiry into the Mutiny in the Castle Barracks, NL 9939, RIN Mutiny Papers, NAI, p. 4.

89. Tan, 'Maintaining the Military Districts', points out that a large majority of demobbed soldiers in Punjab were fit only for semi-skilled civilian jobs. None, for instance, could be found to fill the vacancies in the Railway Department for want of education. This stood in stark contrast to the post-1945 scenario. The technological transformation of the armed forces during 1940-5 meant that many more mechanics, drivers, radio operators, trained seamen and airmen, etc., had been produced by the armed forces during the Second World War. The expectations of these men were substantially different from those entertained by the uneducated peasants which made up most of the Indian Army in 1918.

APPENDIX A
MILITARY PARTICIPATION RATIO OF FOUR MAJOR REGIONS IN 1943

1. Punjab led the field with 25.5 per cent of its recruitable population enrolled to form 39.3 per cent of the Army.
2. Madras came second with 7.8 per cent of its recruitable population enlisted to form 15.4 per cent of the Army.
3. The United Provinces was third with 7 per cent of its recruitable populace forming 14.9 per cent of the Army.
4. Bombay was fourth with 3.5 per cent of its recruitable population forming 6.3 per cent of the Army.

SOURCE: (Historical Section, 601/10751/H, From 'A Statement showing the proportion of the Army recruited from various provinces as at 1/3/1943'.

APPENDIX B
A LIST OF FILMS PRODUCED DURING THE WAR

01. *Sailors of India* (RIN)
02. *She sank a raider* (RIN)
03. *Convoy arrives* (RIN)
04. *India's navy* (RIN)
05. *Young India goes to war* (RIN)
06. *Enemy in sight* (RIN)
07. *All valour* (RIN)
08. *RIN executive officers*
09. *Indian Armoured Corps* (Army)
10. *In the service of humanity* (Army)
11. *Our men of steel* (Army)
12. *Desh seva* (Army)
13. *Watan ki pukar* (Army)
14. *Gunners of Hindustan* (Army)
15. *Tarraqqi* (Army)
16. *Stubborn but sure* (Army)
17. *Future leaders of India* (Army)
18. *Soldiers of the south* (Army)
19. *Mahratta Light Infantry* (Army)
20. *Johnny Gurkha* (Army)
21. *Handy Man* (Sappers and Miners)
22. *Joining up* (RIAF)

23. *Learning to fly* (RIAF)
24. *RIAF squadron* (RIAF)
25. *Women at war* (WAC-I)*
26. *Story of a WRIN*
27. *Let sailors go to sea* (WRIN)**

NOTES: *WAC: Women's Auxiliary Corps India.
**Women's RIN Service.

SOURCE: Historical Section 601/7832/H, Appendix R. These films were first produced in English and later dubbed in local languages.

APPENDIX C
DIFFERENCE IN NAVAL AND MERCHANT RATES 30 SEPTEMBER 1943

(*Rs./month*)

RIN Rating	Merchant Rating	RIN Rate	Indian Merchant Marine	Proposed Merchant Marine
Ordinary seaman	Lascar II	45	-	-
Able seaman	Lascar I	50-5	90-6	133-42
Leading seaman	Tindal	68-78	138-80	204-67
Chief Petty Officer	Deck Syrang	101-11	195-7	289

SOURCE: 601/7450/H (A) Head I.

CONCLUSION

Decolonization vs. *Colonial Over-Stretch: A Resumé*

> . . . there was no positive ideal or symbol to which appeal could be made in the face of growing nationalism. Specialised equipment and the need for education meant that the simple boy from the plough who had never heard of politics would not last much longer; the new kind of Indian officer from the middle classes was bound to tire in time of drinking to the King Emperor's health every night. The outbreak of war in 1939 was the beginning of the end.[1]

This book has not been directly related to the theoretical questions pertinent to 'decolonization'. In fact, while discussing military policy themes within the context of colonial over-extension, I have emphasized the losing of control, rather than its relinquishing, by the British in India between 1919 and 1945. This can only imply that if there was a process of decolonization in the period mentioned above the British had little or no control over it. This book has also not examined the often repeated question: whether the British rulers of India had actually planned and executed a decolonization in the Indian subcontinent. However, this is understandable given the limitations of any research effort. But what cannot be denied is the fact that this book has spanned a period in Indian history known for some important British reform initiatives in India. In conclusion, therefore, I find it productive to refer to the issues of devolution of power and ultimately 'decolonization' with all their limitations in India during the first half of the twentieth century. This conclusion tries to answer a question which arises even if we temporarily, and hypothetically, locate British military policy in the context of 'decolonization': What does 'decolonization' mean to the history of the Indian armed forces and British military policy during the first half of the twentieth century? I am aware that some studies of 'decolonization' would have us believe that the British planned their retreat from Empire in some way or the other towards the end of the colonial period. Some of these studies, with their Whiggish implications, highlight the ostensible merits of imperialism and colonialism. In them 'decolonization' appears as the last chapter of an Imperial policy agenda stretching back to the eighteenth century.

However, and with respect to India, the explanatory value of 'decolonization' diminishes on closer scrutiny. For instance, it is difficult to say with sufficient academic confidence that the British had actually prepared for, or anticipated, what happened in India between 1939 and 1947. In my opinion, a genuine effort towards 'decolonization' would have tried to tackle the problems of communalism, racial discrimination, and demobilization, etc., much more seriously than was actually done. With respect to South Asia the thesis of 'decolonization' should be able to answer many of the uncomfortable questions related to the partition of India, the near complete breakdown of the state during the Civil War of 1946-7, and the large-scale disaffection and disturbances which rocked the Indian armed forces after the Second World War. Furthermore, when historians examine things like devolution of power and a Dominion Status—catch phrases of colonial reform after the Great War—other equally important questions arise. Why and how did the promises made by the British to the Indians during the Great War arise? Were these promises a result of the Indian opposition to colonialism or the lofty intentions of an imperial project or circumstances beyond the control of British colonialism? Were these promises kept in most of the cases? Finally, did the changes in the Indian armed forces during the Second World War occur as a result of a conscious desire of the British to improve them or historical conditions thrust upon Britain's Indian Empire? Hopefully this book has successfully answered some of these questions and in the process challenged the submissions of 'decolonization'. This conclusion has so far mentioned 'decolonization' rather freely but we must see in detail what the term means. This calls for a brief comment on its historiography focused on selected representative works.

Scholars in the West were drawn to the idea of decolonization in the 1970s and 1980s after most of Africa had become free from direct colonial rule in the 1960s. A selective interpretation of this process underpinned the realization, confined largely to the West, that finally the great civilizing mission of the Imperial powers was being accomplished in the task of decolonization. This was a short step from the ideological appropriation of a process in which the imperialist powers had rarely played a positive role. In due course, and as it happens with most concepts, plausible and implausible theories of decolonization based on the ideological orientations of the observers concerned developed. Broadly speaking, there are two kinds of interpretations which seek to identify and explain the process of decolonization. First, we have the projection of decolonization as a long-term phenomenon in British Imperial history reflected in the works of Grimal, Holland, and Rizvi.[2] Second, decolonization emerges as a set of short-term measures taken by the British to overcome their growing economic and political problems in India during the inter-War period and the Second World War years. This approach is taken by Tomlinson.[3]

Let us now briefly study these approaches in the context of the assertions made in this book. But before that, a simple assumption, often found missing from the optimistic theories of decolonization, ought to be considered: evidence of the involvement of a section of the colonized people in local bodies like municipalities in some of the colonies from the nineteenth century onwards is *insufficient* to substantiate the existence of a decolonization process. A viable thesis of decolonization should be able to distinguish between a devolution arising from political expediency and the transfer of power to the colonies due to a principled policy of decolonization. In the context of this book, it is even more important to remember this because, and unfortunately for the protagonists of decolonization, the history of British military policy and the Indian armed forces between the Peel Commission of 1859 and the Chatfield Committee of 1939 does not vindicate their faith in imperialism.

According to one author, the revolt of America and the disintegration of the far-flung Spanish Empire in Central and South America led liberal-minded people in England to apply Turgot's 'biological law' to the history of colonial empires.[4] Before the French Revolution Turgot had set forth the example of a ripe fruit dropping from the tree. By analogy the process was considered inevitable though, it may be added, the comparison was not exactly fair. The enthusiastic liberals probably overlooked the relationship of nurturing between the tree and the fruit as contraposed to the contradiction between the colonial subjects and their masters. It was also considered good policy by some liberals to allow independence to be achieved gradually by peaceful means in the colonies. Though this was certainly not the view of the majority in British ruling circles it is true that the 'White' Dominions like Canada, Australia, and New Zealand evolved within the Commonwealth on these lines. The history of the non-'White' colonies, as we all know, was entirely different although their contribution to the life of imperialism was, in all probability, much greater than that of the former.

The colonial attitude towards the development of self-government in the colonies was inconsistent. The comparative history of 'White' and non-'White' colonies proves this. While even in America the contradiction between the colonial powers and the colonial subjects which broke out into wars of independence can hardly be over-emphasized, in the Asian and African colonies the 'civilizing' Anglo-Saxon mission lingered for long even as historical developments started undermining colonial power and control. In this connection, and with respect to India and other colonies we may add, an author who has examined decolonization in the long-term suggests that although colonialism 'contained the seed of its own destruction' to the generation of the inter-War period 'the day of possible reckoning seemed a long way off'.[5] This is a refreshing and necessary corrective to a careless application of long-term decolonization to the Indian case attempted by writers like Rizvi. The credit given to the British for the process of decolonization in India by Rizvi diminishes further as we explore the basis of Grimal's assertion. The economic backwardness of India under the British was immense and British ministries, Tory and Liberal both, were usually unwilling to ask Parliament for funds needed to develop the colonies. It was not until 1928 that the first Colonial Welfare Act was passed and that too sanctioned an expenditure amounting to a mere million pounds for all the colonies. These facts fortify the economic arguments presented in this book.

Furthermore, the problem was not merely economic because the permanent nature of the colonial *status quo* seemed beyond reproach to the diehard imperialists who constituted the majority of the British ruling classes. Seriously qualifying the thesis of decolonization in the non-'White' colonies, Grimal asserts: 'The only reforms ever considered were those that would link the colonies even more closely to the home country; the only liberal theories considered were those that were unlikely to be implemented.'[6] Chakravarty sums up the British attitude succinctly:

> That the British Empire was a permanent structure and India constituted an organic part of that Empire formed the inner core of the imperial consensus. Despite doses of self-government, it was implied in that assertion that India was to remain a British dependency and that the relationship was to be accepted in the natural order of things.

In the light of developments which have taken place in Indian historiography after 1947 it is difficult to agree with writers like Nicholas Mansergh who opine that the British *never* believed in a system of colonial domination. This absurd assertion can only imply that colonialism was a necessary transition in the march of the uneducated colonies to political maturity.[7] But decolonization is not simple enough to admit such academic recklessness. The progress towards a Dominion Status became increasingly uncertain as the years passed after the Great War. Later the historical movement towards full independence, which remained anathema to the British even during the Second World War, remained slow, with the British trying their best to influence the course of events to the detriment of India's political unity and social cohesion. The entire process of India's separation from the Empire was riven with contradictions because even limited reform in India was designed to simultaneously protect British interests and placate the Indian. In practice this policy was also translated into failure at most stages because the British, who rarely considered the Indians as their cultural and political equals, refused to sacrifice their paramountcy over the Indian political process whereas genuine decolonization would have meant exactly that. In military matters, as this volume claims, sharing power with Indians was more problematic simply because of the nature of colonial rule.

Thus, the British policy towards reform, Indianization, and

recruitment examined in this book was fraught with inconsistency and dominated by an official desire to cling to the military ideologies of the nineteenth century. In this context, and as a comment on the obstinacy with which the British regarded the Indian political scene, Grimal has the following apposite comment to make: 'Britain alone, of course, would decide under which terms this evolution should take place and the stages to be followed, it being fully understood that emancipation on no account implied a complete break with the Empire.'[8]

This was visible as every stage of the Indianization debate and process between the two World Wars. The rather unfortunate and tragic consequences of this attitude have been examined with great insight by another scholar who, in a telling judgement on British policy, asserts that in the decade preceding the Partition of India British short-term tactics worked against their long-term aims.[9] This seriously undermined the process of reform and a rational resolution of India's communal and other problems, many of which were of colonialism's making. However, a recent survey of British and Indian political history in the 1930s and 1940s suggests that London, and often its representatives in New Delhi, actually had no long-term perspective on India and its problems beyond keeping nationalism down and the Raj going. Otherwise India would not have been partitioned so quickly, insensitively, and foolishly in 1947 with such drastic and unprecedented consequences.

Let us now briefly examine the thesis of decolonization formulated by Holland and Rizvi with respect to India. According to Holland, decolonization was the outcome of the erosion of European mastery in rural Asian society. This automatically negates the role of urban protest, also led by the Asian intelligentsia, in finally bringing down colonialism. Furthermore, according to Holland, the process of decolonization was speeded up due to the 'stiffening constraints' imposed upon the European powers in the colonies between 1918 and 1939. These constraints appeared in factors such as population growth, an agrarian crisis, the rise of a colonial bourgeoisie, a religious and national renaissance in the colonial society, and the effects of the Great Depression.

Taking all these facts into consideration, Holland suggests that in a psychological and social state colonialism in Asia was 'dying on its feet' even before the Japanese onslaught of 1941. In projecting this view the author is aware that the decline of colonialism was predicated upon its internal contradictions: 'Decolonisation happened because colonialism as a set of nationally orchestrated systems (by the British, French, Dutch, Belgians and Portuguese) ceased to possess the self-sustaining virtue of internal equilibrium, and this spate of disequilibria can best be observed on a time scale more extended than that provided by the post 1939 decades.'[10]

In other words, decolonization can be viewed as the other side of colonial over-extension surveyed in the introduction to this book and further substantiated in it. My contention is strengthened by another historiographical intervention which makes any model of decolonization more dialectical by suggesting that the British were not in control of the historical process of the Empire in the decolonizing period. In this view the British were not simply actors but were also acted upon by the destiny of the Empire which 'directly and indirectly, entered into the shaping of colonial policy during these years'.[11] This is also the import of more comprehensive studies of decolonization which take into account all the important factors of colonial history influencing British policy before narrating why and how the British finally quit India.[12] As mentioned earlier, it has been the endeavour of this study to place British military policy in India in such a comprehensive framework.

Compared with the above-mentioned approaches to the subject, Rizvi foists a case of long-term decolonization rather uncritically upon India. However, on closer inspection, his assertions end up resembling a sort of colonial discourse. To begin with, his comparison of the 'decolonization' in America with other British colonies does not pay adequate attention to the differences between American, African, and Asian histories of colonization. Furthermore, his contention that a gradual devolution of power over and above mass agitation and civil disobedience would have facilitated a smooth Transfer of Power in India appears to be based on his antipathy to the Indian National Congress more than anything else. Such a view disregards the well-established fact that without Indian pressure even limited reform in colonial India would probably have been impossible. Throughout Rizvi's apology for British policy, and communal separatism in India, can be perceived a haste in reposing total faith in British notions of colonial self-government. His official definition of decolonization stems from this: 'In terms of colonial self-government it meant wider devolution of power for those colonies who seemed capable of governing themselves.'[13] How and where was the capability of self-government to be decided during the colonial period? Who could say with a certain degree of certainty that a particular colony had 'evolved' to a stage of self-government? Political, economic, and social change could easily be postponed indefinitely in such circumstances. This study has shown, especially with reference to military Indianization, that only bold experiments could give policy a progressive orientation. The available Marxist, nationalist, and 'subaltern' perspectives on colonial India and the themes discussed in this book suggest that British policy in general, despite Rizvi's claims to the contrary, would have changed very little in India but for external pressures like Indian opinion and the two World Wars.

In Tomlinson's framework of decolonization the processes of imperialism and decolonization appear concurrent. He claims that even as British imperialism expanded, Britain gave up territory. This is true, and our thesis of over-stretch probably supports the contention, but it is also true that the first half of the twentieth century was specific to the decline of British colonialism. The period saw two World Wars, the emergence of mass and militant nationalism, and unprecedented economic strains on the colonial system. In this context, it would be appropriate to change the idea of the British giving self-government to India into the British being forced to concede some reform to the agitating Indians. Once the question is posed thus, Tomlinson's assertion—that 'decolonization came about through a series of short-term decisions made by British Governments concerned with a limited number of specific objectives and constraints, and underpinned by the broader theme of India's imperial commitment and the financial and political problems of the Raj'—appears more relevant to the themes of British policy studied in this volume.[14]

This book has not consciously viewed the British Raj as the protector of private British economic interests in India. However, any suggestion to the effect that the deepening financial crisis in British India caused some devolution of power is relevant to our exploration of policy reform and economic limitations. However, it is worth remembering here that devolution was rarely enough. As such the concept did not satisfy the majority of Indians who, beginning with self-government and Dominion Status, finally demanded full independence. Of particular relevance to this conclusion is the presentation of British policy as a series of short-term 'expedients . . . not governed by a long-term strategy'.[15] The author further adds: 'The imperial commitment was not cut and dried; it should be thought of more as a series of mental reflex actions in the official mind than as the underlying principle of a coherent policy.'[16] This strengthens the generalizations regarding British military policy made in this book. I also find colonial over-stretch reflected, albeit inadvertently, in Tomlinson's work which recognizes that there were unsustainable imperial commitments shouldered by the GOI. The GOI's revenues were limited and the delicate balance between imperial and domestic commitments could easily be upset: 'To keep itself solvent and secure the colonial Government had to balance imperial commitments against the demands of its subjects. Keeping this equilibrium lay at the heart of the problem of the Raj.'[17] This problem worsened after the Great War when an economic depression made the British realize the prohibitive cost of holding their new Empire in the Middle East. This book has shown how these factors cast a long shadow on military reform in India.

However, some disagreement with Tomlinson persists. For instance, his assertion that the history of the last three decades of the Raj constitutes the history of public finance inclines towards abstraction. Moreover, his claim that the suffering of the Indians during the Great War and their growing demand for reform shifted the Raj towards a 'free market polity', compared with the earlier policy of ruling in collaboration with selected elites, does not square with our study of British military policy. This book has underlined the pronounced reluctance on the part of the British to take educated and 'political' Indians into confidence in military matters. Consequently, much of military recruitment between 1919 and 1939 remained preoccupied with the search to find suitable material from the favoured 'martial races'. In fact, as late as 1938–9, when time had already run out for the British Empire, the Chatfield Committee demonstrated a distrust of the Congress which is difficult to comprehend in the given circumstances. The Congress was then running several Provincial Ministries in accordance with the GOI Act of 1935. The hardening of official attitudes could only set the stage for a confrontation with the Congress during the Second World War and this is exactly what happened.

The genesis of the Esher Committee, with which the inter-War reform of the Indian services began, lay in the Great War, the 'Mesopotamian muddle', and the criticism of the Indian Army during the Afghan War of 1919. However, the appointment of the Nicholson Committee in 1912 suggests that reforming the Army in India was contemplated by British policy before the Great War. The distinguishing feature of the Esher recommendations, compared with the initiative inspired by the Tirah failures, was their being considered in the framework of a future Indian Dominion. By 1923 the Esher recommendations were shelved because of disagreements between London and Delhi on matters discussed by the Esher Committee and the economic crisis of the GOI. This highlights the danger of seeing too much in the Montagu-Chelmsford declarations and their military implications. This study has exposed the contradictions inherent in the Esher recommendations. While Dominion Status continued to elude India during the depressed 1920s, on the most important issues of Army reform the *ECR* remained biased in favour of historical continuities. The relation between social, technological, and military changes in a period of increased mechanization of warfare was not appreciated by the Esher Committee. Consequently, its advocacy of the 'martial races' and its insistence on the recruitment of commissioned officers from the VCO ranks appears old fashioned even by contemporary standards. The attitude towards Indianization, which could succeed only with the help of educated Indians, remained unrealistic in the changing political climate of the 1920s.

The Esher Committee spoke of securing the material contentment of the Army in India but this was done with the aim of reinforcing traditional loyalty in the Indian services. There was no attempt at making the Indian armed forces more responsible and representative in accordance with a Dominion Status. While the demand for Indianization grew, the Esher Committee overruled substantial Indianization. Thus, it failed to anticipate the most important reform issue of the inter-War period. The devolution of power to Indians in the armed forces would have been essential to an Indian Dominion. On this point the Esher recommendations had nothing to offer. Even the idea of developing Indian commissioned officers from selected ranks underscored the desire to preserve British rule in India and keep the 'non-martial' groups out of the Indian Army. It is true that there was widespread discontent in the Indian military establishment after the Great War and implementing the Esher recommendations would have created a less disgruntled soldiery in India. Nonetheless, in the absence of Indianization this would hardly have been consistent with the meaning of devolution, Dominion Status, and decolonization. In the event, and due to reasons surveyed in this volume, the *ECR* became a dead letter. To begin with, it was disliked in India. Finally, post-Great War retrenchment consigned this imperial blueprint to the archive.

Military policy in India, despite the brave pronouncements of 1919, tried its best to exclude educated Indians. Soon after 1918 the British forgot how the Indian middle class had stimulated recruitment during the War. Ironically, the issue almost ignored by the Esher Committee became central to Army reform in India during the 1920s and early 1930s. Chapter 2 of this book emphasizes that between 1921 and 1932 limited Indianization occurred primarily because of Indian pressure. This volume has underlined the fact that at each stage of Indianization the British tried their best to thwart Indian aspirations and protect their vested interests. On the whole, the British attitude towards Indianization was best expressed in the conservative opinion of General Rawlinson. Furthermore, the view of Lord Irwin, as expressed to Lord Birkenhead in 1927, reveals that the British were considering the question of Indianization more out of helplessness than anything else.

Considering all this, critics might rightfully ask whether there was any point in appointing the Skeen Committee. Furthermore, the Indians were disappointed by the Chetwode Committee which belatedly accepted the unpopularity of the Eight Unit Scheme. This disappointment resulted in a greater, and fleshed out, articulation of dissent. A scrutiny of this counter-colonial discourse shows why and how Indianization became a site for a conflict of identities between the colonial state and its subaltern subjects. This conflict remained unresolved for a variety of reasons and by the end of the Round Table Conference it became clear that Indianization had to cross the stage of mischievously designed experiments.

Evading Indianization harmed the Indian services. With the recruitment of Britons falling, not due to Indianization as the apologists would have us believe, the armed forces becoming increasingly and economically unattractive to the public, the War effort faced a serious shortage of officers from 1939 onwards. More significantly, British attitudes failed to promote a mentality of reform and comaraderie within the officer corps. This played havoc with morale in the new services like the RIN. In these services, which truly expanded during the Second World War, the British failed to handle racial discrimination and other service grievances. To overcome officer shortages the British granted Emergency Commissions from 1939 onwards. In the event these 15,000 commissions proved insufficient. Hence, British resistance to Indianization in the inter-War years hampered service expansion during the War. The British, in general, remained mentally unprepared for the changes necessitated by the Second World War. This became an important cause of disaffection in large sections of the Indian armed forces during and after the Second World War.

This study has asserted that military policy in India did not, and indeed could not, favour a comprehensive reform of the colonial military establishment. The British resistance to reform was predicated upon colonial ideology and the related economic and financial difficulties which beset the GOI in this period. In the inter-War years military finances in India deteriorated substantially. The financial arrangements for the Indian armed forces were marked by declining capital expenditure and budgetary instability. With the passing years it became increasingly difficult to meet the standing charges of the establishment. Finally, as the depression worsened and revenues declined, internal savings in the armed forces dictated a second retrenchment in the early 1930s. This happened when the armed forces had not yet recovered from the massive retrenchment of the 1920s.

In these circumstances it was impossible to modernize the Indian services. Undoubtedly, the observations of the Modernization Committee in this regard were most alarming. The worsening service conditions pushed back the recruitment of skilled personnel and officers. In sum, these economies made the services unattractive to potential officers and ranks alike. One way to economize was to reduce the British component of the Indian services and recruit more Indians. This was the point the proponents of Indianization had always made in the interest of Indian revenues. But the official mentality remained unchanged even in extenuating circumstances. After the Round Table Conferences of the early 1930s, London pronounced that reform did not mean the granting of control to Indians. Further, that in the event of war India's case would be considered unsympathetically was underlined by the Garran Tribunal, its definition of imperial danger, and the so-called 'Award' to the Indian taxpayer.

During the inter-War years there was little evidence of London's willingness to relieve India of its imperial burdens. Even during the summer of 1939 the Committee of Imperial Defence placed several new demands upon scarce Indian resources. This issue had featured in the discussions between London and Delhi on the Esher recommendations. Furthermore, as late as 1938, imperial policy makers paid insufficient attention to the fact that Indian cooperation would be invaluable in the coming war against the Axis Powers. The tendency to brush aside the Indian view and underestimate the influence of Indian nationalism in Indian military matters remained buoyant. It was expressed in Chatfield's blimpish reading of the Indian situation. In the Indian armed forces there were seasoned officers like Corbett whose opinion Chatfield could have taken seriously. Similarly, in the Congress there were leaders whose views on the imminent war could have been considered. But nothing of the sort was done. When the War actually broke out in 1939 British policy successfully alienated the Congress. The unfortunate consequences keeping the Congress out of the war effort are too well known to be recounted here.

The Second World War forced the Indian armed forces out of the Roberts era. In the inter-War years recruitment was governed by the 'martial races' theory. From 1939 a change in recruitment became discernible due to the demands of the Second World War. The inevitability of technical recruitment and the enormous demand for manpower overruled the preference for the 'martial races'. New services like the RIN and the RIAF, which grew during the War, played an important role in this change. However, the process of war-driven recruitment posed fresh challenges. For instance, recruitment had to pay attention to local factors influencing the supply of men in the face of deteriorating economic conditions and the Quit India Movement of 1942. In addition, throughout the War the civilian labour market remained more lucrative. To overcome this, the authorities resorted to unprecedented propaganda which proved counter-productive in the long run. Official claims raised expectations in the services to the detriment of colonial authority in 1945-6.

The aspirations of wartime recruits transformed the Indian armed forces and shifted the policy focus to demobilization. It was impossible for the colonial state to contain the historical change affecting the Indian services during 1939-45. The successful demobilzation of the armies of war in 1945-6 would have pacified the discontent in the Indian ranks. In this context, this study has presented a comparison of demobilization after the two World Wars. Comparing the results of demobilization in the 1920s with those of 1945-6 revealed important aspects of a neglected area of military policy in colonial India. In the first half of the twentieth century it was only India's participation in the two World Wars which led to some military changes in the first case and significant social changes in the second. Demobilization after the Great War was difficult because the returning soldiers often felt that the British had betrayed the recruitment promises. In the early 1920s, despite rewards distributed to the demobilized jawans, evidence of discontent remained strong enough to exercise the minds of the policy makers. The salient feature of post-1918 demobilization lay in its emphasis on land because the army of war raised during 1914-18 was largely an extension of the peasant army which had existed in India before 1914. This was the primary difference between the volunteer armies raised in India during the First and Second World Wars.

In the Second World War the proportion of educated and technically skilled men to peasants in the services grew substantially. Therefore, the armies of war raised in 1939-45 were quite different from the enlarged peasant army of 1914-18. During the Second World War more and more men seemed to have joined the armed forces in the hope of finding a better future outside them after the War. But this was not their fault. Our study of recruitment propaganda and the survey of men's aspirations makes this point absolutely clear. Considering this new and unprecedented dimension in the social composition of the Indian armed forces during and after the Second World War, demobilization appeared as a daunting task before British policy. In 1945, after winning the War, the possibility of the British losing the peace in India appeared considerably heightened. The demobilization problem became acute because in 1945 the GOI did not have the land it had in 1918 to distribute amongst those who really wanted it. Finally, in the aftermath of the Second World War, with British policy makers absorbed in dealing with the problems of Partition and Independence, the British wilted under the pressure of demobilizing a largely educated war machine in an underdeveloped colony like India. In the summer of 1945 the epitaph of the Raj was being written when, as Holland notes, 'the great imperial war effort was coming home to roost in the form of disintegrating administration and communal tensions far more intense than anything which had been experienced within the living memory of the Raj'.[18]

It was impossible for the Raj to resolve the contradiction between reform and the imperatives of colonial ideology and finances. This *central failure* of British military policy combined with Indian nationalism caused widespread discontent in the Indian services in 1945-6. Discontent was also inherent in the recruitment drives of 1939-45. The conditions of large-scale unrest in the post-War Indian armed forces were created by British rule in India. The mutinies in the RIN and the RIAF were located in these failures. Sources candidly tell us that while the lessons of the Great War were 'discarded' by British policy, imperial defence also failed to reach its 'complete logical conclusion' before the Second World War.[19] The deficiencies of policy, strategic considerations, and military organization in the 1930s were exemplified by the case of the RIN and the RIAF which remained paper services till 1939.[20] Combined with negligible Indianization these conditions could hardly inspire the Indians.

Involving educated men in services guided by the colonial mentality created a complex problem. Within these services, apart from the economic weakness of the Indian military establishment as a whole, specific service grievances also arose. Besides this, till the end of British rule racial discrimination was practised in the Indian armed forces. Dissent and disaffection were not unknown to the Indian armed forces. However, they do not command a consistent historiography. In 1915 a violent mutiny broke out among the Indian troops in Singapore. Widespread discontent in the Indian Army also surfaced after the Great War. Later, during the Civil Disobedience Movement in 1930, in an incident immortalized by nationalism, two platoons of the Royal Garhwal Rifles refused to fire on nationalist protestors in Peshawar. Scholars have also noted the growing influence of Akali, Arya Samaj, nationalist, and revolutionary politics on sections of the Indian Army after the Great War. During the Second World War the Indian National Army (INA) threatened the loyalty of the British Indian Army. In December 1945 there were 'strikes' in the RIAF on the pattern of the RAF. Following these, the large-scale naval uprising of February 1946 occurred. Secret official reports of the period show that during the Second World War, despite the Allied successes, discontent in the three Indian services had assumed serious proportions. In December 1945 Indian officers *and* men in all Indian services were found sympathetic to the INA.[21]

The naval uprising of February 1946 was a result of this mood. It was caused by a combination of failed demobilization and unaddressed service grievances. In a couple of months after the RIN Mutiny the Naval HQ conducted departmental enquiries into the event by setting up Naval Boards of Enquiry for all the disaffected establishments. On 22 and 23 February 1946, soon after the rebels had surrendered, the uprising was discussed in the Legislative Assembly and on 8 March the Defence Consultative Committee discussed it. In this Committee the C-in-C proposed setting up a RIN Mutiny Commission of Enquiry. Following this, in April 1946, the GOI appointed the RIN Mutiny Commission of Enquiry with the judiciary and the armed forces represented in it. From April to June 1946 the Commission worked in Delhi, Bombay, and Karachi examining 229 witnesses, official documents including several Boards of Enquiry Reports and Morale Reports. The numerous letters, petitions, and memoranda sent to the Commission by the distressed ratings and their testimonies in large numbers before it comprise a severe indictment of British military policy in India.[22]

Our analysis of the available sources suggests that after recruiting relatively educated and upwardly mobile Indians in *significant numbers* during the Second World War the British failed to satisfy their hopes. Most of these Indian volunteers held themselves responsible for British victories especially in Africa and Burma. The number of politically conscious volunteers was also very high. Most of these men refused to settle for anything less than complete equality with the British personnel with whom they worked. And nowhere were British drawbacks more pronounced than in their inability to redress service grievances and racial discrimination. A similar loss of administrative will later underscored the Partition of India. But what are systems and policies without the men who make them? At the end of the Second World War the British in India were a tired and cynical lot.[23] With rare exceptions, most of them wanted to leave a subcontinent poised on the brink of an unprecedented civil war. In 1945 Britain won the War with US help, but lost the peace in India.

NOTES

1. P. Mason, *A Matter of Honour*, London, 1974, p. 470.
2. H. Grimal, *Decolonization in the British, French, Dutch and Belgian Empires 1919-1963*, London, 1978; R.F. Holland and G. Rizvi (eds.), *Perspectives on Imperialism and Decolonization*, London, 1984; R.F. Holland, *European Decolonization 1918-1981: An Introductory Survey*, London, 1985.
3. B.R. Tomlinson, *The Political Economy of the Raj 1914-1947: The Economics of Decolonization in India*, London, 1979.
4. Grimal, *Decolonization*, pp. 2-3.
5. Ibid., p. 5.
6. Ibid., p. 3.
7. Mansergh quoted in Grimal, *Decolonization*, p. 50.
8. Ibid.
9. A.I. Singh, *The Origins of the Partition of India 1936-1947*, Delhi, 1987, p. 250.

10. Holland, *European Decolonization*, p. 2.
11. M. Kahler, *Decolonization in Britain and France: The Domestic Consequences of International Relations*, Princeton, 1984.
12. R. Albertini, *Decolonization: The Administration and Future of the Colonies 1919-1960*, New York, 1971, pp. 59-78.
13. Rizvi in Holland and Rizvi (eds.), *Perspectives on Imperialism*, op. cit.
14. Tomlinson, *The Political Economy of the Raj*, Introduction.
15. Ibid., p. 27.
16. Ibid.
17. Ibid., p. 28. Tomlinson, on p. 111 of the same work, observes: 'If Indians refused to use their increased power to play a part in the imperial system, Britain could and would return to coercion'. Further 'Dominion Status for India was a fine phrase, but London policy makers were, in practice, only prepared to hold to it so long as India's commercial, currency and military policy options were predetermined by other influences over which British interests had the whip hand.'
18. Holland, *European Decolonization*, p. 63.
19. Secret War Department History 1939-45, Head I, General State and role of the armed forces of India prior to September 1939, File 601/7169/H, 15/3/1944 (HS).
20. RIN Memorandum on the general state of the service at the outbreak of War in 1939, OSD/CLO/ii (HS); *Reorganisation of the RIM: Report of a Departmental Committee*, GOI publication, 1927 (CSL); *Progress Report of the armed forces for 1937-38*, 601/10848/HS tells us that till 1939 all important recommendations regarding the development of the services made in the 1930s still existed on paper.
21. Report of the Deputy Director (Morale) Lt. Col. M. Haq Nawaz, General HQ (India), Appendix J of the RIN Mutiny Commission of Enquiry Report, RIN Mutiny Papers (NAI). Most works on the British period mention the erosion of British control over the services during the Second World War. For details see Longer, *Red Coats to Olive Green*; Farwell, *Armies of the Raj*; Heathcote, *The Indian Army*; Cohen, *The Indian Army*; Menezes, *Fidelity and Honour*; and Omissi, *The Sepoy and the Raj*. The influence of nationalism on Indian troops is noted by Evans, *Thimayya of India*; Ghosh, *The Indian National Army*; Chaudhuri, *An Autobiography*; Thorat, *From Reveille to Retreat*. Evans's biography of Thimayya mentions an interesting fact in the context of declining British control over the Indian Army towards the end of the Raj. After the Second World War an opinion poll revealed that 70 per cent of Gurkhas preferred serving under Indian officers *and not in the British Army*. This came as an unpleasant surprise to many British officers who were used to valorizing a special relationship with the 'loyal' Nepalis.
22. This generalization is based on the RIN Mutiny Commission of Enquiry

Report, the various Boards of Enquiry Reports, and other files in the RIN Mutiny Papers collection like the Karachi Statements (File No. 14).

23. Most British officers refused to change with the times. The *Naval Memoirs* of Admiral J.H. Godfrey, VII, 1943-6, India, Churchill Archives Centre, Churchill College, Cambridge, p. 100, mentions that many senior British officers in the naval establishments treated Indians with open contempt. At one time 'three such oafs at Bombay' disgraced the Royal Navy and were a 'continuing and admitted source of embarrassment to Admiral Somerville, Commander-in-Chief, Eastern Fleet' and senior officers of the RIN establishment.

Bibliography

PRIMARY SOURCES

HISTORICAL SECTION, MINISTRY OF DEFENCE, R.K. PURAM, NEW DELHI

The Army in India and its Evolution, Including an Account of the Establishment of the RAF in India, Calcutta, 1924.

Report of the Army in India Committee, 1922-23 (ECR).

Report of the Indian Sandhurst Committee, Simla, 1927.

SECRET 1112-B, Committee of Imperial Defence. Papers prepared for the use of the Chiefs of Staff in their annual review of Imperial Defence (1933), Whitehall 1933, Copy No. 52, F-460 45816/MOI, Committee of Imperial Defence Papers 1933-37, General Staff Branch.

SECRET 1113-B, Committee of Imperial Defence, Imperial Defence Policy, Previous Paper No COS 307, Annual Review (1933) by the Chiefs of Staff Sub-Committee, Copy No. 72, October 1933, 45816/MOI.

SECRET 1181-B, Committee of Imperial Defence, Imperial Defence Policy, Annual Review by the Chiefs of Staff Sub-Committee, 1935 (Prepared in connection with discussions with Dominion Prime Ministers, 29 April 1935, Whitehall) CID Papers 1933-37, 45816/MOI.

SECRET 1311-B, Committee of Imperial Defence Papers, Copy 51 Preparedness for War of Great Britain in relation to certain other powers by May 1937, Annexure A, COS 551, CID, Chiefs of Staff Sub-Committee, comparison of the strength of Great Britain with that of certain other nations as at May, Report, Whitehall, 9 February 1937.

SECRET 1183-B, Committee of Imperial Defence, Imperial Defence Policy, Summary of decisions prepared by the Secretary CID, period 2 June 1934 to 1 June 1935, Whitehall, 1 June 1935, Copy No. 54, CID Papers.

Progress Reports on the Armed Forces for 1929-30, 1930-31, 1933-34, 1935-36, 1936-37 & 1937-38. On the distribution of the Army and the RAF in India, their preparedness for War and for the maintenance of law and order within India 601/10848/H, Secret, Delhi.

SECRET Report of the Expert Committee on the Defence of India, 601/12808/H, 1938-39.

GOI, Army Department General Staff Branch Organization Proceedings B, February 1921.

GOI, Army Department Organization Proceedings, December 1923, No. 601/10798/H.

Confidential Simla Records-3, No. 601/10482/HAD. Case No. 29147, 1927, Nos. 333-341 and Appendix.

Simla Records 10790, 601/10790/H, Secret File No. 31908 II MOI, 1935, GOI, Army Department General Staff Branch, Proceedings B, February 1935.

Committee on the Indianization of the Officer Ranks of the Indian Army (Secret) 18/8/1939 (Report and related matters).

Army Department Proceedings A, March 1927, 601/10482/H.

War Department History-2, Expansion of the armed forces, statistical material supplied by AG's Branch, 601/9074/H.

Monograph on Recruitment for the Defence Services in India by Col. Day, 1946, 601/7832/H.

Proceedings of a Conference to consider India's recruitment D/19, 20 and 21 March 1942, 601/7016/H.

F 174, AOC/ADM/108, I.A.F. Public Relations, Air HQ Directive-3/11/1944 and Air Vice Marshal on the synopsis of a film on the RIAF.

F 182, AOC/ADM/116—Personnel Grievances in the RIAF.

General State of the RIN on the Outbreak of the War in 1939 and RIN Expansion Head 2, 601/7450/H (A) Head I.

RIN Manpower Review 1939-45 SECRET MONOGRAPH approved by the FOCRIN, 601/7188/H.

Recruiting Statistics Most Secret Material used for answering starred questions 112, 127 in Assembly 17/2/1943, War Department, No. 240, 1943, 601/10751/H.

Annual Recruiting Report 1945-46, Defence Department 601/7640/H.

Report of an Informal Meeting of Official Members of the Reconstruction Committee (Labour and Demobilisation) Agenda 1942, 601/7029/H.

TOP SECRET Demobilisation when Germany out, 1944, 601/10609/H.

Demobilisation and Resettlement Planning, Vol. I, 1944-45, 601/10605/H.

Secret Paper Military Finance Department, Sub: Reduction of Defence Expenditure during post-War years, 11401-C, D/12/9/1944.

Reflections on the paper from [Secret C-in-C's (India) Secretariat] Inter Service meeting Minutes of an extra-ordinary meeting held on 6 November 1944 to consider paper 11401-C.

Chiefs of Staff (44) 636 & COS (44) 642 Report on the size and composition of the post-War forces in India and Auchinleck's directive in Appendix A (Top Secret) 601/10605/H, File No. 2

Report of the 288th & 289th meeting of the War Committee 18-19/4/1945, 601/10605/H, Vol. II.

Demobilisation—Paper received from Demobilization Planning, Head 14, 1945, 601/7130/H.

Outline Post War Plan, Air Force Requirements, 601/9710/H.

Demobilization Plan 287—March, May, July, Aug., Sept. and Nov. 1947, 601/8018/H.

Demobilisation of the Indian Army, Monograph in Adjutant General's Branch, Combined Inter-Services Historical Section (India & Pakistan), General Editor Bisheshewar Prasad, Se. No. 365.

Progress Report for the Armed Forces for 1937-38, 601/10848/H.

Secret War Department History 1939-45, Head 1, General State and Role of the Armed Forces of India prior to September 1939, 601/7/169/H, 15/3/1944.

Bisheshwar Prasad (ed.), *Adjutant General's Branch, Monographs, Vol. III, War System of Accounting & Honours and Awards*, Combined Inter-Services Historical Section (India & Pakistan)

NATIONAL ARCHIVES OF INDIA, JANPATH, NEW DELHI

Marine Regulations, India, Vol. I, Part I: Discipline; Part II: Finance, Calcutta, 1886.

Marine Regulations, India, Vol. I, Pay and Allowances and Non-Effective Pay, GOI, Finance Department, Calcutta, 1918.

Marine Regulations, India, Pay and Allowances, Leave, Passage, Pension and Medical rules of the Royal Indian Marine, Vol. I: All Orders issued upto 31 December 1931, GOI, Marine Department, Calcutta, 1931.

The RIN Mutiny Commission of Enquiry Report, July 1946, Se. No. 7, RIN Mutiny Papers (RMP)

Karachi Statements, Se. No. 4, RMP.

Report of the Board of Enquiry into the causes of the Mutiny in HMIS Talwar, NL 9930, RMP.

Report of the Board of Enquiry into the causes of the Mutiny in Castle Barracks, NL 9939, RMP.

Report of the Board of Enquiry into the Mutiny in HMIS Shivaji, Lonavala, NL 9950, RMP.

Report of the Board of Enquiry into the Mutiny in HMIS Akbar, NL 9907, RMP.

Report of the Board of Enquiry into the Mutiny in HMIS Cheetah, NL 9908, RMP.

Report of the Board of Enquiry into the Mutiny in HMIS Narbada, NL 9942, RMP.

Summary of the Report of the RIN Mutiny Commission of Enquiry, Se. No. 18, RMP.

Disturbances in Bombay arising out of the RIN Mutiny, Home Department Political, File No. 5/12/1946, Hom-Pol, 1946.

Disturbances in Bombay—Subhas Bose Day (23-25/1/1946), File No. 5/13/1946, Home Department Political, 1946.

Fortnightly Reports for Bombay, Files 18/10/1939-18/2/1946, Home Department Internal, Index of Fortnightly Reports.

Home Political, 12/2/1945, Poll (I), 1945, GOI (Internal), Sub: Weekly Reviews of Labour Situation (Nos.1-49 summarising Information during 1945) forwarded by the Department of Labour, previous references F 12/2/1944 & later references.

Political (I) GOI, Home Department Political (I) Branch, 14/10/1945, Sub: Reduction on termination of hostilities of temporary posts and expenditure occasioned by war conditions, previous references from 1938 onwards to 1944, later references till Jan. 1946.

SECRET SIMLA RECORDS 1, File No. 303, Se. Nos. 1-48, 1921, GOI, Home Dept. Political, 1921.

Home Dept. Political, 1922, Part B, Deposit Proceedings, File No. 225/11, Subject: Expenditure on military propaganda.

Grant of funds for military propaganda, File No. 225 V, Poll, Home Dept. Political, 1922.

Delhi Records 1919, GOI, Home Dept. Political, Deposit Proceedings, May 1919, No. 47.

SIMLA RECORDS 1919, GOI, Home Dept. Political, Deposit Proceedings, July 1919, No. 37.

SECRET SIMLA RECORDS 1920, GOI, Home Dept. Political, Deposit Proceedings, January 1920, No. 76. Papers relating to the subject of preserving the troops from Disloyalty.

Delhi Records 1919, GOI, Home Dept. Political, Deposit Proceedings, July 1919, No. 51. Report on the Political Situations in the Punjab for the second half of July 1919, in connection with the recent disturbances.

SIMLA RECORDS 1920, GOI, Home Dept. Political, Deposit Proceedings, February 1920, No. 52. Weekly Reports of the Director, Central Intelligence for the month of January 1920.

SIMLA RECORDS 1920, GOI, Home Dept. Political, Deposit Proceedings, August 1920, No. 110. Weekly reports of the Director Central Intelligence for the month of August 1920.

Military Department War Diaries.

Morley Collection [Microfilm].

Zetland Collection [Microfilm].

Cariappa Papers.

Birkenhead Papers [Microfilm].

Montagu Papers [Microfilm].

CENTRAL SECRETARIAT LIBRARY, NEW DELHI

Military Handbook of General Information, 1908.

Report of the Indian Retrenchment Committee, 1922-23, Delhi, 1923.

Gazetteer of the Bombay City and Island, Vol. II, Bombay, 1909.

Report of the Committee of Experts (Chetwode Committee) set up according to the Round Table Conference Resolutions to work out the details of an Indian Sandhurst, 1931.

Report (Final) of the Army Sub-Committee of the Central Retrenchment Advisory Committee 1932.

Reorganisation of the IMM: Report of a Departmental Committee, GOI publication, 192?.

GOI Department of Commerce, Report on the scheme for the establishment of a training ship in India, by Captain M.B. Sayer, RNR, Calcutta, 1926.

UNITED SERVICES INSTITUTE OF INDIA,
KASHMIR HOUSE, NEW DELHI

Handbook for the Indian Army: Jats, Gujars and Ahirs, first compiled under the orders of the GOI by Major A.H. Bingley, 7th Duke of Connaught's own Rajputs, 1904. Revised in the same language by Lt. Col. R.C. Christie, M.C., Recruiting Officer, Delhi, 1937.

Handbook for the Indian Army: Punjabi Musalmans, compiled for the GOI by Lt. Col. J.M. Wikely, 7th Cavalry, Late Recruiting Officer for Punjabi Musalmans. Revised 1927, 2nd edn. 1935, New Delhi, 1936.

Handbook for the Indian Army: Hindustani Musalmans and Musalmans of Eastern Punjab, compiled under orders of the GOI by Major W. Fritz G. Bourne, 10th Jats, Late Recruiting Officer for Hindustani Musalmans, Calcutta, 1914.

Handbooks for the Indian Army: Gurkhas, compiled under orders of the GOI by Lt. Col. Eden Vansittart, 2nd Bn., 10th Gurkha Rifles, Calcutta, 1906. Revised edition with minor changes by Captain Morris, 1933.

Handbook for the Indian Army: Kumaonis, compiled at the request of the GOI by Lt. Col. A. Latham DSO, late 18th Gharwal Rifles, 1933, rpt. New Delhi, 1941.

Handbook for the Indian Army: Garwhalis, by Captain J. Evatt 39th (The Garwhal Rifle) Regiment, 1894, revised by Lt. Col. Henderson, 18th Royal Garhwal Rifles, Calcutta, 1924.

Handbook for the Indian Army: Dogras, revised edition by Lt. Col. W.B. Cunningham, M.C., 2nd Bn. 17th Dogra Regiment, Calcutta, 1932.

CAMBRIDGE UNIVERSITY LIBRARY, CAMBRIDGE, UNITED KINGDOM

India in 1927-28, A statement prepared for presentation to Parliament in accordance with the requirements of the 16th Section of the GOI Act (5 & 6 Geo. V, Chap. 61), Calcutta, 1928.

India in 1928-29, A statement prepared for presentation to Parliament . . ., Calcutta, 1930.

India in 1929-30, A statement prepared for presentation to Parliament . . ., Calcutta, 1931.

India in 1930-31, A statement prepared for presentation to Parliament . . ., Calcutta, 1932.

India in 1931-32, A statement prepared for presentation to Parliament . . ., Calcutta, 1933.

India in 1932-33, A statement prepared for presentation to Parliament . . ., Delhi, 1934.

India in 1933-34, A statement prepared for presentation to Parliament . . ., Delhi, 1935.

India in 1934-35, A statement prepared for presentation to Parliament . . ., Delhi, 1937.

Indian Round Table Conference, 12th Nov. 1930-19th Jan. 1931, Proceedings, London, 1931 [Cmd. 3778].

Report on the Indian Round Table Conference (Third Session), 17 Nov. 1932-24th Dec. 1932, London, 1933 [Cmd. 4238].

Report of the Tribunal on Certain Questions in regard to Defence Expenditure in dispute between the Government of India, The War Office and the Air Ministry, London, 1933 (Garran Tribunal) [Cmd. 4473].

Report of the Royal Commission on the War in South Africa, Volume II, with Minutes of Evidence, 1904 [Cd. 1791].

Report of His Majesty's Commissioners appointed to inquire into the Military preparations and other matters connected with War in South Africa, 1903 [Cd. 1789].

CHURCHILL ARCHIVES CENTRE, CHURCHILL COLLEGE, CAMBRIDGE

Esher, 2nd Viscount, Reginald Baliol Brett (1852-1930) Member of CID and intimate of Edward VII and George V. Diaries, correspondence and papers: *Army in India Committee, Table of Meetings, Names of witnesses & Subjects Discussed.*

The *Naval Memoirs* of Admiral J.H. Godfrey [FOCRIN, 1943-46].

Lt. Gen. Thomas William Corbett's Papers.

Publications of the Navy Records Society, Vol. III; The Jellicoe Papers, Vol. II; The Jellicoe Papers: Selections from the private and official correspondence of Admiral of the Fleet Earl Jellicoe, Volume II, 1916-1935, ed. A. Temple Patterson, London, 1968.

NEHRU MEMORIAL MUSEUM & LIBRARY (NMML),
TEEN MURTI, NEW DELHI

Parliamentary Papers (PP), Vol. 5, Shannon, 1970.

Parliamentary Papers (PP), Vol. 11, Shannon, 1970.

Legislative Assembly Debates I, II, Official Report, 1921.

Legislative Assembly Debates, V, Part II, Official Report, Delhi, 1925.

Legislative Assembly Debates, I, Official Report, Delhi, 1928.

Times of India, December-March 1945-6.

Bombay Chronicle, December-March 1945-6.

People's Age, February-March 1946.

Young India, 1919-31, Vol. III, 1921.

SECONDARY SOURCES

Albertini, R., *Decolonization: The Administration and Future of the Colonies 1919-1960*, New York, 1971.

Banerjee, S., *The RIN Strike*, New Delhi: PPH, 1954.

Barnett, C., *The Collapse of British Power*, London: Eyre Methuen, 1972.

Beaumont, R., *Sword of the Raj: The British Army in India 1747-1947*, New York: The Bobbs-Merrill Company Inc., 1977.

Best, G., *War and Society in Revolutionary Europe, 1770-1870*, Suffolk: Fontana, 1982.

Bhatia, H.S., *Military History of British India (1607-1947)*, New Delhi: Deep & Deep Publications, [illegible]

Bond, B., *British Military Policy between the Two World Wars*, Oxford: Clarendon Press, 1980

———, *War and Society in Europe, 1870-1970*, London: Fontana, 1972.

———, *The Victorian Army and the Staff College, 1854-1914*, London: Leo Cooper, 1972.

Bond, B. and I. Roy (eds.), *War and Society*, Vol 2, London: Croom Helm, 1977.

Bristow, R.C.B., *Memories of the British Raj: A Soldier in India*, London: Johnson, 1974.

Cadell, P., *History of the Bombay Army*, London: Longmans Green & Co., 1938.

Callender and Hinsley, *The Naval Side of British History 1485-1945*, London, 1952.

Candler, E., *The Sepoy*, London: John Murray, 1919.

Chakravarty, S., *The Raj Syndrome*, New Delhi: Penguin, 1991.

Chandler and Beckett (eds.), *The Oxford Illustrated History of the British Army*, London: OUP, 1994.

Chandra, A., *Indian Army Triumphant in Burma*, Delhi: Atma Ram & Sons, 1984.

Chaudhuri, J.N., *An Autobiography as Narrated to B.K. Narayan*, New Delhi: Vikas, 1978.

Chaudhuri, N.C., *Thy Hand Great Anarch India: 1921-1952*, London: Chatto & Windus, 1987.

Cohen, S.P., *The Indian Army*, New Delhi: OUP, 1990.

———, 'The Untouchable Soldier: Caste, Politics and the Indian Army', *Journal of Asian Studies*, Vol. XXVIII, 3 May 1969.

Deshpande, A., 'Sailors and the Crowd: Popular Protest in Karachi, 1946', *Indian Economic and Social History Review*, Vol. 26, No. 1, 1989.

———, 'Limitations of Military Technology: Naval Warfare on the West Coast, 1650-1800', *Economic and Political Weekly*, Vol. XXVII, 25 April 1992.

———, 'The Bombay Marine: Aspects of Maritime History 1650-1850', *Studies in History*, Vol. 11, No. 2, N.S., 1995.

———, 'Hopes and Disillusionment: Recruitment, Demobilisation and the Emergence of Discontent in the Indian Armed Forces after the Second World War', *Indian Economic and Social History Review*, Vol. 33, No. 2, 1996.

———, 'Crowd Intervention in Indian History: An overview of popular resistance coterminous with the 1946 RIN Mutiny', *Mainstream*, 22 February 1992.

———, 'Remembering the RIN Revolt: Popular Celebration of Nationalism Fifty Years Ago', in *Mainstream*, 24 February 1996.

Dewey, C.J., *Arrested Development in India*, New Delhi: Manohar, 1988.

Dutt, B.C., *Mutiny of the Innocents*, Bombay: Sindhu Publications, 1971.

Ellinwood, Dewitt C. and Cynthia Enloe, *Ethnicity and the Military in Asia*, London: Transaction Books, 1981.

Ellinwood, Dewitt C. and S.D. Pradhan (eds.), *India and World War I*, New Delhi: Manohar, 1978.

Evans, H., *Thimayya of India*, New York: Harcourt Brace & Company, 1960.

Farwell, B., *Armies of the Raj*, London: Viking, 1989.

French, P., *Liberty or Death: India's Journey to Independence and Division*, London: HarperCollins Publishers, 1997.

Gamble, A., *Britain in Decline*, Boston: Macmillan, 1981.

Gandhi, M.K., *An Autobiography*, Ahmedabad: Navajivan Publishing House, 1927.

Ghosh, K.K., *The Indian National Army*, Meerut: Meenakshi Prakashan, 1969

Gibbs, Norman, 'British Strategic Doctrine 1918-1939', in M. Howard (ed.), *The Theory and Practice of War*, London: Cassell, 1965.

Gopal, S., *British Policy in India 1858-1905*, Madras: Orient Longman, 1984.

Gourgey, P.S., *The Indian Naval Revolt of 1946*, Chennai: Orient Longman, 1998.

Graham, G.S., *The Politics of Naval Supremacy: Studies in British Maritime Ascendancy*, Cambridge: CUP, 1965.

———, *Great Britain in the Indian Ocean: A study of Maritime Enterprise 1810-1850*, Oxford: OUP, 1967.

Grimal, H., *Decolonization in the British, French, Dutch and Belgian Empires 1919-1963*, London.

Gupta, P. S. (posth.) and A. Deshpande (eds.), *The British Raj and its Indian Armed Forces, 1857-1939*, New Delhi: OUP 2002.

Heathcote, T.A., *The Indian Army: The Garrison of British Imperial India 1822-1922*, London: Newton Abbot, 1974.

———, *The Military in British India: The Development of British Land Forces in South Asia, 1600-1947*, Manchester: Manchester University Press, 1995.

Hennel, R., *A Famous Indian Regiment-Kali Panchwin, 1768-1923*, Delhi: B.R. Publishing Corporation, 1927, rpt. 1985.

Hobsbawm, E.J., *Industry and Empire*, Harmondsworth: Penguin, 1983.

———, *The Age of Empire*, London: Cardinal, 1987.

———, *Age of Extremes: The Short Twentieth Century 1914-1991*, New Delhi: Viking, 1995.

Holland, R.F., *European Decolonization 1918-1981: An Introductory Survey*, London: Macmillan, 1985.

Holland, R.F. and G. Rizvi (eds.), *Perspectives on Imperialism and Decolonization*, London: Frank Cass, 1984.

Horn, D.B. and M. Ransome, *English Historical Documents 1714-1783*, Vol. X, London, 1957.

Howard, M., *The Continental Commitment: The Dilemma of British Defence Policy in the Era of the Two World Wars*, London: Temple Smith, 1972.

Howard, M. (ed.), *The Theory and Practice of War*, London: Cassell, 1965.

Jeffery, K., 'An English Barrack in the Oriental Seas'? India in the Aftermath of the First World War', *Modern Asian Studies*, Vol. 15, No. 3, 1981.

Junior, R.P.S., *British Rearmament in the Thirties: Politics and Profit*, Princeton: Princeton University Press, 1977.

Kadian, R., *India and Its Army*, New Delhi: Vision Books, 1990.

Kahler, M., *Decolonization in Britain and France: The Domestic Consequences of International Relations*, Princeton, 1984.

Katari, R.D., *A Sailor Remembers*, New Delhi, 1982.

Kaul, B.M., *The Untold Story*, Bombay: Allied Publishers, 1971.

Kennedy, P., *Strategy and Diplomacy 1870-1945: Eight Studies*, London: Fontana, 1983.

———, *The Rise and Fall of the Great Powers*, New York: Random House, 1987.

Kiernan, V., *European Armies from Conquest to Collapse, 1815-1960*, London: Fontana, 1982.

Longer, V., *Red Coats to Olive Green*, New Delhi: Allied Publishers, 1974.

———, *Forefront for ever: History of the Mahar Regiment*, New Delhi: Allied Publishers, 1981.

Low, C.R., *History of the Indian Navy (1613-1863)*, Vols. 1 & 2, New Delhi: Manas Publications, 1877, rpt. 1983.

Mackenzie, C., *Eastern Epic, vol. 1, Sept. 1939-March 1943, Defence*, London: Chatto & Windus, 1951.

MacMunn, G., *The Martial Races of India*, London: Adam & Charles Black, 1932.

Mansergh, N. (ed.), *The Transfer of Power 1942-47*, Vol. 6, New Delhi: Oxford & IBH Publishing Company, 1976.

Mason, P., *A Matter of Honour: An Account of the Indian Army, Its officers and men*, London: Jonathan Cape, 1974.

Mare, P.A., *How to become an Officer in the RIN*, Calcutta: Government of India Publication, 1938.

Marwick, A., *War and Social Change in the Twentieth Century*, London: Macmillan, 1974.

Marwick, A. (ed.), *Total War and Social Change*, London: Macmillan, 1988.

Menezes, S.L., *Fidelity and Honour: The Indian Army from the Seventeenth to the Twenty-First Century*: New Delhi: Viking, 1993.

Mollo, B., *The Indian Army*, Dorset: Blandford Press, 1981.

Narain, Maj. Gen. P. (Retd.), *Subedar to Field Marshal*, New Delhi: Manas Publications, 1999.

Omissi, D., *The Sepoy and the Raj*, London: Macmillan, 1994.

Omvedt, G., 'The Satara Parallel Government 1942-47', New Delhi: NMML Seminar, 1980.

Pandey, S.R., *From Sepoy to Subedar*, Delhi, 1970.

Parker, G., *The Military Revolution: Military Innovation and the Rise of the West, 1500-1800*, Cambridge: CUP, 1988.

Peden, G.C., *British Rearmament and the Treasury 1932-39*, Edinburgh: Scottish Academic Press, 1979.

Perkins, R., *Regiments of the Empire: A Bibliography*, Devon: Newton Abbot, 1989.

Prasad, B. (ed.), *Official History of the Indian Armed Forces in the Second World War: Expansion of the Armed Forces and Defence Organisation 1939-45*, New Delhi: Orient Longman, 1956.

———, *Official History of the Indian Armed Forces: Volume on the Royal Indian Navy*, New Delhi: Orient Longman, 1956.

———, *Adjutant General's Branch, Monographs, Vol. III: War System of Accounting & Honours and Awards*, New Delhi: Orient Longman, 1957.

Pruthi, R. and R. Devi, *Armed Forces in British India*, Jaipur: Pointer Publishers, 1998.

Ray, N.R. et al. (eds.), *Challenge: A Saga of India's Struggle for Independence*, New Delhi: PPH, 1984.

Reddy, K.N., 'Indian Defence Expenditure: 1872-1967', *Indian Economic and Social History Review*, Vol. VII, No. 4, 1970.

Reynolds, D., *Britannia Overruled: British Policy and World Power in the 20th Century*, London, 1991.

Rosen, S.P., *Societies and Military Power: India and Its Armies*, Oxford: OUP, 1996.

Roskill, S., *Naval Policy between the Wars*, London: Collins, 1968.

Rothwell, V.H., 'Mesopotamia in British War Aims', *Historical Journal*, Vol. XIII, No. 2, 1970.

Sareen, T.R., *Select Documents on the Indian National Army*, Delhi, 1988.

Sarkar, S., *Modern India 1885-1947*, New Delhi: Macmillan, 1983.

———, 'Popular Movements and National Leadership, 1945-47', *Economic and Political Weekly*, Annual Number, April 1982.

Saxena, K.M.L., *A history of the departments of the Indian Army*, New Delhi: Sterling Publishers, 1974.

———, *The Military System of India 1900-1939*, New Delhi: Reliance Publishing House, 1999.

Sharma, Major Gautam, *Indian Army through the Ages*, New Delhi: Allied Publishers, 1966.

Sharma, Lt. Col. Gautam, *Nationalisation of the Indian Army, 1885-1947*: New Delhi: Allied Publishers, 1996.

Seal, A., *The Emergence of Indian Nationalism: Competition and Collaboration in the Later Nineteenth Century*, New Delhi: S. Chand & Company Ltd., 1971.

Singh, A.I., *The Origins of the Partition of India 1936-1947*, New Delhi: OUP, 1987.

Singh, S., *Under Two Ensigns*, New Delhi: Oxford & IBH Publishing Company, 1985.

Sinha, B.P.N. and S. Chandra, *Valour and Wisdom: Genesis and Growth of the Indian Military Academy*, New Delhi: Oxford & IBH Publishing Company, 1992.

Subrahmanyam, S., *The Career and Legend of Vasco Da Gama*, New Delhi: OUP, 1997.

Sundaram, L., *India's Armies and their costs*, Bombay: Avanti Prakashan, 1946.

Tan, Tai Yong, 'Maintaining the Military Districts: Civil-Military Integration and District Soldiers' Boards in the Punjab, 1919-1939', *Modern Asian Studies*, Vol. 28, No. 4, 1994.

Thorat, S.P.P., *From Reveille to Retreat*, New Delhi: Allied Publishers, 1988.

The Tiger Strikes, Director of Public Relations, Govt. of India, Calcutta, 1942.

Tomlinson, B.R., *The Political Economy of the Raj 1914-1947: The Economics of Decolonization in India*, London: Macmillan, 1979.

Toye, H., *The Springing Tiger: Subhas Chandra Bose*, Bombay: Jaico, Publishing House, 1984.

Trench, C.C., *The Indian Army and the King's Enemies, 1900-1947*, London: Thames & Hudson, 1988.

Wickremesekera, C., *'Best Black Troops in the World': British Perceptions and the Making of the Sepoy 1746-1805*, New Delhi: Manohar, 2002.

Index